$2.50

Plançon

THE SUPPER OF THE LAMB

ROBERT FARRAR CAPON

✤

The Supper of the Lamb

A CULINARY REFLECTION

✤

Doubleday & Company, Inc.
Garden City, New York
1969

TO MY WIFE:

the lightning behind all this thunder

PREFACE

Once upon a time, there was a musician who complained that half the notes he wanted to play were not on the piano. They lay, he claimed, between the keys where he could never get at them. Accordingly, he took up fiddling, which has no such limitations, and lived happily ever after.

This is a book on cooking; but like the musician, it concentrates more on the cracks and interstices of the culinary keyboard than on the conventional notes themselves. It, too, involves considerable fiddling around—some of it rather low, but some of it very high indeed. Nevertheless, I commend it to you in all seriousness. From it, you may learn things you never knew, or be confirmed in prejudices you have always held—or even come away with a recipe or two to add to your collection. In any case, you will find it a leisurely and unhurried book: The outlandish recipe with which it begins lasts the whole work through and provides, not so much an outline, as a fixed star under which the length and breadth of cooking is explored.

As I look it over in its finished form, two matters seem to require a word of explanation. For the first, only those recipes which fit logically within the framework of the book occur in the text itself. All the others have been assembled in the appendix in the usual order, together with page references to the ones previously given. No recipes, however, have been included for mere completeness' stuffy sake: I have given you only what I know and like. It is, after all, my book.

The second matter is the fact that I seem never to have settled in my mind the question of the sex of the reader. Some of my comments are obviously only for women's ears; others will make little sense except to men. I thought for a while about going through the book and straightening this out, but decided against it. It is just such narrow-mindedness about sex that has nearly deprived us of the heights and depths of the sexuality which is our glory. I offer it to you, therefore, as the first androgynous cookbook and spare myself the labor of revision. We are all true men—or women—here. *Vive la difference,* and let it lie where it falls.

Port Jefferson, New York
August 1968

CONTENTS

THE SUPPER OF THE LAMB

ONE

❖

Ingredients

Let me begin without ceremony.

LAMB FOR EIGHT PERSONS FOUR TIMES

In addition to one iron pot, two sharp knives, and four heads of lettuce, you will need the following:

FOR THE WHOLE

1 leg of lamb (The largest the market will provide. If you are no good with a kitchen saw, have the chops and the shank cut through. Do not, however, let the butcher cut it up. If he does, you will lose eight servings and half the fun.)

FOR THE PARTS

I (A)

Olive oil (*olive* oil)
Garlic (fresh)

Onions, carrots, mushrooms, and parsley
Salt, pepper (freshly ground), bay leaf, marjoram
Stock (any kind but ham; water only in desperation)
Wine (dry red—domestic or imported—as decent as possible)
Broad noodles (or spaetzle, potatoes, rice, or toast)

I (B)

Olive oil (again)
Garlic
Onions
Salt, pepper (keep the mill handy), and thyme (judiciously).
  Orégano is also possible, but it is a little too emphatic when
  you get to *III*.
Wine (dry white—even French Vermouth—but not Sherry. Save
  that. Or drink it while you cook.)

II

Spinach (a lot)
Cheese (grated: Parmesan or Cheddar; or perhaps Feta—any-
  thing with a little sharpness and snap)
Mayonnaise (not dietetic and not sweet)
Sherry (only a drop, but Spanish)
Bread (homemade; two loaves) and butter (or margarine, if
  you must)

III

Oil (peanut oil, if you have any; otherwise olive)
3 eggs
Onions
Shredded cabbage (bean sprouts, if you have money to burn)
Sherry (if you have any left)
Stock (as before, but only a little)
Rice (cooked, but not precooked)
Soy sauce (domestic only in desperation)

IV

Onions, carrots, celery, turnip
Oil, fat, or butter
Barley (or chick-peas or dried beans—or all three)
Water
Salt, pepper, and parsley (rosemary?)
(Macaroni and shredded cabbage are also possible. A couple
   of tomatoes give a nice color.)

If prepared correctly, it is all delicious.

Permit me now to wipe my hands and introduce myself.
I am an author who has always intended to write about
cooking, but who has never gotten started in a way that
didn't carry him out of the field in two paragraphs or less.
This time, as you can see, I have outwitted the muse. My
beginning, if confusing, is the most auspicious thus far.

Next, my qualifications.

First, I am an amateur. If that strikes you as disappointing,
consider how much in error you are, and how the error is
entirely of your own devising. At its root lies an objection
to cookbooks written by non-professionals (an objection, by
the way, which I consider perfectly valid, and congratulate
you upon). It does not, however, apply here. *Amateur* and
*non*professional are not synonyms. The world may or may
not need another cookbook, but it needs all the lovers—
amateurs—it can get. It is a gorgeous old place, full of clownish
graces and beautiful drolleries, and it has enough textures,
tastes, and smells to keep us intrigued for more time than
we have. Unfortunately, however, our response to its loveliness
is not always delight: It is, far more often than it should be,
boredom. And that is not only odd, it is tragic; for boredom
is not neutral—it is the fertilizing principle of unloveliness.

In such a situation, the amateur—the lover, the man who

thinks heedlessness a sin and boredom a heresy—is just the man you need. More than that, whether you think you need him or not, he is a man who is bound, by his love, to speak. If he loves Wisdom or the Arts, so much the better for him and for all of us. But if he loves only the way meat browns or onions peel, if he delights simply in the curds of his cheese or the color of his wine, he is, by every one of those enthusiasms, commanded to speak. A silent lover is one who doesn't know his job.

Therefore, the man who said "beauty is in the eye of the beholder" was on the right track, even if he seemed a bit weak on the objectivity of beauty. He may well have been a solipsist who doubted the reality of everything outside himself, or one of those skeptics who thinks that no valid judgments are possible—that no knife can in reality be pronounced sharp, nor any custard done to perfection. It doesn't matter. Like Caiaphas, he spoke better than he knew. The real world which he doubts is indeed the mother of loveliness, the womb and matrix in which it is conceived and nurtured; but the loving eye which he celebrates is the father of it. The graces of the world are the looks of a woman in love; without the woman they could not be there at all; but without her lover, they would not quicken into loveliness.

There, then, is the role of the amateur: to look the world back to grace. There, too, is the necessity of his work: His tribe must be in short supply; his job has gone begging. The world looks as if it has been left in the custody of a pack of trolls. Indeed, the whole distinction between art and trash, between food and garbage, depends on the presence or absence of the loving eye. Turn a statue over to a boor, and his boredom will break it to bits—witness the ruined monuments of antiquity. On the other hand, turn a shack over to a lover; for all its poverty, its lights and shadows warm a little, and its numbed surfaces prickle with feeling.

Or, conclusively, peel an orange. Do it lovingly—in perfect

quarters like little boats, or in staggered exfoliations like a flat map of the round world, or in one long spiral, as my grandfather used to do. Nothing is more likely to become garbage than orange rind; but for as long as anyone looks at it in delight, it stands a million triumphant miles from the trash heap.

That, you know, is why the world exists at all. It remains outside the cosmic garbage can of nothingness, not because it is such a solemn necessity that nobody can get rid of it, but because it is the orange peel hung on God's chandelier, the wishbone in His kitchen closet. He likes it; therefore, it stays. The whole marvelous collection of stones, skins, feathers, and string exists because at least one lover has never quite taken His eye off it, because the *Dominus vivificans* has his delight with the sons of men.

But enough. The amateur is vindicated; let me proceed with my other qualifications.

For the second one, put down that I like food. As a child, I disliked fish, eggs, and oatmeal, but when I became a man, I put away childish things. My tastes are now catholic, if not omnivorous. My children call me the walking garbage pail. (On my own terms, of course, I refuse the epithet: All that I take is stored lovingly in an ample home—it becomes not waste, but waist. On their meaning, however, I let it stand: I am willing to try anything more than once.)

Admittedly, there are some delicacies that give me pause— prairie oysters, for example, or the eye of the calf in a *tête de veau*. But since I have never tasted them, my apprehension may be only the disenchantment wrought by distance. Even the surf is frightening when you lie in bed and *think* about it. In any case, it is part of my creed that there are almost no foods which, given the right cook, cannot be found delectable. Just so long as they are not corrupt—no, that is too sweeping: It will cost me pheasant and venison—just so long as they are not *gracelessly* corrupt, there is, somewhere in the world, an eye that can conceive them in loveliness, and a recipe that can deliver the goods. I am convinced that even shoe tongues, if cooked *provençale* or *à la mode de Caen,* would be more than sufferable.

Third qualification: I like drink. Without any exceptions of time, place, or circumstance, man and boy, I have never tasted wine or spirit for which I could not find a kind word or at least an hour's culinary employment. (I have tasted some pretty mean stuff; but with enough garlic in the recipe, a show of decency is usually possible—anything is better than water in a stew.) To the best of my recollection, I have never thrown away a bottle of anything. If wine is too bad, it can be used to cut vinegar for salads; and there is no spirit so poor but that a stronger one cannot be used to cover it. *In extremis,* bitters will absolve anything.

Admittedly, there are spirits so pronounced that they are unrepentant. Chief among them is *marc,* or *grappa*—brandy distilled from the leavings of the vintage. As it happens, though, I have no desire to cover it with anything. I find it delectable—full of nostalgia and the remembrance of the first afternoon on which I drank it. It is redolent of earth and stems and the resurrected soul of the grape, all combined with an overpowering suggestion of freshly painted radiators in a shoe store—which, you will concede, must be the very essence of unforgettability.

Every rule has its exception, however. While I have never thrown any liquor away, there is one bottle in my house which, after ten years, is still half full. It contains a synthetic Kirsch manufactured by an insecticide company (sic). (Precisely.) It was given to me, seven-eighths full, by a chemist friend who was employed by the firm at the time. He drank just enough to discharge his obligation to his superiors and then with a straight face bestowed the rest on me. It was purely and simply terrible, and ten years have not altered that judgment. Every now and then, however, I take another sip, partly to remind myself of what a paragon of awfulness it is, but partly to prove that for all its faults, it is still not undrinkable. In a real world, nothing is infinitely bad. My bottle of bogus Kirsch bears witness that there is no bottomless pit in any earthly subject—that to be good or bad is not as much of an achievement as to *be* at all. Even the devil, insofar as he exists, is good. What he does wrong with his existence is all small compared with what God does right about him. The Kirsch in my closet is a little hell; by an imitation of the divine courtesy, its being is precious to me, even when its manners are not.

My remaining qualifications—peculiarities, if you prefer—follow more briefly.

On cookbooks. I have Henri-Paul Pellaprat on my shelf, but Fannie Farmer in my heart. You may locate my culinary politics slightly to the right of the latter, but well to the left of the former. In my own terms, I describe myself as an Anglican, or moderately high-church, cook.

On equipment. I dislike gadgets. The thought of an electric knife short-circuits all the connections in my brain. I do not collect corkscrews, but I have a mania for sharp knives (though not for knife sharpeners) and for large pots. I own enough ironware to anchor a twenty-eight-foot cruiser in a twenty-knot wind. To the best of my knowledge, nothing in my house is coated with Teflon.

On the act of cooking. I despise recipes that promise results without work, or success without technique. I have eaten too many short-cut piecrusts to trust anyone who tells women that pastry made with oil is just as good as the "hard" kind. Mere facility, of course, is no more a guarantee of good taste in cooking than it is in music; but without it, nothing good is possible at all. Technique must be acquired, and, with technique, a love of the very processes of cooking. No artist can work simply for results; he must also *like* the work of getting them. Not that there isn't a lot of drudgery

in any art—and more in cooking than in most—but that if
a man has never been pleasantly surprised at the way custard sets or flour thickens, there is not much hope of making
a cook of him. Pastry and confectionery will remain forever
beyond him, and he will probably never even be able to get
gravy to come out the same twice. Interest in results never
conquers boredom with process.

For all that, however, boredom is not unconquerable. Delight in the act of cooking is one of the oldest and nearest
things in the world. We have not made mud pies for nothing.
If a cook is willing simply to look at what he is doing, there
is hope. And if he should ever be fascinated by the fact
that cornstarch and flour do the same thing differently, there
is more than hope. There is a slight but distinct foretaste of
victory. *Chaudfroid of boned squab, fong wong gai,* and
paklava are just over the next line of hills.

Finally, my prejudices. I avoid, when possible, mild hams,
New York State wines, thin bacon, vodka, and all diets. I
think turkey is, if not overrated, at least overserved. I enjoy
cocktails (other than cute ones) but I dislike them before
dinner, and think them gauche after. (Some of them, like the
martini, are marvelous inventions, but man has yet to find a
civilized use for them.) I am also against margarine, "prepared" foods, broiled grapefruit, marshmallow sweet potatoes,
and whipped cream in pressurized cans.

On the other hand, I am wild about peanut butter and
canned fruit cocktail (even the kind that tastes like the
can). I will eat as much process cheese as I am handed,
and I have been known to put mayonnaise on cooked pears.
I am also a notorious stealer of Franco-American spaghetti
from the plates of unsuspecting children, and (probably)
the foremost canned ravioli *maven* on the east coast.

Having thus insulted not only my home state, but also the
standard menu of American Christendom, and the drinking
habits of an entire nation—having, in short, alienated all

possible readers (those who do not find me a snob will call me a boor)—I think we are ready to begin. Continue at your own risk; you have been more than adequately warned. I am an excuse for a cook, writing a book that is an excuse for. . . . But why should I warn you about everything?

TWO

❖

The First Session

Let me concede a point to the reader. You no doubt feel that, whatever else may be forthcoming in this book, I owe you at least an attempt to make good on the obviously pretentious and apparently ordinary recipe with which I began. You are right; I intend to address myself to it immediately. I must ask, however, that you permit me to do it at my own rate. These things take time.

For the moment, therefore, set aside the leg of lamb. If you are a hardy soul, and do not mind getting cold fingers cutting up meat, return it to the refrigerator; alternatively, if comfort is a consideration with you, let it warm up a bit on the kitchen counter. In any case, we do not need it yet. I must teach you first how to deal with onions.

Select three or four medium-size onions—I have in mind the common, or yellow, onion normally available in the supermarket. The first movement (IA) of my recipe is simply a stew; small white onions, while more delicate as a vegetable in their own right, are a nuisance to cut up for inclusion in something else. The labor of peeling is enlarged beyond

reason, and the attempt to slice up the small slippery balls
you are left with can be painful.

Next take one of the onions (preferably the best-looking),
a paring knife, and a cutting board and sit down at the
kitchen table. Do not attempt to stand at a counter through
these opening measures. In fact, to do it justice, you should
arrange to have sixty minutes or so free for this part of the
exercise. Admittedly, spending an hour in the society of an
onion may be something you have never done before. You
feel, perhaps, a certain resistance to the project. Please don't.
As I shall show later, a number of highly profitable members
of the race have undertaken it before you. Onions are excellent
company.

Once you are seated, the first order of business is to address
yourself to the onion at hand. (You must firmly resist the
temptation to feel silly. If necessary, close the doors so no
one will see you; but do not give up out of embarrassment.)
You will note, to begin with, that the onion is a *thing*, *a*
being, just as you are. Savor that for a moment. The two
of you sit here in mutual confrontation. Together with knife,
board, table, and chair, you are the constituents of a *place*
in the highest sense of the word. This is a *Session*, a meeting,
a society of things.

You have, you see, already discovered something: The
uniqueness, the *placiness*, of places derives not from abstractions like *location*, but from confrontations like man-onion.
Erring theologians have strayed to their graves without learning what you have come upon. They have insisted, for example,
that heaven is no place because it could not be defined in
terms of spatial co-ordinates. They have written off man's
eternal habitation as a "state of mind." But look what your
onion has done for you: It has given you back the possibility
of heaven as a place without encumbering you with the ir-
relevancy of location.

This meeting between the two of you could be moved to

a thousand different latitudes and longitudes and still remain the *session* it started out to be. Indeed, by the motions of the earth, the solar system, the galaxy, and the universe (if that can be defined), every place—every meeting of matter —becomes a kind of cosmic floating crap game: Location is accidental to its deepest meaning. What really matters is not where we are, but who—what real beings—are with us. In that sense, heaven, where we see God face to face through the risen flesh of Jesus, may well be the placiest of all places, as it is the most *gloriously* material of all meetings. Here, perhaps, we do indeed see only through a glass darkly; we mistake one of the earthly husks of place for the heart of its mattering.

But back to the onion itself. As nearly as possible now, try to look at it as if you had never seen an onion before. Try, in other words, to meet it on its own terms, not to dictate yours to it. You are convinced, of course, that you know what an onion is. You think perhaps that it is a brownish yellow vegetable, basically spherical in shape, composed of fundamentally similar layers. All such prejudices should be abandoned. It is what it is, and your work here is to find it out.

For a start, therefore, notice that your onion has two ends: a lower, now marked only by the blackish gray spot from which the root filaments descended into the earth; and an upper, which terminates (unless your onions are over the hill, or have begun to sprout because you store them under a leaky sink trap) in a withered peak of onion paper. Note once again what you have discovered: an onion is not a sphere in repose. It is a linear thing, a bloom of vectors thrusting upward from base to tip. Stand your onion, therefore, root end down upon the board and see it as the paradigm of life that it is—as one member of the vast living, gravity-defying troop that, across the face of the earth, moves light-and airward as long as the world lasts.

Only now have you the perspective needed to enter the onion itself. Begin with the outermost layer of paper, or onionskin. Be careful. In the ordinary processes of cooking, the outer skin of a sound onion is removed by peeling away the immediately underlying layers of flesh with it. It is a legitimate short cut; the working cook cannot afford the time it takes to loosen only the paper. Here, however, it is not time that matters, but the onion. Work gently then, lifting the skin with the point of your knife so as not to cut or puncture the flesh beneath. It is harder than you may have thought. Old onion skins give up easily, but new ones can be stubborn.

Look now at the fall of stripped and flakèd skin before you. It is dry. It is, all things considered, one of the driest things in the world. Not dusty dry like potatoes, but smoothly and thinly dry, suggesting not accidental dessication, not the withering due to age or external circumstance, but a fresh and essential dryness. Dryness as an achievement, not as a failure. Elegant dryness. Deliberate dryness. More than that, onion paper is, like the onion itself, directional, vectored, ribbed. (It will, oddly, split as easily across its striations as with them: Its grain has been reduced by dryness to a merely visual quality.) Best of all, though, it is of two colors: the outside, a brownish yellow of no particular brightness; but the inside a soft, burnished, coppery gold, ribbed—especially near the upper end—with an exquisiteness only hinted at on the outside. Accordingly, when you have removed all the paper, turn the fragments inside-up on the board. They are elegant company.

For with their understated display of wealth, they bring you to one of the oldest and most secret things of the world: the sight of what no one but you has ever seen. This quiet gold, and the subtly flattened sheen of greenish yellow white onion that now stands exposed, are virgin land. Like the incredible fit of twin almonds in a shell, they present themselves to you as the animals to Adam: as nameless till seen

by man, to be met, known and christened into the city of
being. They come as deputies of all the hiddennesses of the
world, of all the silent competencies endlessly at work deep
down things. And they come to *you*—to you as their priest
and voice, for oblation by your heart's astonishment at their
great glory.

Only now are you ready for the first cut. Holding the onion
vertically, slice it cleanly in half right down the center line,
and look at what you have done. You have opened the
floodgates of being. First, as to the innards. The mental diagram
of sphere within sphere is abolished immediately. *Structurally,*
the onion is not a ball, but a nested set of fingers within fingers,
each thrust up from the base through the center of the one
before it. The outer digits are indeed swollen to roundness by
the pressure of the inner, but their sphericity is incidental to
the linear motion of flame inthrusting flame.

Next, the colors. The cross-section of each several flame
follows a rule: On its inner edge it is white, on its outer,
pigmented; the color varying from the palest greenish yellow
in the middle flames, to more recognizably onion shades as
you proceed outward. The centermost flames of all are frankly
and startlingly green; it is they which will finally thrust upward into light. Thus the spectrum of the onion: green through
white to green again, and ending all in the brown skin you
have peeled away. Life inside death. The forces of being
storming the walls of the void. Freshness in the face of the
burning, oxidizing world which maderizes all life at last to the
color of cut apples and old Sherry.

Next, pressure. Look at the cut surface: moisture. The incredible, utter wetness of onions, of course, you cannot know
yet: This is only the first hinted pressing of juice. But the
sea within all life has tipped its hand. You have cut open
no inanimate thing, but a living tumescent being—a whole
that is, as all life is, smaller, simpler than its parts; which
holds, as all life does, the pieces of its being in compression.

To prove it, try to fit the two halves of the onion back together. It cannot be done. The faces which began as two plane surfaces drawn by a straight blade are now mutually convex, and rock against each other. Put them together on one side and the opposite shows a gap of more than two minutes on a clock face.

Again, pressure. But now pressure toward you. The smell of onion, released by the flowing of its juices. Hardly a discovery, of course—even the boor knows his onions to that degree. But pause still. Reflect how little smell there is to a whole onion—how well the noble reek was contained till now by the encompassing dryness. Reflect, too, how it is the humors and sauces of being that give the world flavor, how all life came from the sea, and how, without water, nothing can hold a soul. Reflect finally what a soul the onion must have, if it boasts such juices. Your eyes will not yet have begun to water, nor the membranes of your nose to recoil. The onion has only, if you will, *whispered* to you. Yet you have not mistaken a syllable of its voice, not strained after a single word. How will you stop your senses when it raises this stage whisper to a shout?

Now, however, the two halves of the onion lie, cut face up, before you. With the point of your paring knife, carefully remove the base, or bottom (or heart) much as you would do to free the leaves of an artichoke or of a head of lettuce. Take away only as much as will make it possible to lift out, one by one, the several layers. Then gently pry them out in order, working from the center to the outside. Arrange them in a line as you do, with matching parts from the separate halves laid next to each other, making them ascend thus by twos from the smallest green fingers, through white flames, up to the outer shells which sit like paired Russian church spires.

Then look. The myth of sphericity is finally dead. The onion, as now displayed, is plainly all vectors, rissers and thrusts.

Tongues of fire. But the pentecost they mark is that of nature, not grace: the Spirit's first brooding on the face of the waters. Lift one of the flames; feel its lightness and rigidity, its crispness and strength. Make proof of its membranes. The inner: thin, translucent, easily removed; the outer, however, thinner, almost transparent—and so tightly bonded to the flesh that it protests audibly against separation. (You will probably have to break the flesh to free even a small piece.) The membranes, when in place, give the onion its fire, its sheen, soft within and brighter without. But when they are removed, the flesh is revealed in a new light. Given a minute to dry, it acquires a pale crystalline flatness like nothing on earth. Eggshell is the only word for it; but by comparison to the stripped flesh of an onion, an eggshell is only as delicate as poured concrete.

Set aside your broken flame now and pick up a fresh one. Clear a little space on the board. Lay it down on its cut face and slice it lengthwise into several strips. (You will want to tap it lightly with the edge of the knife first. There is a hollow crisp sound to be gotten that way—something between a *tock* and a *tunk*. It is the sound of health and youth, the audible response of cellularity when it is properly addressed. Neither solid nor soft, it is the voice of life itself.)

Next take one of the slivers and press it. Here you will need firmness. If you have strong nails, use the back of the one on your middle finger; if not, steamroller the slice with a round pencil. Press and roll it until it yields all the water it will. You have reached the deepest revelation of all.

First, and obviously, the onion is now part of you. It will be for days. For the next two mornings at least, when you wash your hands and face, your meeting with it will be reconvened in more than memory. It has spoken a word with power, and even the echo is not in vain.

But, second, the onion itself is all but gone. The flesh, so crisp and solid, turns out to have been an aqueous house of cards. If you have done your pressing well, the little scraps of membrane and cell wall are nearly nonexistent. The whole infolded nest of flames was a blaze of water, a burning bush grown from the soil of the primeval oceans. All life is from the sea.

And God said, Let the waters bring forth abundantly. . . . And God saw that it was good. This juice, this liquor, this rough-and-ready cordial, runs freely now on board and hands and knife. Salt, sweet, and yet so much itself as to speak for no other, it enters the city of being. What you have seen, to be sure, is only the smallest part of its singularity, the merest hint of the stunning act of being that it is, but it is enough perhaps to enable you to proceed, if not with safety, then with caution.

For somehow, beneath this gorgeous paradigm of unnecessary being, lies the Act by which it exists. You have just now reduced it to its parts, shivered it into echoes, and pressed it to a memory, but you have also caught the hint that a thing is more than the sum of all the insubstantialities that comprise it. Hopefully, you will never again argue that the solidities of the world are mere matters of accident, creatures of air and darkness, temporary and meaningless shapes out of nothing. Perhaps now you have seen at least dimly that the uniquenesses of creation are the result of continuous creative support, of effective regard by no mean lover. He *likes* onions, therefore they are. The fit, the colors, the smell, the tensions, the tastes, the textures, the lines, the shapes are a response, not to some forgotten decree that there may as well be onions as turnips, but to His present delight—His intimate and immediate joy in all you have seen, and in the thousand other wonders you do not even suspect. With Peter, the onion says, Lord, it is good for us to *be* here. Yes, says God. *Tov. Very* good.

Fair enough then. All life is from the sea. It takes water to hold a soul. Living beings are full of juices.

But watch out.

I once gave a dinner party at which I conned my wife (then hardly more than a bride) into garnishing a main dish (I think it was a mixed grill) with fried parsley. *Persil frit* is one of the traps that is laid to teach humility to men beset by culinary presumption. I had spent the better part of a morning off devising a way of making attractive bunches of parsley for frying, and I had finally come up with what I still consider (apart from the disaster that followed) the perfect presentation of persil frit. I took bread sticks and, with a coping saw, carefully cut them into three-quarter-inch lengths. Then, ever so gently, I bored out the centers with a small twist drill. This provided me with a number of neckerchief slides, as it were, into each of which I thrust a sufficient number of parsley sprigs to make a snug fit. Since my wife had bought excellent parsley, they made magnificent little sheaves of green.

Unfortunately, however, I neglected to tell my wife that, in spite of all this artsy-crafty ingenuity, I had never prepared, cooked, eaten, or even seen fried parsley before. What she trustingly accepted from me as a manageable fact was nothing but a conceit. We sow, on bright, clear days, the seeds of our own destruction.

For a young thing she had done more than well. Hors d'oeuvres, soup, and fish had come off beautifully—but at an expense of spirit to which I was blind. The working cook of a major meal operates under pressure, and the ivory tower gourmet should never forget it. The mixed grill was in the broiler, the french fryer was heating on the stove, and my wife, tense but still game, picked up my little parsley masterpieces and dropped them into the fat.

What followed was the nearest thing we have ever had to a kitchen fire, and one of the nearest to a marital disaster.

Parsley: freshness: water. All life is from the sea. Water: heat: steam. When the bouquets hit the fat, the whole business blew up. Steam: sound: fury. And grease all over the kitchen. Fury: wife: tears. All waters return to the sea.

I spent the fish course in the kitchen mending my fences, trying to bluff my way out. To this day, I remember nothing about the rest of the meal. Except one thing. The parsley was glorious. It fries in ten seconds or so and turns the most stunning green you can imagine. It was parsley transfigured, and I shall never forget it. It is just as well. My wife has never cooked it again.

Between the onion and the parsley, therefore, I shall give the summation of my case for paying attention. Man's real work is to look at the things of the world and to love them for what they are. That is, after all, what God does, and man was not made in God's image for nothing. The fruits of his attention can be seen in all the arts, crafts, and sciences. It can cost him time and effort, but it pays handsomely. If an hour can be spent on one onion, think how much regarding it took on the part of that old Russian who looked at onions and church spires long enough to come up with St. Basil's Cathedral. Or how much curious and loving attention was expended by the first man who looked hard enough at the insides of trees, the entrails of cats, the hind ends of horses and the juice of pine trees to realize he could turn them all into the first fiddle. No doubt his wife urged him to get up and do something useful. I am sure that he was a stalwart enough lover of things to pay no attention at all to her nagging; but how wonderful it would have been if he had known what we know now about his dawdling. He could have silenced her with the greatest riposte of all time: Don't bother me; I am creating the possibility of the Bach unaccompanied sonatas.

But if man's attention is repaid so handsomely, his inattention costs him dearly. Every time he diagrams something instead of looking at it, every time he regards not what a thing *is* but what it can be made to *mean* to him—every time he substitutes a conceit for a fact—he gets grease all over the kitchen of the world. Reality slips away from him; and he is left with nothing but the oldest monstrosity in the world: an idol. Things must be met for themselves. To take them only for their meaning is to convert them into gods— to make them too important, and therefore to make *them* unimportant altogether. Idolatry has two faults. It is not only a slur on the true God; it is also an insult to true things.

They made a calf in Horeb; thus they turned their Glory into the similitude of a calf that eateth hay. Bad enough, you say. Ah, but it was worse than that. Whatever good may have resided in the Golden Calf—whatever loveliness of gold or beauty of line—went begging the minute the Israelites got the idea that *it* was their savior out of the bondage of Egypt. In making the statue a matter of the greatest *point*, they missed the point of its *matter* altogether.

Berate me not therefore for carrying on about slicing onions in a world under the sentence of nuclear overkill. The heaviest weight on the shoulders of the earth is still the age-old idolatry by which man has cheated himself of both Creator and creation. And this age is no exception. If you prefer to address yourself to graver matters, well and good: Idolatry needs all the enemies it can get. But if I choose to break images in the kitchen, I cannot be faulted. We are both good men, in a day when good men are hard to find. Let us join hands and get on with our iconoclasm.

There is a Russian story about an old woman whose vices were so numerous that no one could name even one of her virtues. She was slothful, spiteful, envious, deceitful, greedy, foul-mouthed, and proud. She lived by herself and in herself; she loved no one and no thing. One day a beggar came to her door. She upbraided him, abused him, and sent him away.

As he left, however, she unaccountably threw an onion after him. He picked it up and ran away. In time the woman died and was dragged down to her due reward in hell. But just as she was about to slip over the edge of the bottomless pit, she looked up. Above her, descending from the infinite distances of heaven, was a great archangel, and in his hand was an onion. "Grasp this," he said. "If you hold it, it will lift you up to heaven."

One real thing is closer to God than all the diagrams in the world.

THREE

❖

The Burnt Offering

You see, I hope, how hard it is to rush past even a single detail. The world is such an amiable place. There is a distinct possibility that a properly attentive cookbook might never get through even one recipe. Nevertheless, things are not quite as bad as all that.

Lamb for Eight Persons Four Times is not simply a recipe. It is a way of life. It does indeed produce thirty-two servings from a single leg of lamb, but at the same time, it opens the door to a school of cooking that has produced some of the greatest dishes in the world. The fundamental approach of this school involves the wholesale and deliberate manufacture of leftovers, the creation of all of one's dishes from carefully precarved and precooked meats. It insists that there is a sharp distinction to be observed between ordinary and extraordinary eating—between ferial and festal dining, if you will. To the extraordinary or festal cuisine are relegated all roasts, joints, chops and steaks, and, in general, any meats that are cooked in large pieces and carved at the table. To the ferial cuisine belong all the rest—the dishes which take a little, cut it up small, amd make it go a long way.

The reason for the distinction is obvious: economy. A roast or joint, presented whole to a table of hungry diners, will hardly survive the ordeal. Meat lavishly presented demands proportionate consumption. Even with a carver of surpassing skill you will be lucky if you serve eight people *once* from a whole leg of lamb. (And if you let a duffer with an electric knife at your roast, forget about *lamb* for eight altogether. Someone is going to have to fill corners with peanut butter.) Accordingly, if it is the cook's intention to make her joint last beyond the first sitting, she will have to forgo its festal presentation. She will prepare it ferially—cooking it, but never letting anyone but herself get his hands on it. Which brings us to the first principle of the ferial or ordinary cuisine.

It is: *Never serve anybody a whole anything.* As you can see, it is rooted in the hard-earned wisdom of the ages. It goes back to that primeval cook who first discovered the culinary version of Parkinson's Law: Appetite rises to meet food supply. She found that her family would eat a whole leg of mutton as readily as a half—and with very little additional gratitude. Accordingly, she cooked the leg in two installments, seasoned it highly, sauced it liberally, and advised them to keep the gratitude coming, unless perhaps they would like her to try quartering it. She won, of course. Witness the grudging acknowledgment of her triumph in the Jewish aphorism: When a poor man gets to eat a whole chicken, they're both sick. But she was magnanimous in victory: A generosity of sauce kept pace with her stinginess of meat. The glory of ordinary cooking began to dawn.

The second principle of the ferial cuisine is an extension of the first: *If you can possibly do so, contrive to make even a part of anything come to the table twice.* In its pure form, of course, this can be used as a cloak for a miserly disposition —it can condemn a family to a perpetual diet of leftover meat and last season's tomatoes. But then, any principle, applied with sheer consistency, borders on madness. In its more temperate form, this second axiom serves not to diminish, but to extend the pleasures of the table.

A chicken, for example, will see the inside of your soup pot, not only *after* it has been served, but before. You will make a first soup from the whole—or only slightly dismembered —bird, and on that day, your family will taste no chicken at all. (Why do you think matzoh balls were invented?) You will serve them only the soup—and not even all of that, since a little must be set aside to make tomorrow's sauce. But when the day of the bird itself finally arrives, your refusal to serve it the first time around becomes a crown of glory. For what you have to work with is not run-of-the-mill leftovers (two wings and a back), but a whole moist, tender bird, ready to give itself liberally to any one of a hundred ways of preparing it.

Should your family, however, begrudge you your victory— should they rail against you, calling you Soup-waterer or Chicken-stretcher, several rejoinders are possible. For the first, remind them that if it's festal cooking they want, they had better provide you with a more festal food allowance. For the second, ask them when they last had a roast that could stand comparison with your lightly sherried chicken in supreme sauce with mushrooms. (Sherry is essential to ferial cooking. It provides the perfect lift for the dish, and the perfect squelch for the smart alecks who are always throwing festal cooking in your face.) Finally, point to the pot now simmering once more on the stove, and remind them that out of today's discard of bones and stems, they will all have mushroom soup tomorrow, provided they stop carping and behave. (A good ferial cook, like a judo expert, always keeps her opponents off balance. She is all confidence and bold response. Her only real enemy is self-doubt.) Once you have regained the upper hand, however, be gracious. Offer them a drop of your Sherry.

The ferial cuisine, you see, was the poor man's invention

out of necessity, but it is light years away from poor cooking. The poor man may envy the rich their houses, their lands, and their cars; but given a good wife, he rarely envies them their table. The rich man dines festally, but unless he is an exceptional lover of being—unless he has the soul of a poet and a saint—his feasts are too often only single: They delight the palate, but not the intellect. They are greeted with a deluxe but mindless attention: "What was it, dear, sirloin or porterhouse?" Every dish in the ferial cuisine, however, provides a double or treble delight: Not only is the body nourished and the palate pleased, the mind is intrigued by the triumph of ingenuity over scarcity—by the making of slight materials into a considerable matter. A man can do worse than be poor. He can miss altogether the sight of the greatness of small things.

One or two final comments on the distinction between the ferial and the festal cuisine. First, the excellence and exquisiteness of the dishes is in no way involved. It is not that festal cooking is best and ferial second-best. Some of the most discerning palates in history have pronounced a good *boeuf Bourguignon* or *tripe Niçoise* the full equal of any steak in the world. Many, many of the dishes that now rest secure in the *haute cuisine* are simply worthy specimens of ferial cooking at its best.

Even more important, however, the distinction must never be thought of as depending on the "richness" or fattening qualities of the foods involved—as if the festal ones were full of calories and the ferial ones dietetic. The calorie approach is the work of the devil. He has persuaded otherwise sane men that festal eating should not alternate with ferial eating at all, but with dieting—an activity which, while it uses food, hopes that it can keep food from having anything significant to do with us. The modern diet victim sees his life at the table not as a delightful alternation between pearls of great price and dishes of lesser cost, but as a grim sentence which condemns him to pay for every fattening repast (even the sleaziest) with a meal of carrot sticks and celery. Not that there is anything wrong with raw vegetables, or with eating less if you want to—but to allow such considerations to become the rule of man's eating is simply the death of dining.

In fact, of course, the insane distinction of fattening/dietetic cannot be squared with the rational one of festal/ferial. The first fastens its attention, not on food, but on little invisible spooks called calories; only the second honestly addresses the real matter at hand. Consequently, the dieter has no way of distinguishing good food from bad. Take éclairs, for example. The world is full of them, mostly awful. Any true eater, ferial or festal, will be able to give you an accurate judgment as to which of them are worth meeting and which should be avoided. The dieter, however, has lost all criteria for judgment. That éclairs are fattening is his sole piece of information. If he is in a mood to diet, he will pass up the best éclair in the world without even a backward look; and if he is in a mood to eat, he will devour a corner-bakery, cardboard-and-corn-starch monstrosity as if it were something out of Brillat-Savarin. He is a man who, for all practical purposes, has lost his taste. He will choose tough steak in the presence of elegant stew, and canned stringed beans when he might have dined on mashed parsnips drenched in butter. All because he has fabricated a set of distinctions which has nothing to do with the subject.

Ferial cooking—the cooking of most people on most of the days of the year—neither is nor can be dietetic. The truth of the matter is that it costs more to diet than to get fat. It is the festal roasts and chops which are low in calories, and the everyday mountains of rice, potatoes and gravy which are high. It was the poor man who first invented sauces. He could not afford to roast his pig whole, so he ate it in installments, floating the pieces in lakes of gravy to keep them from looking lonely on the expanses of pasta he had to eat to keep body and soul together.

Both the ferial and the festal cuisine, therefore, must be seen as styles of unabashed *eating*. Neither attempts to do anything to food other than render it delectable. Their distinction is grounded, not in sordid dietetic tricks, but in a choice between honest frugality or generous expense. Both aim only at excellence; accordingly, neither is suitable for dieting. Should a true man want to lose weight, let him fast. Let him sit down to nothing but coffee and conversation, if religion or reason bid him do so; only let him not try to eat his cake without having it. Any cake he could do that with would be a pretty spooky proposition—a little golden calf with dietetic icing, and no taste at all worth having.

Let us fast, then—whenever we see fit, and as strenuously as we should. But having gotten that exercise out of the way, let us *eat*. Festally, first of all, for life without occasions is not worth living. But ferially, too, for life is so much more than occasions, and its grand ordinariness must never go unsavored. But both ways let us eat with a glad good will, and with a conscience formed by considerations of excellence, not by fear of Ghosts. If this book has any culinary point to make, it is that the ferial cuisine must once more be exalted among us. Between the dietmongers and the prepared-food hawkers, we are in danger of losing the greater part of our heritage. Herewith, therefore, a little prayer for the return of sanity to our tables.

V. The poor shall eat and be satisfied.
R. They that seek after the Lord shall praise
him; your heart shall live forever.

O Lord, refresh our sensibilities. Give us this day our daily taste. Restore to us soups that spoons will not sink in, and sauces which are never the same twice. Raise up among us stews with more gravy than we have bread to blot it with, and casseroles that put starch and substance in our limp modernity. Take away our fear of fat, and make us glad of the oil which ran upon Aaron's beard. Give us pasta with a hundred fillings, and rice in a thousand variations. Above all, give us grace to live as true men—to fast till we come to a refreshed sense of what we have and then to dine gratefully on all that comes to hand. Drive far from us, O Most Bountiful, all creatures of air and darkness; cast out the demons that possess us; deliver us from the fear of calories and the bondage of nutrition; and set us free once more in our own land, where we shall serve thee as thou hast blessed us—with the dew of heaven, the fatness of the earth, and plenty of corn and wine. Amen.

With that, the philosophy of Lamb for Eight Persons Four Times is complete. It remains only to apply it specifically to the joint at hand.

As you have no doubt guessed, my leg of lamb is intended to be cooked in several installments, and served as four distinct meals. For the first, a stew will be made of the chops cut from the upper end of the leg. The reason for suggesting that you cut them off yourself is that the butcher will normally not be quite generous enough. Something very like one third of the leg should go into the stew. (The remaining dishes can disguise a shortage of meat better than this one—especially since I allow no potatoes, dumplings, or other forms of edible blotting material to be cooked with my stew.)

The other two thirds of the leg will then be browned and braised (or possibly even poached, if you want to employ the two-soup gambit on a leg of lamb). Once cooked, it will be completely dismantled, and the meat divided into three portions (two generous and one skimpy), and stored for the subsequent meals. Finally, the bones will be returned to the stock pot, where they will either strengthen the first soup or make a second *de novo*. In any case, your lamb will provide you long company—and not a minute of it boring.

On then with the recipe.

Select three or four medium onions, peel them, and slice them up. (Does such haste now seem somehow blasphemous? Good. Chapter Two was not in vain.) Peel and crush a few cloves of garlic (six would be excessive). Permit me a digression here. There is a Chinese trick with garlic which you should learn. It involves the use of a knife called the *choy doh* —which is the small cleaver which the cartoon Chinese chef invariably carries. It makes short work of garlic. Any heavy-bladed knife will do for the job, however—but the more like a cleaver, the better.

Place the unpeeled clove of garlic on your onion board (by now, you realize that onions not only deserve, but demand a board of their own), take your cleaver, and hit the clove lightly but firmly with the side of the blade. Properly administered, the blow should crush the garlic just enough to loosen the papery outer skin. Flick that away with your fingers, and then smash the clove once more—viciously this time— with the flat of the cleaver. If you do this correctly, the garlic will be crushed to a fare-thee-well and will need no further chopping or mashing. If you do it incorrectly (bringing the blade down at an odd angle to the board), you will have crushed garlic all over the place. Without precision, it squirts. The trick is enough of a timesaver, though, to be worth a little untidiness in the learning—especially if it persuades you that fresh garlic is no more trouble to use than powdered.

Next, scrape a carrot and slice it thinly. Take as many mushrooms as you think fit—more than a pound would be pretentious, even if not excessive—and cut them up any way you like. (In a dish of this sort it is not necessary to do much to the mushrooms. If, as a child, you were frightened by the germ theory, you may want to run a little water over them; but peeling or scrubbing is merely high church. I would suggest, however, that even if you leave them whole you break off the stems—they will provide you with a small soup on a later day. Remember, this is not simply a recipe; it is a way of life.) Finally, *using a sharp knife*, cut up a reasonable quantity of parsley. (Chopping away with a dull knife will give you, not an ornament to your stew, but an unpleasant green pulp, most of whose goodness never reaches the pot. It is crushed to death on the cutting board.)

Now place each of your prepared vegetables in some kind of container. (Coffee cups, jar lids, saucers, and cereal bowls are all possibilities) and cover each with plastic wrap. (You see, I hope, that I am no mere antiquarian, insisting on barefoot walks through unimproved sculleries. I am as grateful for real progress as any modernist. More so, perhaps. Anything that preserves freshness for the pot is on the side of the angels.)

Now, however, set aside your vegetables for a moment and turn to the leg of lamb. Using your handiest and sharpest knife, cut off all the chops and cast a judicious eye over the result. If what is left on the leg proper looks more like three quarters than two thirds of the whole, take off another generous piece (a slice an inch thick would not be too much). In any case, you will probably make this additional cut quite without my telling you to. As you proceed down the leg, its progressively more elegant meatiness will tempt you to make more of a stew than you first planned.

Next, take a sharp, pointed knife and remove all the bones from the meat you have sliced off. (Put the rest of the leg back in the refrigerator.) Trim and cut up the meat into the neatest pieces you can manage. Remember, however, that this is a *ferial* stew; it cannot possibly hope to be made up of perfect little cubes of meat. The only rule is: Everything goes into the pot. Big pieces, little pieces, infinitesimal pieces— fat, bones, and all. (If you are squeamish about fat, you may omit the larger pieces; but I hope you will not make a fetish of getting every scrap of it off the meat.)

Now then. You are ready at last for the crucial operation; the *sine qua non* of any stew, festal or ferial. Put a little olive oil in the bottom of a heavy (deep, too, if possible) iron skillet, and place it over a high fire until it begins to smoke. Then add the cut lamb, bones and all, and brown well. *Use no flour.*

It sounds absurdly simple; but it is the point at which nine tenths of the stews in the world go wrong. The trouble is that few cooks realize how long it takes to brown meat thoroughly. (One note on a culinary heresy: People who flour their meat and brown it in butter are entitled to their religion. We live in a pluralistic society. I think it only fair to note, however, that such people have never gotten around to browning *meat*. All they have done is darkened some butter and scorched a little flour. The meat inside remains untouched. Accordingly, their stews never know the savor of the true burnt offering; in their haste they settle for the dubious pleasure of eating charred wheat.)

Even for a little stew like this, therefore, it will take fifteen minutes or so to do a good job of browning the meat. (Remember once again, this is *ferial* cooking—what it saves in money, it spends in time and fuel. It is, like most frugalities, penny wise and pound foolish. But it does aim at excellence, and as long as it gives good stew, its minor extravagances can hardly be faulted.)

What leads most cooks into turning off the fire too soon is the fear of drying out the meat. Now clearly, there are dishes to which this fear is entirely appropriate; stew, however, is not one of them. It matters not how many juices run out of the meat during browning because they go nowhere but into the pot. Any drying that occurs is only temporary. The water that escapes as steam will be restored shortly by the stock and wine to be added. Your meat's lost soul will be replaced by a second and better one.

Do not be afraid, then, when some of the tinier scraps of lamb shrivel into brown crumbs. Turn the heat down a bit so as not to blacken them, but don't turn it off. Your larger cubes of meat, of course, will behave like candidates for a festal stew—they will brown on the outside, and seal their juices within. But even in the face of some shriveling, keep the burner going.

In the meantime, add the sliced onions and carrot and let them brown too. (These should go into the skillet, not at the beginning, but only when the meat has turned a good color by itself. Added at the start they release so much moisture that they cool the pan and slow the browning of the meat; worse yet, once the moisture is gone they will blacken before the meat browns, and give a bitterness to your stew.) Add them later, therefore, and give them a little time to reach a nice color. Then put in the mushrooms and the garlic. (Why do I put the garlic in so late? It is a personal prejudice. I happen to like my stew made with the soul of the garlic, not with its cremated remains. Of course, if you prefer dishes that taste like overdone garlic bagels, go ahead and put it in earlier.) In any case, stir and turn everything until it is all browned to perfection. Then, and only then, turn off the fire.

That, as I said, is the sine qua non of a stew. There is, however, one more step, without which even the sine qua non itself will come to nothing. It is the solemn rinsing of the skillet. Remove the meat to the pot in which you intend to cook the stew. (Even if you have done the browning in an iron skillet deep enough to accommodate all the ingredients, I would advise against using it for the long cooking that is to follow. If your ironware has a well seasoned surface, three hours of stewing will strip it down to bare metal and undo months, if not years, of care. If, on the other hand, it is one of those overwashed pans with no real surface at all, it will

make your stew taste like rusty nails.) Empty the skillet,
therefore, and rinse it out enough times to release all its color
and flavor. If you are using water for your stew, add a cupful
at a time to the skillet, turn on the heat, and while it boils,
scrape and stir to loosen the browning from the bottom of the
pan. Repeat this process until you have used up all the liquid
you intend to put in the stew. It makes no difference if you
are using wine and stock: Every drop of liquid must rinse the
skillet before it goes into the pot. You did not dry and brown
these juices to wash them down the sink.

(A word about the liquid itself. Unless you are physically
prevented from doing so, always use stock or wine, especially
in a ferial stew. We are working here with an admitted
minimum of meat. To add water to it is to strain it, to demand
of it a cruel exertion, to have it arrive at the table worn out
with overwork. This is no festal dish, with enough meat in it
to make meals for a week. This is a poor dish, whose meat is
to be pitied and spared. Accordingly, any liquid that goes into
it should be of a charitable and kindly sort—a *bonum diffu-
sivum sui*—which knows how much more blessed it is to give
than to receive. Stock then; not water. And, no matter what
else, wine. A gallon of good California red in the kitchen
closet will do more for your cooking than all the books in the
world.)

We are almost at an end. To your now brimming stew pot,
add the parsley, some freshly ground black pepper, a bay
leaf, a generous pinch of marjoram (thyme and orégano are
also possible, of course, but marjoram has finesse), and lastly,
salt. Use it sparingly. You can always put more in later, but
it's the devil's own work to get it out if you overdo it—all that
business of cooking potatoes in the stew to soak up the salt—
in the process you lose half your liquid. (Incidentally, that is
why I am against ferial stews with potatoes or dumplings in
them. Once again, it is a case of overworking a small quantity
of meat. In the festal cuisine, of course, I am heartily in

favor of the idea. I am a dumpling man, though; when it comes to potatoes and stew, I prefer to have them meet on my plate—not before.)

One last word about the cooking. Remember that a ferial stew must boast as much liquid as is consistent with good flavor. Therefore, while your pot simmers, check the level of the gravy from time to time, and taste it often. If it seems robust enough to take a little more liquid, add stock or wine. Don't be afraid of overdoing here. You can always reduce the liquid. Should it taste a bit thin—if you begin to hear again in your mind's ear cries of Soup-waterer and Chicken-stretcher —leave the lid off for a while. When the gravy evaporates to the desired richness, replace the cover and proceed as before. The more solemn cookbook authors will no doubt warn you against this; except for grave cause, they allow nothing, not even bouquet, to leave the pot. But I lay no such strictures upon you. It gives the house a marvelous smell.

By my first principle, even a whiff of reality is worth the price.

FOUR

The Generous Ox

We have arrived at the marvel of *meat*—at delectabilities which we deny only at the price of making ourselves small. Lamb has set our feet in a large room. It is time to stop, draw a deep breath, and look around.

First, therefore, a parable.

Once upon a time, there was a wise man who gave a dinner party. To it he invited, among others, a handsome widow and an eligible bachelor. His purpose was to combine a little matchmaking with his wining and dining; but his friends, on hearing the candidates in action, questioned his wisdom.

The widow spent the evening complaining that her family was tired of eating nothing but beef, lamb, pork, veal, and poultry. She claimed that menu-planning was about to drive her out of her mind unless someone came along quickly and invented a new animal.

The bachelor, however, was a gentleman of a progressive turn of mind and took off after this remark in a burst of quasi-scientific argument. He pointed out that nature, far from being insufficiently bountiful, was entirely too lavish to suit anyone with a taste for technology and efficiency. He stated flatly that if he had had anything to do with the creation of the natural order, he would have insisted on something a good deal less splashy than this uneconomical riot of flora and fauna that now passes for a world. He would have contented himself with the invention of a single species of animal, perhaps, and of one kind of vegetation—just to keep the carbon dioxide cycle going. Beyond that, however, only the most burdensome necessities could have led him to create more.

To the guests at the table, it seemed as if their host had taken leave of his senses: Two more unsuitable candidates for matrimony would be hard to find. Everyone was surprised, therefore, when, immediately after dessert, the pair rose, excused themselves and left the party together—apparently deeply engrossed in each other. The host simply smiled. On being questioned, he explained the attraction in the following way.

What they had in common was a total lack of what he called the *sensus lusus*, or playful spirit—the sense by which the ordinary man is glad that veal is not beef, and that the world does not require him to choose between chicken and duck; the sense, in short, by which he relishes the elegant superfluity, the unnecessary variety of the world. The host had anticipated (correctly) that under their apparent differences of opinion, they would be the first to sense the deep and abiding mirthlessness which united them. He had no doubt but that they would shortly marry and live efficiently ever after.

He pointed out, however, that public as well as private benefits would stem from his matchmaking. The union between them would, he felt, prove so satisfying that all normal human converse would seem light and frivolous. He looked forward confidently to the day when they would voluntarily withdraw themselves from circulation, and decline dinner invitations altogether. He expected that they would soon become nutrition faddists of the first water, who would stay at home and live on instant breakfasts and pills. At that point, he hoped, his friends would be duly grateful. The Creator, of course, had seen to it that they were born too late to get their sticky fingers into the pie of creation, but he was responsible for keeping them away from other people's dinner tables.

As it turned out, his friends had more cause for gratitude than anyone then suspected. They did indeed marry, and they devoted themselves to the development of a nutrition pill, which, if taken once a day, obviated the necessity of any attention to food at all. Their pill is of course a menace, but only to the equally mirthless and mad; for the sane, the mercy is complete: The wretched couple don't *give* dinner parties either. Anyone with an ounce of playfulness is sure to be spared the anguish of their company.

It is a good place to begin.

Think first of the widow with her clamor for a new animal. What can her complaint against beef, lamb, *et al.* mean except that she had never looked at any of them? If she had, she would have realized that beef, for example, far from being a single animal, is a whole menagerie of delights. Shin, plate, rump, and chuck are individual worlds of flavor. Rib, sirloin, and filet are separate provinces of texture. Even the fat of the animal changes its nature as it moves from place to place in the noble beast: varying from the hard and heavy layers that surround a standing roast to the exquisite, almost buttery globules of suet that lie around the kidneys. Ah! Kidneys! And all those other distinct species of goodness so aptly named *variety* meats: tongue, brain, sweetbreads, tripe, heart, liver, and, last of all, the oxtail, which, when glorified with a little Madeira and good bread, can wag any meal into an occasion of joy.

Add to that only the consideration that each of these

seventeen uniquenesses (which by no means exhaust the animal even in its natural state) can be prepared in five, ten or fifty ways; that what is left will make sausages in abundance, and soups whose variety is limited only by the length of a man's life; and that every dish takes on a special color from the occasions on which it is served (a hot steak and kidney pie at a formal dinner is one thing; the same pie eaten cold on the next day as a workingman's lunch is quite another)—add only these considerations, and the argument against the widow is complete. Another animal indeed! The woman is a hopeless case. If she cannot see a hundred marvels in the ox that licketh up the grass of the field, there is no reason to expect her to see a single wonder anywhere, though the Creator provide her a hundred new animals a month. The girl is bored. Additional goodness cannot help her; inattention has immunized her against even what she has.

On the other hand, take her new-found husband. He reminds me of a panelist I once heard on a late night talk show. His subject was Unidentified Flying Objects, and the possibility of life on other planets. The question raised was whether the purported sightings meant that we are being visited by intelligent extraterrestrial tourists. (I should go on record here as feeling ill at ease with the whole subject. Not, mind you, because I am prejudiced against the idea of unearthly intelligences—I am not—but because I think too many of the earthly contributors to the debate are mirthlessly beyond the help of whatever additional goodness such visitors might possess.) Witness the panelist in question. He argued that the sightings involved too many different kinds of space craft to be the work of intelligent beings. True rationality, he insisted, would never produce two versions of anything where one would do.

His brand of reasoning would, if followed, render us all certifiable in a matter of weeks. It would tell the man who can afford three cars that he must, to be truly intellectual, buy three sedans—all Buicks and all black; that if he eats eggs, it is unnecessary to eat them any other way than boiled; and that, if he roasts his lamb, he must, day after day, whittle away at it in its original state until the last tired scrap is laid to rest.

A curse on them all! May an endless variety of worms feed sweetly upon their thrifty little efficiencies. Hell is the only place fit for such dismal crampings of the style of our being. Earth must not be entrusted to such people. Their touch is death to all that is counter, original, strange and spare about us. In their hands, the joy of our randomness and oddness is crushed under the millstone of monotonous consistency. God may be simple, but simplicity makes a bad god.

Economy is not one of the necessary principles of the universe; it is one of the jokes which God indulges in precisely because He can afford it. If a man takes it seriously, however, he is doomed forever to a middle-income appreciation of the world. Indeed, only the very poor and the very rich are safe from its idolatry. The poor, because while they must take it seriously, they cannot possibly believe in it as a good; and the rich, because, though they may see it as a good, they cannot possibly take it seriously. For the one it is a bad joke, for the other, a good one; but for both it is only part of the divine ludicrousness of creation—of the *sensus lusus* which lies at the heart of matter. And that is why all men should hasten to become very poor or very rich—or both at once, like St. Paul, who had nothing and yet possessed all things. The world was made in sport, for *sports;* economy is worth only a smile. There are more serious things to laugh at.

O the sad frugality of the middle-income mind. O the humorless neatness of an intellectuality which buys mass-produced candlesticks and carefully puts one at each end of every philosophical mantelpiece! How far it lies from the playfulness of Him who composed such odd and needless variations on the themes of leaf and backbone, eye and nose! A thousand praises that it has only lately managed to lay its cold hand on the wines, the sauces, and the cheeses of the world! A hymn of thanksgiving that it could not reach into the depths of the sea to clamp its grim simplicities over the creatures that swim luminously in the dark! A shout of rejoicing for the fish who wears his eyeballs at the ends of long stalks, and for the jubilant laughter of the God who holds him in life with a daily *bravo* at the *bravura* of his being!

Into outer darkness then with the pill-roller and his wife. They have missed the point of the world; they are purely and simply mad. Man invented cooking before he thought of nutrition. To be sure, food keeps us alive, but that is only its smallest and most temporary work. Its *eternal* purpose is to furnish our sensibilities against the day when we shall sit down at the heavenly banquet and see how gracious the Lord is. Nourishment is necessary only for a while; what we shall need forever is *taste*.

Pills indeed! Some day, no doubt, the dreadful offspring of that hapless couple will invent flavorless capsules which, when swallowed, will give the user a complete command of any desired language. Let us hope only that when he does, the sane among us will lobby for a law to keep such people from writing poems. Language is no utilitarian abstraction; English, French, Greek, and Latin are concrete delights, relishings by which the flavor of words and syntax are rolled over the tongue. And so in their own way are all the declensions and conjugations of beef, lamb, pork, and veal. Food is the daily sacrament of unnecessary goodness, ordained for a continual remembrance that the world will always be more delicious than it is useful. Necessity is the mother only of clichés. It takes playfulness to make poetry.

What can I tell you, therefore, about meat? How best excite your sense of the gloriously unnecessary abundance in which we stand? There is so much that I must be careful.

Mere enumeration of recipes, however excellent, might leave you as unsatisfied as the widow, unless your eyes could be opened to see the bounty of small things. On the other hand, further philosophizing might do no more for you than it did for her future mate, who fell to worshiping idols instead of loving realities.

What then? Is there anything between the glitteringly general and the exhaustingly particular that will serve to sharpen your eye for variety and your taste for distinctions—to quicken your appreciation of the poetry that has been made out of meat? Ah, yes. There is the category of the minutely and shimmeringly specific, of the little things which make great differences—of the graces and ornaments that separate the cooks from the scullery maids. Three things there are which the earth cannot bear, yea, four which are to be feared as the shadow of death: A painter who will not look, a sculptor with a dead thumb, a musician with a tin ear, and a cook with a wooden palate. Let Ithiel therefore listen.

There is, for example, the Swedish trick of basting a roast leg of lamb with a cup of coffee (complete with sugar and cream). You simply add it early in the cooking and continue basting all the way through. Add water if it begins to dry out, and, near the end, add a glass of wine, if you like (Port is good). It adds a strangely nutlike flavor to the gravy, a flavor which obviously would never have been discovered by any nutrition expert or Home Ec major. Somebody was just playing around.

(One word here about adding wine to any dish. It should always be put in early enough to allow the alcohol to boil out. There is nothing worse than soups, stews or sauces that taste like firewater. Let the hot-buttered-rum boys scald their throats and ruin their digestions on their own time—let the rest of us enjoy our cooking Sherry cooked.)

Playing around. Man has thrown just about everything into the pot with his meat, and no doubt a good ninety per cent of his bright ideas have long since been mercifully forgotten. But he has not played in vain. Let a woman learn only a handful of basic finishes for her meat, and she will become a *cook* instead of a housewife. Butter and cream, for example. What chicken is there—what veal, what pork—indeed, what shrimp, scallops, oysters, or clams, that will not come to a glorious end if, five minutes before they leave the stove, they are graced with a lump of butter and as many tablespoons of cream as can be spared? Add to that only a note that the grace itself can be graced with a little Sherry—or with Tabasco, or Worcestershire, or meat glaze, or soy sauce—and you have proof positive against boredom in your cooking.

(Do not tell me it is expensive. We live in an age in which saving is a subterfuge for spending. No doubt you sincerely believe that there is margarine in your refrigerator because it is more economical than butter. But you are wrong. Look in your bread drawer. How many boxes of cute snack crackers are there? How many packages of commercial cookies reeking of imitation vanilla badly masked with oil of coconut? How many presweetened breakfast cereals? Tell me now that you bought the margarine because you couldn't afford butter. You see—you can't. You bought the bread drawer goodies because you were conned into them; and you omitted the butter because you were conned out of it. The world has slipped you culinary diagrams instead of food. It counts on your palate being not only wooden, but buried under ten coats of synthetic varnish as well. Therefore, the next time you go to check out of the supermarket, simply put back one box of crackers, circle round the dairy case again, swap your margarine for a pound of butter and walk up to the checker with your head held high, like the last of the big spenders. This is no time for cost-counters: It is a time to be very rich or very poor—or both at once.)

(And but me no buts about the cream, especially if you can still buy unhomogenized milk. To be sure, those who are utterly at the mercy of the supermarket will be forced to buy their cream straight, or in the slightly dishonest form of half and half. But if you can get plain milk with cream floating on top, you are practically guaranteed a reputation as a cook. To begin with, your children will normally hate the cream; therefore, you can skim every quart of milk you use. Secondly, you can get cream of any desired weight by skimming lightly or deeply. And third, you can splash it about with a lavish hand. Fried anything can be treated to a little top of the bottle with no examination of conscience whatsoever. Once again, it is a time to be rich enough—or poor enough—to play. You have nothing to lose but your homogenized chains.)

One other basic finish: Olive oil, onion, garlic, tomato, and wine. It is the sauce that flows from one of the great watersheds of Western cooking: Provence, Italy, and the Mediterranean coast. What is in your frying pan? Chicken? Veal, pork, or lamb? Bluefish, flounder, shrimp, or crab? When it is cooked, add a few tablespoonfuls of olive oil (unless there is enough in the pan already), half an onion, chopped, and a crushed clove of garlic. Cook them briefly till they acquire a color suitable to the rest of the dish, add a mashed, peeled, fresh tomato (or the equivalent from a can) and a glass of dry wine (white for lighter meats, red for heavier, but don't make a fetish of it). Then boil it vigorously for a minute or two, and fish out the meat piece by piece and put it on the platter. When the sauce is well reduced, check the seasoning and pour it over the meat. Behold, you are ready to retire your can opener forever.

It is the finish to end all finishes. It can be put on anything, and almost anything can be added to it. You need taste, of course, but beyond that your hand is free. Parsley, rosemary, orégano, thyme; basil, tarragon, marjoram, dill; mushrooms, olives, peppers, truffles; Tabasco, Worcestershire, lemon, soy; sausages, anchovies, tongue, ham. Twenty variations and you have hardly begun. But see what you have achieved, even at that. There are 313 weekdays in the year. Divide 20 into 313, and you get 15.65. Therefore, given this one sauce only, it is obvious that with fewer than sixteen varieties of meat you can dine for an entire year without repeating yourself. But I gave you seventeen distinctions without even leaving the subject of beef. Shed a tear for the handsome widow with the middle-income mind; utter a curse on the tin ear and the wooden palate; open your eyes to the elegant oddness of the world—and then go and do something minor and monumental with your meat before you take it out of the pan.

FIVE

※

Wave Breast and Heave Shoulder

I owe you something more, however—something darker—on the subject of meat: The minor leads inexorably to the monumental. Lamb has set our feet in a large room indeed. Man not only dines; he also kills and sacrifices. The room in which he relishes the animal orders lies between slaughterhouse and temple. There are death's heads at each end of the table of the world.

No doubt we would just as soon forget them. Most cookbooks are content to sit in the kitchen and sing songs. Blood is not pretty. But no book which tries to see the whole picture —to speak not only about cooking, but to say what cooking is about—can afford to let it slide by out of mind. Man is not simply gourmet, he is carnivore and offerer as well. No matter that we are able to ignore his butchering by specialization and his priesthood by sophistication. Our home ground remains what it always has been: bloody ground and holy ground at once. Inattention explains nothing.

Go back, therefore, and look.

Once we were children,
Filling long car trips with games:
Animal, Vegetable, Mineral;
Testing the textures of creation,
    savoring the styles of its coinherence.

Mineral:
The stony reciprocities of the ribs and shanks of earth.
Granites; lavas:
    the fiery combining of elements in the bowels of the
    planet; the casting of the shell of the world; vast batho-
    liths, volcanic stones; granularity, glassiness; rock *qua*
    rock.
Slate; marble:
    the crust of earth chilled, cracked and heaved, renewed
    heats; pressures beyond imagining; juxtaposition of tex-
    ture and texture; rock recombined, metamorphosed; rock
    as forged.
Quartz and all crystals:
    perpetual structurings in seas and depths; shapes, faces,
    angles, planes; fire and water bringing forth abundantly,
    yet with no hint of life; the geometry of stone.
Sandstone; shale:
    the sedimented floor of the world; the patient settling of
    layer upon layer beneath the face of the deep; rock as a
    million leaves in the book of time.
Then, Water:
    cloud, trickle, torrent, flood; long rain gnawing the face
    of earth, advancing the coinherence by which off-scoured
    mountains feed alluvial floors; plains, deltas; fertility,
    fatness.
Vast interchanges:
    but distant, bloodless, neat.

Man offers no expiation for the death of hills.
The endless waters wash the world
Clean.

Higher, therefore.

Vegetable:
>the shooting, green, upthrusting world, the kingdom of
>seed, birth, life; no longer stone to stone, but soil to bud
>to green to leaf to yellow, orange, red, brown—and brown
>leaf to ground, to mold, corruption, rot—to soil again.

And for the first time,
>the reek of death; the stench of homelier, organic reci-
>procities; subsiding cabbage, festered lily; more than
>matter altered: freshness putrified, life lost;

Untidy mutualities
>by which, through a billion years and deaths, the white
>and rinsèd sands become black ancient earth, and vege-
>table fertility distracts the pitying mind from vegetable
>death.

Not wholly, of course, but tolerably;
>it lies closer to us than the grinding of valleys, yet
>remains leavable, assignable to compost pit or dump—the
>smell unforgettable but not graceless, the sense of having
>killed not long remembered.

Onions die quietly,
Cabbages shed no blood;
All plants forgive:
By the waters that comprise them
They wash man's hands
And let him walk away.

But for the last time.
The next kingdom brings him home.

Animal:

    cat: mouse; lion: antelope; ferret: hen; and, lastly, *man:*
    lamb, ox, pig, goat, duck, pheasant, quail, deer.

Interchange in dead earnest:

    a world in which no sparrow falls unknown, but where
    —so much for the neatness of our diagrams—it is the
    Father's will that sparrows fall,

No world of quiet, eroding stones,

    of meekly rotting cabbages,

But one of groaning births and screaming deaths,

    a savage, coinherent tissue where, in no mutual courtesy,
    the lion's whelp is fattened by the lamb.

Red in tooth and claw, we come at last

    to a fierce and painful city, to the bloody, unobliging
    reciprocity in which life lives by death, but still insists
    that death is robbery.

But more,

We come *home:*

    to butchered lamb and ox, headless chicken, stuck pig;
    to deaths not alien, to agonies unkindly kin, to our own
    screams echoed, our own eyes mirrored, parts nearly
    human pierced, and blood as plainly red as any man's.

It is a world easily protested,

    easily left for vegetarian schemes, dull apocalypses
    where the saints eat pills;

But it stands despite the antiseptic dreams,

Recalling us to what we are.

This blood,

This universal convulsion of twitching death,

    insists upon the breadth of our humanity, animal among
    animals; breaks the angelic pretense, the paltry pre-
    millennial hope by which man turns his back on flesh,
    and leaves himself too little to be saved.

In the mystery of the end, of course,
> man hurts not nor destroys in all the holy mountain,
> and lion lies down with lamb.

But before the end,
> it cannot be, unless the lion becomes a docile bag of air
> that is no lion at all—a king of beasts with nothing fit for
> general resurrection but an empty skin: a mangy, risen
> rug unfit to grace the Supper of the Lamb.

There is no way around the killing here
> that is not less than human in the end; man is what
> he is: hunter, butcher, carnivore; save him without that
> and you save nothing—manskins stuffed with sacred saw-
> dust reach no New Jerusalem; the trip is not worth the
> baggage left behind.

Raise him indeed,
> but raise him in the time of resurrection—and raise him
> *Man*—with flesh, bones and all things appertaining to the
> perfection of man's nature.

Give him
Eyes to relish twelve-jeweled walls,
Ears still soft to songs,
And risen toes
> to run along the golden, jointed stones.

Raise him not for what he is not
But bring him home himself:
> with hands still pierced by grim exchanges, glorious scars;
> and with a heart still ready for astonishment at Lion and
> Lamb

In their unimaginable concourse.

Good then.
The whole tissue kept:
> each man owning the honest interchange by which he
> steals his livelihood; each woman's hand intimate with

the crack of wrung neck and severed spine; the lion un-
emasculated; lambs still rife with woolly deaths; and all
terrible complacencies pronounced
Meet and right,
Bloody
Yet good.

But not enough.
Go back, therefore,
And look again.

In the Law of the Lord,
Leviticus, the eighth chapter, the fourteenth verse: Aaron
and his sons laying hands upon the bullock's head, blood
poured at the bottom of the altar to make reconciliation;
the caul above the liver, and the two kidneys and their
fat—all burnt by fire for a sweet savor.
Smoke, incense,
wave breast, heave shoulder, rams of consecration, the
pomegranate and the golden bell, sounding upon the
hem of the robe round about; priest and temple, death
and holocaust, always and everywhere.
Why?

It is tempting
simply to write it off as barbarism, nonsense, superstition;
to fault it and forget it;
But the fact of blood still stands,
reproving materialist and spiritualist at once; gainsaying
worlds too small and heavens too thin.
This superadded killing,
this sacrifice, these deaths which work no earthly interchange, this rich, imprudent waste
Witnesses

The City's undiminishable size:
Man wills to make of earth,
> not one Jerusalem but two; this sacramental blood de-
> clares the double mind by which he wills to lift both
> lion and lamb beyond the killing to exchanges unaccount-
> able and vast.

Man's priestliness therefore
> bespeaks his refusal of despair; proclaims acceptance of
> a world which, by its murderous hand, subscribes the
> insupportable dilemma of its being—the war of lion and
> lamb having no other, likely outcome here than two im-
> possibilities:

The one,
> a pride of victors feeding on the slain; but leaving the
> lion as he was before, trapped in ancient reciprocities by
> which at last all power falls to crows;

And the other,
> a hymn to despair no victim will accept; it is not enough,
> in this paroxysm of martyrdoms, to stand upon the ship-
> wrecks of the slain and praise the weak for weakness; the
> lamb's will, too, was life; he died refusing death.

Sacrifice therefore
Not written off, but recognized,
> a sign in blood of the vaster end of blood; a redness
> turning all things white; an impossibility prefiguring the
> last exchange of all.

The old order, of course,
> unchanged; the deaths of bulls and goats achieving
> nothing; Aaron still ineffectual; creation still bloody;

But haunted now by bells within the veil
> where Aaron walks in shadows sprinkling
> blood and bids a new Jerusalem descend.

Endless smoke now rising
Lion become priest

And lamb victim
The world awaits
The unimaginable union
By which the Lion lifts Himself Lamb slain
And, Priest and Victim,
Brings
The City
Home.

SIX

❖

The Tin Fiddle

Well, you say. How do we get back to mere cooking after *that?*

It is easier than you think. For one thing, cooking is anything but mere; and for another, the road from temple to kitchen is quite plain. It lies through the subject of knives.

We commonly define man as *homo sapiens,* the knowing animal. Yet long before he left traces of his knowing, he was busy, as men have always been, misplacing tools. It is by the hammers and the axes he never quite could keep in sight, that *homo faber,* man the maker, betrays his presence in the depths of history. The oldest fingerprints in the world are those on tools; and of all tools, the knife reigns supreme.

No doubt it was not the first. In all likelihood, man bludgeoned and tore creation before he carved and sliced it; but precisely because he was man, it could not have been long before he acquired a preference for sharp stones over dull ones. With that, the knife was invented. The rest was only a matter of materials.

Equally certainly, the knife is not the last tool. We have

gone so far beyond it now that we forget its supremacy. Our implements have grown so complex that the word tool suggests machinery before it does hand tools—and, among hand tools, it suggests wrenches and screwdrivers (tools for fixing machines) before it does knives. But for all that, the knife remains more common than them all—the one tool used by more people, more of the time, than any other. All the kitchens, and half the pockets in the world, are filled with knives. With your permission, I shall work my way through the pockets before proceeding to the kitchen. The digression is profitable.

I grant you that I have overstated the case: Not all men have pocketknives. I was carried away by the force of my upbringing. I was raised, you see, in a tradition in which it was considered improper for a man to be without a knife on his person. (Seriously. I hound my sons to carry one, just as my father hounded me, and his father him, and so on, world without end.) My grandfather had a number of *dicta,* all of which were aimed at delineating how a gentleman should comport himself. One of them was: *No gentleman should ever be without a pocketknife.* You would have to have known him to appreciate the full paradoxicality of the statement. He had the most elegant manners of any man I ever met, but he was ready for anything—fish or cut bait, figuratively or literally— at a moment's notice. I give you one more of his *dicta* to help you take the full measure of the man: *A gentleman should be able to prepare a light supper without removing his jacket.* Obviously, you would have loved him.

Both my father and grandfather preferred what they (expectedly) called gentlemen's knives: thin, graceful ones with pearl or gold handles. For myself, I have for years carried a large Swiss Army knife (the kind that has not only blades, but saws, scissors, screwdrivers, tweezers, a file, an auger, a can opener, and—again, expectedly—a corkscrew). In my father's eyes, such a knife, while admittedly fascinating and obviously useful, was gauche. It tried to be too many things at once (my father was a stickler for using only real tools, and for using them right)—and it was too bulky for a gentleman's pocket. I suppose it marks me as the degenerate son of a great house, but as long as I carry a knife at all, and keep it sharp, I hardly think my forebears will disown me.

I feel the day coming, though, when the pressure of my upbringing will force me to lay aside my portable Swiss workshop. They taught me too well. Deep in my subconscious lies the proposition: *An old man without a thin, gold pocketknife is not a real old man.* He is a man who missed his calling: no ancient priest of creation, but a superannuated acolyte who never earned the badge of his profession. My ownership of a gold knife, therefore, is only a matter of time. I could not think myself ripe without it.

What is true of my family, however, may not be true of yours. Many men are so taken up with the world of machines that they think it idle to carry a pocketknife. After all, you say, chocolate bars are scored to break easily, cigars are now manufactured with holes in their heads, and the post office efficiently breaks all package strings before they reach the addressee. Who needs a knife?

Your points are well taken. Let me direct your attention, however, to some factors you may have overlooked. First, while chocolate bars can be eaten without a knife, many of life's more satisfactory alfresco delicacies are intractable—even inaccessible—unless you have one. Candy never relieves the monotony of long family car trips half as well as an impromptu dispensation of sausages and cheese. Pepperoni, touristen-wurst, landjaeger, cervelat, salami—name what you like—any of them, thrown whole into the back seat along with Daddy's pocketknife, will provide more wholesome diversion than chocolate ever could. If your children are contentious, of course, it will tend to bring out the worst in them. But then, with contentious children, so will anything else. At least it keeps them fighting with each other, and not with their parents.

Your two other points may be dealt with more briefly. For the first: Not all cigars have holes in their heads; until they do, no wise man should go through life (unless he has elegantly sharp teeth and a miraculous bite) chomping the ends off expensive cigars. For the second: My only answer is that you have never received a package from me. What I tie up stays tied forever, unless you have a knife. You will sooner find a piece of postal clerk caught under my string than you will find the string missing from my package.

For the rest, however, let me simply ask you: How, without a pocketknife, do you pick a piece of privet blossom for a present to your second youngest daughter? How peel an orange to prove the goodness of creation? How amaze your friends with your ability to splice rope on a deserted beach? How open the clams you dig of an idle afternoon? (Even with a pocketknife, it isn't easy; but it is something a gentleman should practice till he masters.) And lastly, how is the race of men to survive boring lectures, conferences, and committee meetings without a knife with which to whittle away the time? We give gold watches when men retire. To keep them sane, we should give them gold pocketknives when they start out.

So much for the digression.

At the root of many a woman's failure to become a great cook lies her failure to develop a workmanlike regard for knives. After all, unless she has the tools and the talent with which to bone, skin, slice, and split, she must revert to the condition of her ancestors. The progress of the race, of course, enables her to serve prefried fish fillets and diced vegetables in butter sauce, but she herself regresses a million years. Her frozen vegetables are bludgeoned from the freezer with any club that comes to hand. (I have seen women use milk bottles, chair legs and even, ironically, the handle of a knife.)

Once freed from the ice, the package is torn open with bare hands and thrown in the pot. Her results may be satisfyingly modern. But her methods! She is hardly better than her primeval grandmother.

Accordingly, if she is to mend her ways—if Fannie Farmer is not to have died in vain—she will have to acquire enough knives to liberate her from slavery to "prepared" foods, and enough skill to be able to cut what she wants the way she wants it. (You think it unimportant? Think again. When was the last time you saw supermarket "Italian style" veal cutlets that were anything like as thin as they should be? How often have you given up trying to make good *roulade* of beef simply because the store cuts it so thick that each serving is the size of an overstuffed jelly roll? And, above all, how often have you paid through the nose for stew meat, when you could have cut it raw from the end of your own roast and gotten two meals for the price of one? If none of those questions strikes home, you are either no cook at all, or else a whiz with a knife. In any case, you are the exception that proves the point: The quality of butchering being what it is, the woman who wants to cook well needs a sharp knife and a good eye.)

But it takes more than saying so to bring it off. It comes as no surprise to anyone that the good eye takes time to acquire; but, unless you are wise in the ways of the world, you will be surprised how hard it is to find a decent kitchen knife. Not because good ones are unavailable, but because there are so many bad ones around that the odds are against you. If you take what comes to hand, the chances are you will get a knife that is too small, or the wrong shape, or that will not hold an edge. In any case, it will cost more than it is worth.

How can that be, you wonder? How can it happen here in the land of the better mousetrap, where quality merchandise always sells and the makers of shoddy goods invariably wind up poverty-stricken? Ah, yes! I shall spare you the chapters on aesthetic principles, personal integrity, popular taste, and political morality which a sufficient answer requires. I give you only a new category by which to examine the assumptions of your question. It is the concept of the Tin Fiddle.

Take the modern American bread knife. You undoubtedly own one: shining stainless steel, slightly curved blade, and *serrated edge*. They are sold, I suppose, by the millions. Yet if you remember your childhood—your grandmother's house perhaps—or if you were lucky enough to pick one up at a junk shop or a rummage sale, you have seen another, older kind of bread knife: stained carbon steel, straight blade, and, most important of all, a *wavy* edge. Now *there* was a bread knife. It held an edge. Better yet, its long straight blade came down flush with the board for a full eleven inches. Best of all, with two wipes on a stone and six on a steel, it would slice bread fresh from the oven. (Any knife that will not cut hot bread is not a bread knife at all. If it will not let you have bread at its best, how can it be worthy of the name?)

Now, what happened to that knife? I own an old one: It is on its third handle. But the only modern copy of it I have ever seen was useless. It had a wavy edge, all right, but the blade was curved, the steel was hopeless, and the whole thing was too short. Why can't the vast technological resources of America bring us up at least to the level of our grandmothers? That is where the tin fiddle comes in.

It is as if there were a conspiracy among violin makers (for whatever reasons) to provide the public only with violins made of metal. With enough control of the market, and with advertising sufficient to arouse the public's interest, they could reach the point at which no new wooden violins were available.

It would meet with opposition, of course. Nobody who remembered having heard a wooden violin would think the tin one as good. No professional violinist would willingly play a tin fiddle. And there would be an active market in old wooden violins. All that notwithstanding, however, the tin ones would sell. With enough manipulation, the only thing available to the man in the street would be an instrument no professional would use: partly because some people never pay enough attention to hear any difference; but mostly because the people who really care about doing things well are not numerous enough to cut much mustard in the marketplace.

The serrated bread knife, therefore, is a tin fiddle, a con-job foisted off on the nonprofessional public. So too are at least half the knives on the market, as well as a good percentage of the rest of the kitchen equipment sold for home use. (Details later. I have a number of tin fiddles earmarked for smashing.) Accordingly, if you care—if you are serious about getting a knife which can become the friend that every good cook deserves—you will have to shop carefully before you buy. You will also have to pay for what you get.

To begin with, good steel is seldom cheap, and without that, no knife can ever be the joy it should be. (A word about stainless steel. Its two advantages are obvious: It is good-looking and it is hard. For the first, it cannot be faulted; the second, however, is not quite the asset you might think. The hardness of stainless steel insures your getting a sharp knife from the factory; once that edge goes, though, it is the devil's own work to get it back. Carbon steel, on the other hand, while it looks less than elegant, is just soft enough to respond nicely to a few wipes on a steel. If you never sharpen your own knives, you will no doubt prefer stainless ones; but if you are the constant whetter of edges you ought to be, only carbon steel blades will keep you happy.)

In any case, however, good steel takes a bit of hunting for. Fortunately, there are makers who turn out excellent knives, some exclusively for kitchen use, some as formal carving sets; and with good advice and the right money you can get what you need. Perhaps the best course, however, at least for cooking knives, is to go to a restaurant supplier, and pay a good stiff price for the best he has in the size and shape you want. If you have a husband who is a tool enthusiast, by all means send him. Few men can resist a display of knives—just watch the flow of pedestrians past a cutlery store window. If your husband is the true man you think he is, he will probably buy you, not one knife, but a whole arsenal. With a little luck, he may even take on the job of keeping them sharp.

But steel is only half the story. The other half is shape. The knives normally available to the American housewife are so uniformly the wrong size and design that a tin-fiddle-style conspiracy is the only possible explanation for the situation. We buy them because we can find nothing better, but they stunt our growth as cooks. The better companies, of course, have begun to resolve the predicament, but it is still rare to go into somebody's kitchen and find tools worthy of the food to be prepared.

Admittedly, there is room for diversity of opinion on the subject of knives. My wife, for example, swears by a wicked-looking, broad-bladed carbon steel butcher knife; I lean toward the choy doh, or Chinese cleaver. Perhaps the best advice is to let yourself be guided by real professionals and expert amateurs: Within the bounds of your preference, use only knives that are acceptable to people who care about knives. I do, however, make one suggestion unequivocally. Try using a short (4½-inch) French chef's knife as your ordinary paring and slicing tool. (The Swiss make particularly nice ones.) Unless I am completely wrong, you will soon send your husband back to the restaurant supply house for another. *That's* a knife for you.

One word about cleavers. They are, of course, more danger-ous than other knives, and no one who is fundamentally un-handy should be allowed within hailing distance of them. Then too, the larger sizes are meant for use only on pro-fessional butcher blocks; they can demolish an ordinary counter board in short order. Even granting all that, however, I still cannot conceive of a kitchen without one. (Don't stint here—don't buy a cute "household" job. Get a small professional one, or try to find a Chinese choy doh.) If you use it for nothing more than cutting up fryers and dismembering turkey carcasses, it will be worth ten times its cost; and if you learn all its tricks, it will be priceless. Properly edged and skillfully used, a cleaver will prepare whole meals without the assistance of another knife.

But it does more. It bolsters your ego as a cook. Parting chickens with aplomb, you begin to believe you really might make it. And so does everyone else. A woman with cleaver in mid-swing is no mere woman. She breaks upon the eye of the beholder as an epiphany of power, as mistress of a house in which only trifles may be trifled with—and in which she defines the trifles. A man who has seen women only as gentle arrangers of flowers has not seen all that women have to offer. Unsuspected majesties await him.

In the end, however, sharpness is everything in a knife. Correctness of shape and quality of steel come to nothing unless the edge is given loving care. Blessed is the woman whose husband surreptitiously touches up her knives. It may cost her a few surprise cuts now and then, but they are a small price for perfection. Thrice blessed, though, is the woman who does the job herself.

To do it well, she will need a good stone and a good steel: the stone for intermittent, major whettings; and the steel for the all-important six strokes or so before any job at all. As I have said, the best equipment is professional equipment: a long, well-handled stone, and an even longer, heavy steel. Nonetheless, many carving sets come with decent, if short, steels. If you have a good one, root it out of its velvet-lined case in the sideboard and make it earn its keep in the kitchen drawer. Put it to work—all the time. (In place of a butcher's stone, the hardware store will sell you a scythe stone at very little cost. It has no handle or guard, of course, so you will have to watch what you are doing. But it does the job nicely.)

Above all, however, learn the right way to sharpen knives. Watch anyone who does it well. It takes a little nerve to do it properly—drawing the blade *toward* you—but it is the way it's done by those who do it all the time; and it's done that way because it works: The experience of the race should not be allowed to go for naught. Your reward will be tools that help instead of hinder, that invite use rather than despair. Raw meat will not render you inoperative; you will approach ripe tomatoes as a virtuoso approaches difficult passage work: with confidence and delight in doing. You will become the Isaac Stern of the cutting board.

You will also be provided with an instant rejoinder to anyone who presumes to lecture you on housewifery as an abject capitulation to the feminine mystique. Simply let him see you presiding over your kitchen with steel in one hand and butcher knife in the other. Execute six well-drawn strokes, and his words will turn to ashes in his mouth. He was ready only for a maladjusted prisoner of the pantry; you have showed him instead one of the priestly archtypes of the race. Mystique indeed! He has hardly scratched the surface.

Before leaving the subject of knives, however, there are two matters of omission to be dealt with. I have not given you an orderly list of the knives I consider necessary in a proper kitchen, and I have not given myself an opportunity to speak out against the insensitivity of electrifying the domestic cutting process.

First then, the List.

One good carving set (knife, fork, and steel) for state occasions. This will be adequate for small roasts and modest birds. It will not do, however, for standing ribs of beef or for large turkeys (unless you're willing to settle for less than magnificent slices of breast). For great roasts, use your longest kitchen knife.

One large (large for you, not for the butcher—8–10 inches will do nicely) broad-bladed butcher knife, for heavy-duty kitchen work on meats.

One large (8–10 inches) French chef's knife, for general use, but especially for vegetables. (Until they learn better, most women choose, and use, knives that are too small to do the job with efficiency and élan. Think big. Great cooking is not the work of small minds.)

One wavy bread knife—if you can find it. Otherwise talk someone into willing you one.

One cleaver (7 inches, about 1 pound), for a thousand uses. Just be careful.

One small (4½ inches) French chef's knife, for paring, boning and incidentals.

One very long (11–12 inches) straight-bladed carving knife. This is commonly called a roast-beef slicer, and several companies make good ones. It has a pointed end. The slimmer, shorter, round-tipped version is called a ham slicer. If you can only afford one, take the larger. Think big.)

Last, one large-size slotted vegetable parer—the kind with the open metal handle and the freewheeling blade. (You see, I am not against gadgetry altogether—especially when it is as effective as this, and enables you to fob off onto ten-year-olds the job of peeling carrots and potatoes.)

Just be sure that the knives have the best possible handles consistent with good steel. Good composition handles will last almost forever if they are not burned, but wooden ones are a problem. Some of the best knives have distinctly inferior handles, so don't hesitate to shape them a little more to your liking, if you can. Above all, though, keep wooden-handled knives out of the automatic dishwasher. It is a wonderful machine, but it will crack wood in a matter of weeks. Wash your good knives by hand, along with the pots.

(I hope it is also clear that when a fine blade loses its handle, it is not to be retired, pensioned off, or—God forbid—discarded. Move heaven and earth if necessary, but find someone who will make you a new one. Abandoning a knife without a handle is like forsaking a friend just because he is poor. It takes a defect in character to go through with it.)

That knives should be used on boards, and not sink or counter tops, goes without saying. Let me go further, therefore, and suggest that your cutting boards be numerous: a chopping block, if you can manage it, then a bread board, a fish board, and an onion board. Except for the chopping block, these can succeed each other in a kind of hierarchy. A new board is always a bread board; a retired bread board becomes a fish board (for filleting and skinning); and a retired fish board becomes an onion board. The principle is simple: At any given period in its life, a board will come into contact with nothing stronger than that for which it is named. A retired onion board, accordingly, becomes firewood. None of them, obviously, should ever see the inside of a dishwasher.

Finally, however, my protest.

I am against the electric knife personally, and against the electric knife sharpener absolutely.

To take the latter first, it is one of the greatest tin fiddles on the market. The only people who use it are people who don't care about knives. To begin with, it is not a sharpener, but a grinder. A well-treated knife, however—one kept abreast of its destiny by stone and steel—will never need grinding. (My father had a carving knife which he kept razor-sharp for thirty-five years with nothing but a steel. There was not a scratch on the blade. My knives are as sharp as his were, but not as beautiful. We are descended, you see, from men whom we shall be lucky if we match. There were giants in the earth in those days.)

The electric grinder is a dull tool. Its angles are usually too steep for a long-lasting edge, it turns over a burr large enough to stop peas, and, in the hands of anyone but a genius, it will, in six short months, turn a die-straight edge into a series of gruesomely notched curves. Add to that the fact that it literally eats knives, and you have more than enough reasons for never bothering with it. Anyone who can use it well is already intelligent enough not to use it at all.

The electric knife, however, is a more complex problem. I grant you that there are people who carve better with one than without. So far I allow it. I would rather see a roast sliced by electricity than mangled by a clown with a dull knife. I have watched beautiful roasts dismantled by inept carvers, and I know the anguish it involves. It would be less painful—and neater—to see them kicked apart with a pointed shoe. I have also eaten Smithfield ham in great half-inch-thick slabs hacked off by a knife whose last sharpening took place at the knife factory. Anything that will spare mankind the torture of chewing its way through tough meat to searing thirst is on the side of the angels.

But for myself, I beg to be excused from the general stampede of progress. By one of the ironies of fate, I do in fact own an electric knife. After brief use, it was placed on permanent loan to a friend. Not that it did not do what it was supposed to do—it did; and it was admirably ingenious in the bargain. It is just that, having learned the trade from experts, I found it gross, noisy, and unnecessary. When my father or grandfather carved, knife and hand were an inseparable unity; the whole process a silent display of grace. I could as soon imagine them with wires connected to their brains, as see them wanting cords to run their knives. I grew up with *artists*, you see—with philosophers who remembered that everything new is not necessarily better than everything old. The electric carving knife, therefore, makes no more sense to me than a motor-driven palette knife or a steam-powered violin bow. When Isaac Stern changes his ways, it will be time enough for me to think about mending mine.

It isn't stubbornness. It's just that, once you've seen giants, you don't forget so easily.

✥

SEVEN

Living Water

Meanwhile, back at the stove . . .

You no doubt feel that it is high time for a speedy return to the pot of lamb stew that was left simmering at the end of Chapter Three. If I assess your mood correctly, you judge that the intervening chapters, with their excursions into meat, metaphysics, and metalware respectively, should have been more than enough to allay the author's apparently morbid dread of proceeding too hastily through a recipe. After all, you say, what we have in hand here is a very minor stew indeed. Why will he not simply thicken the gravy as he pleases, and get on with it?

Let me say, first, that I understand your impatience. I am as much a product of the age of hurry, of the era of instant results, as you are. I, too, have been saddled with a conscience that winces at delay and feels obliged to apologize for anything longer than a laundry list. I understand—but I do not agree. The feet-on-the-stove stance of this book is a deliberate attempt to cure myself, and anyone else who will listen, of the nasty habit of worrying the world to pieces like a terrier with a rag. What we are up to here is not the hasty shaking loose of a culinary result, but a patient rumination on cooking itself. There are more important things to do than hurry.

That, of course, has always been true—even when most men had to work so hard that contemplation seemed a luxury. The day after tomorrow, however, it will be truer still. If the prophets of automation and cybernation are right, leisure, not labor, is going to be the normal condition of man. Men will become philosophers, artists, and poets just to stay sane: Contemplation will be the only defense against drowning in our own spare time. Even now, the doctrine of justification by work is difficult to defend. Jobs are shorter and more boring than they used to be. It's hard to believe that five hours of a day of button-pushing and paper-shuffling are the heart and soul of human existence. Heaven help us, then, in the bright new day of the guaranteed income and the twenty-hour week. The grim old religion of salvation by rushing will go bankrupt altogether, and we shall go straight out of our minds—unless we learn to sit still.

The habit of contemplation, therefore—the ability to sit down in front of something and care enough to let it speak for itself —cannot be acquired soon enough. Accordingly, I invite you, too, to put your feet up on the stove. If some true believer in the gospel of haste comes along and asks us why we are wasting time, we shall tell him we are busy getting the seats of our pants properly shined up for the millennium.

Such as it is, that is all the apology anybody gets for my postponing the thickening of the stew a while longer. Its juices have been given short shrift: Stock and wine must not be neglected.

Admittedly, the Scriptures begin and end with water. There is a river in Eden, and there is a river in the Heavenly Jerusalem: All life comes from the sea. Equally certainly, without water, no life is possible in between. No man can praise it enough. It is the root of freshness, the sign of purity, the means of grace. Most of all, it is the element that makes earth Earth, the principal ornament of the round world, the blue mantle of what must be a stunning planet indeed.

But for all that, plain water is not the world's best gift to a stew. What is needed in cooking is living water, water elated to new eminences, water transformed into *stock*. To be sure, there are dishes best cooked in plain water. Rice, for example, while delicious when prepared with stock, is even better cooked with nothing but water and salt—provided, of course, you are a lover of the taste and smell of plain rice. It is possible to overdo the use of stock—I have eaten meals which tasted as if they had been floated to the dining room on a river of consommé. Too much of a good thing is as bad as too little.

Abuses, however, should not be allowed to dictate use. Indeed, while on the subject of abuses, it ought to be said that Americans, by and large, use too much water in their cooking. All foods are full of juices. A handful of lettuce, for example, dropped into a hot, lightly oiled pan and cooked covered for three or four minutes will be found to have drowned in its own liquor. (Just add a little salt and pepper—and a drop of vinegar or lemon juice—and you have an excellent vegetable. Lettuce, for all its reputation as a tasteless doily on which to serve shrimp, is full of surprises.) If, however, you were to take that same handful of lettuce and boil it in a cup of water, its essential juices would be hopelessly diluted—fit at the end only for the kitchen sink. As for the lettuce itself, half its flavor would have gone down the drain.

Lettuce is perhaps an extreme example, though it is amazing how many vegetables can be cooked with little or no added water at all. Even the hardest ones—like carrots and turnips—if sliced thin enough will be twice as flavorful for having been gently wilted rather than boiled to death. The rule for deciding how much water to use is simple: Generally speaking, any cooking water you throw away is excess water;

if you use that much less, your food will have that much more taste. This is the secret of the Chinese method of cooking vegetables: No liquid is thrown away; therefore no flavor is lost. Nor is it only an oriental device—it is known in Western cooking as the Greek method. It is also the reason why boiled potatoes never taste as good as the steamed ones you eat like apples at a clambake. (Which brings up another fascinating fact. Not only do vegetables have enough water to cook themselves, most of them also have enough salt. Approached in the true contemplative spirit—given a chance to speak for themselves—they are self-sufficient. There is no reason for the oceans of brine in which we usually drown them.)

In the case of a stew, however, the goal is to have a generous amount of liquid left at the end of the process. The pot liquor is not thrown away but served. How sad, then, if it began as mere water, if it represents only a dilution of the juices of the meat. Let me illustrate by reference to what is probably the worst-made sauce in America today: unthickened roast-beef pan gravy—the *jus* from beef *au jus*.

You are no doubt familiar with the traditional method. The roast is removed to the platter, and the pan is placed over a top burner. A little water is added, and the pan is scraped and stirred until all the color and flavor are released. So far, so good. At this point, the wise gravy maker would stop. If he were to taste his product, it would probably be excellent— strong, dark, and salted to perfection. The scant half cup or so would serve no more than two. But it would be worthy of any two in the world.

Unfortunately, however, the economics of family life weigh in on him. He thinks of his potato-eating sons, of his bread-dunking daughters, of his own habit of spooning gravy straight from sauce boat to mouth, and of his wife's insistence on some leftover juice for the next day's cold roast beef. He must make two cups of gravy at least, if even half of these demands are to be met. Enter here, therefore, the irretrievable error. He reaches for the kettle, and floods the pan with water.

The American kitchen tragedy begins its inexorable denouement. Natural color and saltiness pale to insignificance; original flavor fades to a distant echo of itself. To revive the color, he reaches for a bottle of caramelized gravy additive; to adjust the seasoning, he pours in salt. But rescuing the flavor is now a double problem: He must not only make it taste like beef again; he must also do something to kill the college dining hall taste of the commercial gravy stretcher he threw in. At this point, he may well panic. Beef extract, bouillon cubes, Worcestershire, A-1, ketchup, garlic and even curry may follow each other in frantic succession. He is trapped. If he uses none of them, he gets tasteless gravy; if he uses some or all, he gets only another one of Daddy's memorable palate-shockers to add to his list of things that seemed like a good idea at the time.

His error, of course, was all that water. He worked the modest juices of his beef to death. If only he had used stock: a good grade of canned bouillon (one without too much extraneous spice and zip—he should not avoid Worcestershire simply to run afoul of clove); or, better yet, a homemade veal (or chicken) stock. You are surprised? White stock in beef gravy? Set your prejudices aside. I give you my own method.

To your roasting pan, add a full quart of mild veal stock (recipe later), turn the fire up high, scrape, stir and boil until it is reduced to half the original quantity. Skim the fat and serve. The color? Beautiful. White stock is no longer white after this treatment. Reducing in an open pan continually browns the stock itself at the edges. If the pan was a good color to begin with, the gravy will be beautiful. The seasoning? Perfect. The stock you added was, as all cooking stocks should be, undersalted (in anticipation of reduction); a little pepper is all you will need. No more fake stove-top virtuosity; no wild pulling of bottle after bottle off the shelf like E. Power

Biggs gone mad at the console of the mighty Wurlitzer. Just gravy made once, and right. And the flavor? Well, I leave my case in your hands. Unless you are hopelessly conditioned to commercial tastes, it will make your heart leap. Imagine! Beef gravy; natural, plentiful, and good!

Stock, therefore, not water—whenever it is a matter of meat.

For guidance, I give you this simple working rule: *Any liquid added to a meat dish should be at least tolerable as a soup to begin with.* Soup itself, of course, is another subject. It is stock raised to the height of its natural eminence, and, except for broths, bouillons and consommés, it is stock rejoicing in the pleasure of other creatures' company. But even the thickest soup will be better for having been started with a base of good stock. Pepper pot, for example, should begin with chicken. Oxtail with brown stock, and minestrone (yes, I know it can be made with water) should start with anything you have left in the freezer. Such soups have body willy-nilly; what they cry out for is a soul, and mere water cannot provide it. Made with a good gelatinous stock, they will pass the crucial test for great soup: Mere thickness is not enough; a soup has fulfilled its destiny only when it can be served cold in slices.

Accordingly, what is needed is a practical system for keeping stock on hand all the time. It should be as available as tap water, and only slightly less convenient to use. Fortunately, between the better grades of canned products, and the almost unlimited resources of the home freezing compartment, you should have no difficulty keeping yourself in stock at all times.

Take the commercial varieties first. Perhaps the best product on the market is plain beef bouillon as put out by the large soup manufacturers. Campbell's makes a particularly fine one, and, on the whole, it is better (and cheaper) than any brown stock that can be made in the home—unless you are willing to spend inordinate amounts of time at it. It has the virtue of being mostly beefy, and its seasonings are moderate so as not to prejudice the eventual flavor of any dish. For general cooking, it is vastly to be preferred to canned consommé, which, however excellent is its own right, is simply too jazzy for most foods. (I will insist, of course, that no one who cares about cooking should go to his grave without having tried his hand at real homemade brown stock. There is a meat-bone-and-marrow goodness which even the best commercial product misses. You have probably tasted it once or twice in a good French restaurant. It would be a shame not to know how to achieve it yourself.)

After canned bouillon, however, the quality of commercial stocks declines rapidly. There are, to be sure, canned chicken stocks, but they are nowhere near as good as what can be made at home, and, more important, they are no cheaper, and hardly more convenient. Unlike brown stock, the white variety is quick and cheap. It is simply a matter of boiling bones and freezing the result. In an emergency, of course, a couple of cans of chicken broth are an asset, but if you manage your freezing compartment well, you will seldom need them. White stock is as easy as duck soup.

Next, in descending order, are the other short cuts to stock. Dehydrated soups: The brown ones are either terribly oniony or terribly commercial, if not both at once. The white ones are better (you can, for example, remove the dry noodles from a package of chicken noodle soup mix and boil up only the dehydrated chicken part of it), but they are out of balance: too little chicken flavor and too much seasoning. Bouillon cubes are another step down. They contain far too little beef or chicken to qualify for much besides the retrieving of otherwise hopeless disasters. Read the labels. If you have a taste for hydrolized plant protein, they are just the thing for you. If not, go back up the ladder a bit. Commercial meat glazes—Bovril, for example—are more or less in the same category.

They have, admittedly, more meat in them, but they are exceedingly salty, and the flavor of the beef tea made by dissolving a teaspoonful in a cup of hot water moves one to something less than ecstasy. There is more than a hint of the old glue pot about it. It makes you think sadly of poor old Dobbin.

At the bottom are the so-called gravy mixes. They are simply preparations of the previous sort, adapted to instant use. I place them at the bottom, not because they taste much worse, but because they do more harm. They confirm our bondage to the commercial taste by making it easier to achieve than any other. They insure the continued progress of American cooking toward institutionalism. Two more generations of instant gravy eaters and no one will remember what a domestic kitchen smelled like. Men will be able to walk into a hospital at dinnertime or into the county almshouse at the end of their days and, wonder of wonders, think fondly of Mother.

(About canned gravy I have nothing to say. Like canned spaghetti sauce, it can, of course, become an acquired taste. But then so can a lot of things, some of them rather odd. In any case, as with canned spaghetti, sauce, electric knife sharpeners, and margarine, I consider it a tin fiddle. No one who cares or knows would use it, except on occasions for which C rations would be appropriate anyway. For real cooking, I simply cannot see it. If you will excuse my blind spot, I shall pass on.)

First, a word of general counsel. The making of stock must not be thought of as an occasional act. In every well-regulated household, it will be lifted to the status of a habit. With no exceptions of time or circumstance, leftover bones and meat will be boiled before being tossed to garbage can or dog. If there are too few for immediate processing, freeze them until you have enough. Just remember that the point of domestic stockmaking is not to produce vast quantities, but to garner unique and fleeting goodness in manageable amounts. A pound or so of bone and scrap, plus a quart of water, will yield a cup or two of broth—just right for home freezing. Tucked away in an old plastic one-pint ice cream container, it will be ready at short notice when you want something more complimentary than water to finish off your veal scalloppine. As a matter of fact, huge containers of frozen stock are not only a nuisance to store; the ice picks, hatchets, and hammers needed to make them yield their goodness in a hurry constitute a real menace to life and limb.

Habitual stockmaking, therefore. The remains of two fryers, six lamb chops, one pork loin, or a breast of veal will, in each several instance, give you a singular and authentic liquor for use at leisure. Be sure to cook each kind of leftover separately, unless you have good reason to combine them; it is one of the shortest cuts of all to variety of flavor. Don't be led astray by the hymns of praise to the universal stockpot which you may find in certain fancy writers on the subject of cooking. They conjure up visions of the great restaurant kitchen where a perpetual kettle of leftovers simmers at the back of the stove. Into it are thrown all available bones and scraps, and out of it comes the triumphant dipperful of broth that lifts the dish to perfection.

It is a lovely picture, but it won't work in the home. The volume of business simply isn't great enough. In a restaurant, the perpetual stockpot varies from day to day. On Tuesday, it is beefy from Monday night's banquet of standing ribs *au jus;* on Wednesday, it is redolent of Tuesday's broiled chickens for the Friends of the Village Library. But in your kitchen or mine, it seldom gets enough of anything to lift it out of the small beer category. Worse yet, it is such a minor operation that there is a constant temptation to turn it off for a while and spare yourself the necessity of watching it. With only ordinary forgetfulness, you could easily end up with a festering pot of lukewarm garbage. Small quantities, then, made separately item by item—and each batch frozen immediately.

I once read of a man who was swept off his feet by an article on what were glowingly referred to as the "gourmet uses of the stockpot." He dutifully kept his pot at the back of his stove, and, for a whole week, he added to it bones, scraps, vegetable trimmings, and odd pot liquors. At the week's end, he suddenly renounced cooking altogether. It seems that the article had not been explicit about the necessity of turning on the fire under the pot. He had, in effect, built himself a portable, if slightly runny, compost heap. Pretensions without expertise can be devastating.

With that warning, then, here are the recipes.

BROWN STOCK

Any good cookbook will teach you how to make brown stock the expensive way. I give you here the peasant's method. It is excellent.

Get some cracked, raw bones from the butcher. Beef and veal are best (though you will probably be charged for the veal bones); pork, in combination with the others, is quite possible, but lamb and smoked meats are out. Five pounds or so will do nicely. If they smell a little gamey (you see, I hope, how far I am from being an ivory tower cook), sprinkle some baking soda on them and rinse them well. If there is no fat at all on them, ask for a little suet or pork fat. Spend as little money as possible—the cost of this stock is one of its intellectual delectabilities. Buy no meat at all: Whatever happens to have adhered to the bones will do the trick nicely (but cooked bones and meat, if you have any around, may be added halfway through the roasting process.)

Put the bones and a little suet in a large roasting pan and

cook them for two hours in a hot oven (425°). Turn them occasionally (they smell marvelous). After about an hour, add two carrots and two onions, sliced, plus a little shaved turnip, if you like. Continue cooking until everything is richly browned—until the natural sugars are well caramelized, though not, heaven forbid, burnt. (The roasting of carrots and onions, by the way, is one of the secrets of good color in brown stock. Some cooks even sprinkle in a trace of straight sugar along with the vegetables; but carrots and onions are sweet enough to do the job alone. Just don't let them go black. Nobody needs stock that tastes like cremated marshmallows.)

Remove the bones to the stockpot and cover well (about a quart to each pound of bones) with water which has first been used to rinse the roasting pan. Remember, a good bit of the color and flavor of your stock is in that pan, so rinse it over and over into the stockpot until you have captured it all. Then add a couple of sliced fresh onions, a carrot or two cut up, a little more turnip and a stalk or so of celery. Add very little salt, a large bay leaf, and a couple of peppercorns. Simmer, covered, for three or four hours. Near the end, sample the broth (dip deep—there's usually a lot of fat on top). If it is not strong enough, take the cover off and reduce it slightly. Just remember to judge it as stock, not as finished soup. When done, strain it though a fine sieve (but don't throw away the contents of the strainer), cool it quickly (uncovered) and refrigerate or freeze. Leave the fat on top until you use the stock; it comes off much more easily when cold, and it protects the broth besides.

(By the way, should you ever want to remove the fat from a batch of hot stock, try using one of those tall copper coffeepots whose long spout starts at the bottom. Simply pour your stock into it, wait a few minutes for the fat to float to the top, then pour clear stock from the spout. The first splash, of course, will have some fat in it, so put that in another dish;

so will the last, unless you are careful to stop pouring before the fat reaches the inside orifice or the spout. All in all, it is the best method around—some china manufacturers even make a gravy boat which works on the same principle. If, however, you lack such elegant equipment, do what ordinary mortals do: Select a narrow-mouthed jar too small for the stock in question (a milk bottle, for example), rinse it out with hot water and stand it in a pot. Fill it to the brim with stock, let the fat rise for a minute or so, and then slowly add the rest. The grease will flow off over the top. If you should happen to run out of stock before all the fat runs off, throw in a couple of knives, forks or spoons for added displacement. There is more than one way to skim a pot—even if you have to go back to high school physics to find it.)

Having finished your stock, however, you are now ready for the really astonishing part of the exercise.

HOMEMADE MEAT GLAZE
(Meat Extract)

Take the strainerful of bones and scraps and put them back into the stockpot. Add any scraps of meat you have around: poultry, pork, veal—even leftover hamburger—just stay away from lamb and ham. Meat extract can, of course, be made from the used bones alone, but anything that brings more natural gelatin to the pot is welcome. Cover everything deeply with cold water, *adding no salt at all*, and boil for two or three hours more.

That done, strain once again, this time into a large saucepan. Discard the bones. (They have been worked to death. Even the dog will look down his nose at them now.)

Boil the contents of the pan hard, skimming the froth from the top now and then, until the liquid is drastically reduced. When it is down to about a pint, transfer it to a smaller pan and boil on, over slightly reduced heat. Continue boiling until it reaches the consistency of a thick, blackish-brown syrup (half a cup, give or take a little). Pour this into a heatproof jar, cool, and refrigerate.

You now have, perhaps for the first time in your life, real meat extract—one of nature's marvels. It is, of course, highly concentrated gelatin, but it has been imbued with the heart and soul of meat. Its taste is beautiful. Moreover, in spite of the fact that no speck of salt went into all those quarts of water the second time around, it is salted to perfection. Its consistency is, admittedly, a little forbidding: It is not unlike a young and tender shoe heel. Refrigerated, it will keep in this state for weeks; but, obligingly enough, it melts at the temperature of the mouth. If you are any lover of food at all, you will find yourself whittling off little pieces to dissolve on your tongue at odd times of the day.

Use it ad lib. Its general effect is to give a sauce soul and substance without overpowering the proper flavor of the dish. Experiment. It improves almost anything. A tablespoonful melted in warm Hollandaise imparts a certain roundness and resonance to what is sometimes an excessively light and lemony sauce. A piece dropped on top of a hot fried egg (plus a dash of Tabasco, if you are up to it), is delightful. And in the form of Colbert Butter, it is the perfect accompaniment to steaks, chops, fish, or poultry—not to mention a piece of matzoh at three in the afternoon.

COLBERT BUTTER

To a small saucepan, add 1 tablespoon lemon juice, 1 tablespoon meat glaze, and a generous pinch of tarragon. Warm gently over very low heat until the extract melts, remove from the fire and add 5 tablespoons butter. Cream all together until smooth, and keep refrigerated till needed. You are now ready, at the drop of anyone's culinary gauntlet, for Sole Colbert, Sweetbreads Colbert, Artichoke Hearts Colbert, and Anything-else-you-like Colbert. Spread it on swordfish steak just before serving. Or on broiled bluefish. Or on your breakfast toast, if it looks as if it might go begging. It is simply superb.

Two notes. If you make more meat extract before the first is gone, just pour the new on top of the old. If, on the other hand, your experiment with homemade stock and meat glaze has left you with what looks like an excessive quantity, I suggest Knackwurst Soup (see page 210).

Admittedly, brown stock and meat extract are fussy and long-winded; though, if you made them only once in a lifetime, they would be well worth the price of admission. White stock, on the other hand, is the working cook's dream. It can be made without looking.

WHITE STOCK

Bones, scraps and water (1 quart of water to each pound of solids)

Onion, carrot, celery (sparingly; this is not vegetable soup)

Salt (stingily)

Pepper (one peppercorn to a quart)

1 small bay leaf

Savory, marjoram (just a pinch)

A few specks of garlic (very stealthily—the garlic is supposed to be an undercover agent here)

Simmer for an hour or so, cool quickly (uncovered), and refrigerate or freeze promptly.

The most delectable white stock will, of course, be made from raw veal or chicken bones. If you use boned veal of any kind, insist on the bones with your order. If you ever fillet breasts of chicken, the remnants will make the lightest, loveliest stock in the world. Just keep your eyes open for opportunities and there will be plenty of them.

More usually, however, you will make your white stock from leftovers. If you are not particular, throw in everything that is left of your veal, chicken, pork or turkey. If whiteness is a necessity, however, you will have to remove the browned parts of the meat before boiling. Remember, too, that pork, while it makes delicious white stock, makes a darker product than the others. And remember, above all, to cool white stock uncovered and quickly. Boiling does not entirely defeat certain little organisms. If they are given six or seven hours to recuperate in a lukewarm airless space, they revive mightily and ruin your stock.

Accordingly, be careful about trying to cool large quantities of white stock. Better to parcel it out in smaller pots. One of the most frantic Sunday afternoons of my life was spent trying to get together the ingredients for creamed turkey for fifty people, after the first batch (all eight quarts of it in one pot) had spent Saturday night fermenting merrily in the refrigerator. (I finally found someone with a frozen turkey—we cut it up on his band saw, and made the 7:30 P.M. deadline with not a minute to spare.)

Use your white stock anywhere, anytime. Don't hesitate to add it to dark gravies or soups, don't be afraid to use it for vegetables, and, by all means, don't forget to use it for basting. Faithfully made and diligently used, it will become your culinary right hand, and the daily working odor of your kitchen. I recall it as the smell of my grandmother's house. To this day, steaming veal stock (suitably reduced), served in a flat soup plate with chopped parsley, transports me instantly to her presence. The nose has the longest memory of all—though it helps if the soup plate is white with a green and gold border.

We have come a long way from plain water. There are stocks we have not even celebrated. Court bouillon, the fastest of all: 1 carrot, 1 onion, 1 stalk celery, cut fine, and cooked in butter for 3 minutes; then a quart of water, a tablespoonful of lemon juice, a bay leaf, a few peppercorns, a clove and a sprig of parsley—all boiled for 1 minute only. Fish stock: a slightly longer court bouillon with fish bones and white wine in place of some of the water. And, last of all, the pot liquors: Their uses are limited (not all vegetable waters are complementary to sauces) but I am willing to nominate two of them for awards: turnip liquor and mushroom juice. The turnip is one of the lordliest vegetables in the world; its broth is practically a soup in itself. And the mushroom? Ah! It is the proof of creation *ex nihilo,* the paradigm of the marvelously solid unnecessariness of the world. How anything so nearly nothing could at the same time be so emphatically something—how the Spirit brooding upon the face of the waters could have brought forth this . . . well, words fail, and mystery reigns.

Which, after all, is as it should be: As far as we have come from water, we have further still to go.

❖

EIGHT

Water in Excelsis

Water above the firmament:
> winter rain descending; the roots of *vitis vivifera* clutch-
> ing earth.

Spring warmth:
> water drawn through vinestock, stem, and leaf; tendril,
> flower, fruit.

Summer heat:
> sun fierce upon the hills; in the grape now, water, glucose,
> fructose, tannin, acid; all beneath the thin firmament on
> which the Spirit's brooding leaves behind a bloom of
> yeast; *Saccharomyces ellipsoideus:* the thumbprint of the
> Lord and Giver of life.

Then autumn:
> basket, press, vat; sugar and yeast wantoning; earth's old
> September love revived: $C_6H_{12}O_6 = 2C_2H_5OH + 2CO_2$; fer-
> mentation; the warm must, its jaunty cap set drunkenly,
> rejoices in the pleasure of good company.

Here sing and brawl now
> alcohol, carbonic acid gas, acetic acid, higher alcohols,
> succinic acid, glycerol, and, chief among them,

Water come of age
> in the vast pots of this old Cana, where the Word, in
> silence, orders up new wine.

Finally:
> racking off, barreling, clearing, bottling; the long wait—
> for esters: alcohol and acid reconciled, wine bodied forth
> to roundness and a nose; for oxidation: tannin and al-
> cohol softened, corners smoothed by the Spirit's thumb,
> purple shaded to brown

Until
> (in Heaven it is alwaies Autumne) earth's last best gift
> is brought to sere and velvet elegance,

To Wine indeed

To Water *in excelsis.*

To raise a glass, however, is to raise a question. One honest
look at any real thing—one minute's contemplation of any
process on earth—leads straight into the conundrum of the
relationship of God to the world. The solution is hardly obvious. For something that could not *be* at all without God,
creation seems to *do* rather well without Him. Only miracles
are simple; nature is a mystery. Autumn by autumn, He
makes wine upon a thousand hills, but He does it without
tipping His hand. Glucose, fructose, and *Saccharomyces ellipsoideus* apparently manage very nicely on their own. So
much so, that the resolving of the conflict between the sacred
and the secular (or, better said, the repairing of the damage
done by divorcing them) has been billed as the major problem
of modern theology. Permit me, therefore, glass in hand and
cooking Sherry within easy reach, the world's most interrupted
discourse on the subject. *In vino veritas.*

Take the largest part of that truth first. God makes wine.
For all its difficulties, there is no way around the doctrine of
creation. But notice the tense: He *makes;* not *made.* He did
not create *once upon a time,* only to find himself saddled

now with the unavoidable and embarrassing result of that first rash decision. That is only to welsh on the idea of an unnecessary world, to make creation a self-perpetuating pool game which is contingent only at the start—which needs only the first push on the cue ball to keep it going forever. It will not do: The world is more unnecessary than that. It is unnecessary *now;* it cries in this moment for a cause to hold it in being. It was St. Thomas, I think, who pointed out long ago that if God wanted to get rid of the universe, He would not have to *do* anything; He would have to *stop doing* something. Wine *is*—the fruit of the vine stands in act, outside of nothing—because it is His very present pleasure to have it so. The creative act is contemporary, intimate, and immediate to each part, parcel and period of the world.

Do you see what that means? In a general way we concede that God made the world out of joy: He didn't need it; He just thought it was a good thing. But if you confine His activity in creation to the beginning only, you lose most of the joy in the subsequent shuffle of history. Sure, it was good back then, you say, but since then, we've been eating leftovers. How much better a world it becomes when you see Him creating at all times and at every time; when you see that the preserving of the old in being is just as much creation as the bringing of the new out of nothing. Each thing, at every moment, becomes the delight of His hand, the apple of His eye. The bloom of yeast lies upon the grapeskins year after year because He likes it; $C_6H_{12}O_6=2C_2H_5OH+2CO_2$ is a dependable process because, every September, He says, That was nice; do it again.

Let us pause and drink to that.

To a radically, perpetually unnecessary world; to the restoration of astonishment to the heart and mystery to the mind; to wine, because it is a gift we never expected; to mushroom and artichoke, for they are incredible legacies; to improbable acids and high alcohols, since we would hardly have thought of them ourselves; and to all being, because it is superfluous: to the hairs on Harry's ear, and to the seven hundred and sixty-eighth cell from the upper attachment of the right gluteus maximus in the last girl on the chorus line. *Prosit,* Dear Hearts. *Cheers,* Men and Brethren. We are free: nothing is needful, everything is for joy. Let the bookkeepers struggle with their balance sheets; it is the tippler who sees the untipped Hand. God is eccentric; He has *loves,* not reasons. *Salute!*

But there is more. He creates in a mystery. What He holds intimately and contemporaneously in being, acts, nonetheless, for itself. The secular is not the sacred. Creation exists in its own right, is no parable, no front, no Punch and Judy show in which God plays all the parts, but a vast and raucous meeting where each thing acts out its nature, shouts I am I, as if no other thing had being. The world exists, not for what it means but for what it is. The purpose of mushrooms is to be mushrooms; wine is in order to wine: Things are precious before they are contributory. It is a false piety that walks through creation looking only for lessons which can be applied somewhere else. To be sure, God remains the greatest good, but, for all that, the world is still good in itself. Indeed, since He does not need it, its whole reason for being must lie in its own goodness; He has no use for it; only delight.

Just think what that means. We were not made in God's image for nothing. The child's preference of sweets over spinach, mankind's universal love of the toothsome rather than the nutritious is the mark of our greatness, the proof that we love the secular as He does—for its secularity. We have eyes which see what He sees, lips which praise what He praises, and mouths which relish things, because He first pronounced them *tov.* The world is no disposable ladder to heaven. Earth is not convenient, it is good; it is, by God's design, our lawful love.

Another toast then.

To Da Vinci's notebooks; to Einstein's preoccupations; to Mozart and to Bach, and to the child who hears a canon for the first time in *"Frère Jacques"*; to the singularities of chalk and cheese and to the delectabilities of all things, visible and invisible; *l'chaim* because it is good; *to health,* for no reason but itself; to men because they are men, to women without explanation, and to the good company of every secular thing *in saecula saeculorum.* Toast them with their own watchword: *Here's how!*

So far, so good then. God intimately creative; but things uniquely themselves. The paradox of being, by which the secular stands gloriously free of the sacred—on which it utterly depends. What next?

Ah, mischief. Man is not always content to take reality at such widths and depths. He cuts the wine of paradox with the water of consistency: The mystery of God *and* things is tamed to the simplicity of God *or* things; he builds himself a duller, skimpier world.

If he is a pagan, he abolishes the secular in favor of the sacred. The world becomes filled with gods. To improve his wine, he searches, not for purer strains of yeast, but for better incantations, friendlier gods. He spends his time in shrines and caves, not chemistry. Things, for him, become pawns in the chess game of heaven. Religion devours life.

On the other hand, if he is a secularist, he insists that God must have no part in the world at all. That God has made *Saccharomyces ellipsoideus* competent enough to ferment sugar on its own, becomes, for him, a proof that He never made it at all. Poor man! To be so nearly right, and so devastatingly wrong! To hit so close, yet miss the mark completely. Yeast, without God, to give it as a gift, ceases to be good company. It becomes merely useful—a mechanism contributory to other mechanisms. And those, in turn, to the vast mechanism of the whole. And that, at last, to—well, he is hard put to say just what. He has found the sewing machine and lost the thread of delight. Unique goodnesses are swallowed up in process.

Worse yet, if he is a contemporary theologian, he acquires an irrational fear of natural theology. He distrusts people who claim to see the *vestigia Dei,* the footprints of God, in creation; he blames them for being pagans, filling the world with gods. Poor man, again! The *vestigia Dei* are not irrelevant divinities ruffling the surface of a matter for which they have no sympathy. They are rather the tracks of God's figureskating upon the ice of the world. They are evidences of play, not pilgrimage. He cuts them, not to make a point, but because ice cries out for such virtuosity. They prove He knows what the world is for.

So with all things. Creation is God's living room, the place where He sits down and relishes the exquisite taste of His decoration. Things, therefore, *as things,* are inseparable from God, *as God.* Separate the secular from the sacred, and the world becomes an idol shrouded in interpretations; creation becomes too meaningful to make love to. As religion devoured life for the pagan, so significance consumes the world of the secularist. Delectability goes by the boards, dullness reigns, and earth becomes a sitting duck for confidence men and tinfiddle manufacturers of all sorts. Poor earth, poor stars, poor flesh. Without a Giver, they never become themselves.

We have arrived at an untoastable condition. Turn your glass upside down for a moment. There are demons to be exorcized.

> *Omnes dii gentium daemonia sunt; Dominus autem coelos fecit.* Deliver us, O Lord, from religiosity and Godlessness alike, lest we wander in fakery or die of boredom. Restore to us Thyself as Giver and the secular as Thy gift. Let idols perish and con jobs cease. Give repentance and better minds to all pagans and secularists; in the meantime, of Thy mercy, keep them out of our cellars.

Now we may drink.

To the world, which belongs to those with tongues to taste it: *Na Zdrovie!* To God Who gives the world to those with tongues: *Er lebe hoch!* And to the vast paradox by which the One enjoys the other: *Bottoms up!* Creation deserves the most resounding slap we can give it. *Min skål, din skål, alla vackra flickors skål.* He fathers forth whose beauty is past change. Praise Him!

One might have hoped that, with so gracious a creature as wine, even the most ardent religionists and secularists would have made an exception to their universal custom of missing the point of things. But alas, between teetotalism on the one hand and the habit of classifying it as an alcoholic beverage on the other, they have both lost the thread of delight.

Consider first the teetotalers. They began, no doubt, by observing that some men use wine to excess—to the point at which, though the wine remains true to itself, the drinker does not. That much, I give them: Drunks are a nuisance. But they went too far. Only the ungrateful or the purblind can fail to see that sugar in the grape and yeast on the skins is a divine idea, not a human one. Man's part in the process consists of honest and prudent management of the work that God has begun. Something underhanded has to be done to grape juice to keep it from running its appointed course.

Witness the teetotaling communion service. Most Protestants, I suppose, imagine that it is part of the true Reformed religion. But have they considered that, for nineteen centuries after the institution of the Eucharist, wine was the only element available for the sacrament? Do they seriously envision St. Paul or Calvin or Luther opening bottles of Welch's Grape Juice in the sacristy before the service? Luther, at least, would turn over in his grave. The WCTU version of the Lord's Supper is a bare 100 years old. Grape juice was not commercially viable until the discovery of pasteurization; and, unless I am mistaken, it was Mr. Welch himself (an ardent total abstainer) who persuaded American Protestantism to abandon what the Lord obviously thought rather kindly of.

That much damage done, however, the itch for consistency took over with a vengeance. Even the Lord's own delight was explained away. One of the most fanciful pieces of exegesis I ever read began by maintaining that the Greek word for wine, as used in the Gospels, meant many other things than wine. The commentator cited, as I recall, *grape juice* for one meaning, and *raisin paste* for another. He inclined, ultimately, toward the latter.

I suppose such people are blessed with reverent minds which prevent them from drawing irreverent conclusions. I myself, however, could never resist the temptation to read raisin paste for wine in the story of the Miracle of Cana. "When the ruler of the feast had tasted the water that was made raisin paste . . . he said unto the bridegroom, 'Every man at the beginning doth set forth good raisin paste, and when men have well drunk [*eaten?*—the text is no doubt corrupt], then that which is worse: but thou hast kept the good raisin paste until now.'" Does it not whet your appetite for the critical *opera omnia* of such an author, where he will freely have at the length and breadth of Scripture? Can you not see his promised land flowing with peanut butter and jelly; his apocalypse, in which the great whore Babylon is given the cup of the ginger ale of the fierceness of the wrath of God?

The secularists, on the other hand, are no better. They classify wine as an alcoholic beverage, which makes about as much sense as classifying cheese as a salted food. Alcohol occurs all over the place; bread has its share, rotten apples do very well by it, hard cider is amply provided with it, and distilled spirits are full of it. How foolish, therefore, to encourage people to think of alcoholic content as the principal identifying note of wine. The general classification, of course, is legitimate enough as far as it goes. But it is hardly more than slightly relevant. Apart from an intellectual fascination, I have no *consuming* interest in alcohol; nor, I think, does any sane man. It is tasteless, odorless, indigestible, and, in sufficient doses, blinding. Far from being the only, or even the most notable, ingredient in wine, it is simply one member of a vast committee—and not the most responsible member at that.

Nothing appalls me more than to hear people refer to the drinking of wine as if it were a forbidden and fascinating way of sneaking alcohol into one's system. My flesh creeps when I hear the legitimate love of the fruit of the vine treated as if it were a longer-winded way of doing what the world does with grain neutral spirits and cheap vermouth. With wine at hand, the good man concerns himself, not with getting drunk, but with *drinking in* all the natural delectabilities of wine: taste, color, bouquet; its manifold graces; the way it complements food and enhances conversation; and its sovereign power to turn evenings into occasions, to lift eating beyond nourishment to conviviality, and to bring the race, for a few hours at least, to that happy state where men are wise and women beautiful, and even one's children begin to look promising. If someone wants the bare effects of alcohol in his bloodstream, let him drink the nasty stuff neat, or have a physician inject it. But do not let him soil my delight with his torpedo-juice mentality.

Wine is not—let me repeat—in order to anything but itself. To consider it otherwise is to turn it into an idol, a tin god to be conjured with. Moreover, it is to miss its point completely. We were made in the image of God. We were created to delight, as He does, in the resident goodness of creation. We were not made to sit around mumbling incantations and watching our insides to see what creation will do for us. Wine does indeed have subjective effects, but they are to be received gratefully and lightly. They are not solemnly im-

portant psychophysical adjustments, but graces, super-added
gifts. It was St. Thomas, again, who gave the most reasonable
and relaxed of all the definitions of temperance. Wine, he said,
could lawfully be drunk *usque ad hilaritatem,* to the point of
cheerfulness. It is a happy example of the connection between sanctity and sanity.

Once wine is defined as an alcoholic beverage, however,
sanity is hard to come by. As a nation, we drink the way we
exercise: too little and too hard. Our typical gala dinner
party is a disaster: three or four rounds of martinis followed
by a dinner with two tiny glasses of middling Burgundy. The
food is wolfed without discernment, the wine is ignored, and
the convivialities come on so early that no one is up to the
profundities when they arrive.

How much better if we would forget, at least in our dinnering, the alcoholic idiocy—if we would provide our guests
with long evenings of nothing but sound wine, good food, and
fit company. Try it sometime. Sherry or Cinzano or Dubonnet
—or, best of all, a good rainwater Madeira before dinner. No
gin, no whiskey—and, in the name of all that's holy, no
vodka. More important still, no dips, no crackers, no de-appe-
tizers at all. Only a mercifully brief apéritif, followed by a
long and leisurely meal, with one wine or many, but with
whatever wine there is dispensed with a lavish wrist: a minimum of half a bottle per person, if you are dealing with
novices, or a whole bottle if you have real guests on your
hands. Your party will reach an *O Altitudo,* an *Ecce, quam
bonum!,* to which wine is the only road. Hard liquor is
for strong souls after great dinners; it is the grape that brings
ordinary mortals *usque ad hilaritatem.*

And ordinariness is the right note on which to sum up the
case for wine. It is precisely the foolishness of classifying
wine as an alcoholic beverage that keeps so many of us from
taking it with our lunches, suppers—and even breakfasts, if
you like. Whiskey, gin, and rum are sometime things. A

man who takes them too often courts disaster. But wine is simply water that has matured according to nature's will. It is the ordinary accompaniment of a grown man's food. How sad, then, that the secular conscience sweeps Sherry into the same category as vodka and looks on Zinfandel as liquor. God gave us wine to make us gracious and keep us sane. The light apéritif *en famille,* and the half bottle or bottle split between husband and wife over cold meat loaf and brawling children, are not solemn alcoholic dosages. They are cheerful minor lubrications of the frequently sandy gears of life. Properly underrated—that is, taken for what they are, and not as great problem-solving idols—they are on the side of the angels; they can hardly be overrated at all. *A tà Sante!*

To say much more, however—to provide you with a detailed directory of wines and their uses—is too large a task for any book that does not give itself entirely to the subject. I commend you the standard works. If you want the full treatment, start with the Britannica, and read your way in. Here you will have to be content, or discontent, with personal observations and prejudices.

My own tastes would, I suppose, have to be described as classic or orthodox. I have long since stopped apologizing for them. From time to time, well-intentioned authors write articles which urge novices of wine to ignore everybody's advice and drink what they like. To be sure, there is a substantial grain of truth in that. No man ever knows just how good the best is until he is familiar enough with the mediocre to appreciate the greatness of the achievement. One must drink a lot of wine before one is an expert.

Unfortunately, however, the articles lead some people to think that expertise is simply a matter of letting untutored personal preference have its head. I have little patience, of course, with wine snobs who look down their noses at anything but Romanée-Conti, Montrachet, and the four great Clarets. But I have even less patience with the man who implies that a middle-priced California red is really just as good as Château Latour. It is as if he were to tell me that the strings of the local high school orchestra are in the same league with those of the New York Philharmonic. (No gentleman should ever utter it, of course, but the proper rejoinder to such a man is the remark of the guide to the lady who said she didn't think much of the paintings in the Louvre: "The paintings are not on trial, Madame; you are.")

Accordingly, a balance must be struck. Exercise your own taste; trust it, even when it is less than perfect. Like conscience, it is the only personal guide you have. There is a point in every art beyond which no one can go without at least a modest supply of pretensions. Don't be ashamed, therefore, to be a *pretender* to the kingdom of wine. You cannot come into your own unless you do. On the other hand, however, be sure that your taste, like your conscience, has ample opportunity for instruction. Better men than you or me have drunk wine before us. No one needs instruction more than the man who thinks he needs none.

With that in mind, go to it. Remember, for example, that the wines of France and Germany do not enjoy unearned reputations. If all you know is Chilean Riesling, don't close your mind to the great Rheingaus and Moselles. Or, if your drinking experience is limited to Chianti (however good), don't speak too quickly against Rhônes, Burgundies, and Clarets. Every man will have his lawful preferences, of course, but in great wines, preference is a question of Stern or Heifetz —a matter of informed taste judging between goods, not a choice between good and bad.

Remember, too, that while the great European wines are unquestionably in a class by themselves, American wines can be very good indeed, and many of them, especially the California varietals, get better every year. One important note, however. American wines fall into two categories: California and Eastern. The California growers make their wines chiefly from European grape varieties—that is, from species of *Vitis vinifera,* the classic wine grape—the grape which, from the Bible to the present, has made the world's heart glad. The best California wines, accordingly, are named after the grape varieties themselves. If you want the best, you will buy, not a Burgundy, but a Pinot Noir; not a Claret, but a Cabernet Sauvignon; not a Rhine wine, but a Riesling.

Eastern wine growers, however, do not normally plant European varieties at all. Instead, they make their wines from domesticated strains of the native American grape, *Vitis labrusca*—the so-called fox grape, or slip-skin grape. That is the reason why New York State wines, for example, taste so very different from California or European ones—why they taste, to Americans, more "grapey" than the classic types. We have not been raised on peanut butter and Concord grape jelly for nothing: Quite naturally, the preferences of a large part of the nation lean to the "foxy" taste of wines made from Concord, Delaware, or Niagara grapes.

To me, however, such wines present a problem. For drinking neat, they are passable enough; but for use with food, they lack the graces and subtleties of the classic types. That applies especially to cooking: Concord-flavored sweetbreads are a mistake; a "foxy" fillet of sole is simply tragic. I would almost be willing to make a firm rule that, of domestic wines, only the California ones should ever be allowed to see the inside of a pot. As an Easterner, I wish I could say something kinder; but there it is. I shall never be governor of New York.

As long as I am putting my reputation on the block, let me close by declaring myself on one of the most controversial matters in the world of wine: corkscrews. If you have never considered the subject carefully, you no doubt think that a corkscrew is just a corkscrew, and that one will do as well, or as badly, as another. The truth is, however, that there are more tin-fiddle manufacturers in the corkscrew business than anywhere else. So much so, that you could live a whole lifetime and never come across a good one—unless, of course, you learned what to look for. Herewith, therefore, a short course on how to find a real corkscrew in a world of fakes.

The principal tool you will need to enable you to discern between the useful and the useless in the corkscrew department is an ordinary ⅛-inch-wide paper match. If you can insert such a match lengthwise up through the middle of the screw, or worm, it has passed the first test. Such a screw will grip the cork over the widest possible area. Above all, unlike a screw with a solid shaft running up the middle, it will not act as a drill, tearing holes both in the cork and in your patience.

Next, be sure that the worm passes these other tests: It should be made of wire, not flat metal (which simply cuts what it should be lifting); the wire should be just about ³⁄₃₂ of an inch in diameter, making the whole worm a shy ⅜ of an inch across; the helix formed by the wire should make at least six complete turns along the length of the worm; its working length should be between 2¼ and 2½ inches; and finally, the point of the worm should be sharp, smooth, and *not centered*—it should simply lie in the regular path of the rest of the helix.

If you are a stout fellow, and if this paragon among worms has a good handle attached to it, your shopping is over. All you need to do is insert the screw into the cork, place the bottle firmly on the floor between your feet, put your back into it, and pull. If, however, you were looking for something your wife or child might use, you had better continue your search until you find just as good a worm attached to a screw or lever mechanism which will make the work go easier.

Perhaps the best and most available of these is the (usually) French model which looks (roughly) like a toilet paper tube with two handles set crosswise at one end, and with a worm protruding from the other. The upper handle drives the worm into the cork, and the lower one (via a left-handed thread) lifts upper handle, worm, and cork out of the bottle and into the barrel of the device. It is commonly made of wood, but elegant ones in bone are available. I recommend it because it is one of the few corkscrews which combines useful mechanical advantage with a (normally) good worm. If you want something more stylish, go ahead and look. I wish you luck. The world is full of utterly intriguing corkscrews—most of them just as utterly hopeless.

Just to prove, however, that I am not one of the finest minds of the sixteenth century, I shall also recommend to you the most modern corkscrew of all, the carbon dioxide cork extractor. As you might expect, this one has no worm, but rather a long, hollow needle set at the end of a handle containing a CO_2 cartridge. The needle is simply pushed all the way through the cork, the handle is activated, and the pressure of the gas forces the cork out, Champagne-bottle style. The CO_2 does nothing to the wine, but there is hardly a cork anywhere which it will not unseat. The gadget is particularly useful in the cases of young wives, old corks, or both.

One sad note, however. Once a cork has made up its mind to go *into* the bottle, no corkscrew on earth can persuade it to do otherwise. If you can't lick 'em, join 'em: Push the cork all the way in with a pickle fork, hold it back while you pour the wine into a pitcher, and then glare at the empty bottle in triumph. A good cook must never lose the upper hand.

NINE

❖

The Suspended Solution

At long last (you *have* been patient), I am ready to thicken the stew.

Estimate the amount of liquid in your stew. For every cup, take one tablespoon of butter and one of flour. (If you like your sauce rather more thin than thick, disregard any fractional cups; if vice versa, count them.)

Melt the butter in a pan large enough to hold the liquid easily, stir in the flour, and cook for a minute or so over low heat. Then pour most of the liquid from the stewpot into the saucepan and beat vigorously with a whisk, being careful to scrape the bottom and corners of the pan as it comes to a boil. When thickened, pour it back into the stew, stirring gently until well mixed. Continue cooking for a few minutes, correct the seasoning, and serve. Your stew, so long deferred, stands finally *extra causas*. Greet it as a fellow creature: It is as deliciously unnecessary as you are.

It is worth considering, however, just what it is that you have done. Thickening is perhaps the most ordinary of the finishes of which a dish is capable. It is, often literally, child's play: the exercise by which the eight- or nine-year-old first realizes the visible and palpable magic of cooking. Yet for all its commonness—or, more accurately, precisely because it is common, it is one of the most deeply satisfying processes of all. Only miracle is plain; it is the ordinary that groans with the unutterable weight of glory.

Consider first what actually happens. Flour and fat are combined. Each grain of flour is thus isolated from each other grain by a thin coating of grease. The principle involved is simple enough: When the boiling liquid finally causes the grains of flour to swell, it would be undesirable in the extreme to have them expand in unified and glutinous groups of a thousand or so each. Accordingly, the barrier of fat allows each grain to expand separately from the others, almost as if it had been individually cooked and carefully floated free within the sauce.

It is the smallness of the process that hides the wonder. Imagine, therefore, if you will, a pot of water the size of an ordinary 12- by 15-foot dining room. On this scale, the grains of flour would be the size of small potato dumplings. Now, if you were simply to throw several thousand of these all at once into a roomful of boiling water, you would foment a disaster of monumental proportions. Simultaneous expansion, with no provision for maintenance of separation, would yield lumps of surpassing magnitude. The group adhering to the bottom of the room would swell to an irregular carpet a foot or so thick. Other clusters would detach themselves, but at maturity they would be the size of dining room chairs or sideboard drawers. Vigorous stirring might break them up a bit; but the best you could manage would be a thin liquid in which were floating smashed chair backs, odd seat cushions, torn hunks of carpet, and the assorted contents of all the drawers. No matter how delicious the sauce—no matter how stout a trencherman the giant who ate it up—it would take a bit of doing to put it away.

If, however, you were to drop those tiny dumplings one by one into your dining room-sized stewpot, allowing each to expand before adding the next, you would, by the time you reached the five thousand and first dumpling, have a much more desirable condition. To begin with, each several dumpling would be floating independently of the others. Furthermore, since there would not be room at the top for all of them, they would dispose themselves as best they could throughout the liquid. Your dining room would now be filled floor to ceiling and wall to wall, not with odd lumps and runny liquid, but with a throng of uniform dumplings freely jostling one another in the ambient broth. The whole atmosphere would have been brought to a condition of thick and consistent crowding, to a happy state of Standing Room Only.

There, you see, lies the genius of the first cook who thought of mixing her flour with fat before adding liquid to it. By a spectacular short cut, she achieved separation of granules without the burden of having to deal with granules at all. The world owes her a monument. The next time you stir a sauce or thicken a stew, give it an extra stroke in her honor. The giants in the earth must not be forgotten.

Understanding the principle of thickening, however, takes nothing off the marvel of the process. Consider it further. Take a single grain of flour as it lies coated with hot fat or butter. What lies inside that protective barrier? Ah! It is a vast complexity of cells, a tissue riddled with a thousand interstices. And when liquid is added? Ah, again! By capillary action, it is drawn into the grain along a hundred channels. Each particle of flour, till now so nearly dry, becomes a creature of the sea again, pregnant with the juices of life, waiting for a pentecost of power.

At 212° F., it happens. The entrapped water turns to steam and each grain is exploded by the giant who lived in James Watt's teakettle. The processes involved in sauce making are hardly as dramatic as the driving of great engines, but they testify no less to the brooding of the Spirit upon the face of creation, to the endless speaking of the Word Who mightily and sweetly orders all things.

Unfortunately, we live in an age which is too little impressed by the small and too easily intimidated by the great. It is the stock in trade of atheists and other knockers of the wonder of being to insist that the magnitude of the universe makes all man's musings insignificant. How, they ask, can we seriously think we are of much account in a universe where light travels at 186,000 miles per second, and it takes a hundred light years to go from one galaxy to the next?

Looking into my saucepan as the stock thickens, I find a counterfoil to such astronomical terrorism. Creation is vast in every direction. It is as hugely small as it is large. The number of water-filled interstices in my three tablespoonfuls of flour runs the interstellar distances a fair second; the appeal to size is a self-canceling argument. Plying my whisk, I know that what goes on here is neither less mysterious nor less marvelous than what happens there. We may not have settled the question of whether I am mad to think I matter, but we have definitely eliminated the numbers game as a method of proof. I will listen to any man who wants to argue me down, but, saucepan in hand, I refuse to be snowed.

Philosophizing about sauce making, however, is not enough. For all its commonness, the process is (apparently) one that strikes many cooks as inordinately troublesome: Witness the ease with which the frozen food companies sell the public creamed potatoes as if they were sparing the race some vast labor. Therefore, as a riposte to this low commercial thrust, I propose to give you a few notes about equipment, followed by a list of variant methods of thickening. Armed with these, you will be able to pass the frozen food counter with your head held high.

First of all, you will need a whisk; and, once again, you will have to watch out for tin fiddles. The situation here is not quite as bad as it is in the corkscrew department, but it is bad enough to keep most people in lifelong bondage to lumpy gravy, and in lifelong exile from the company of great sauces. Herewith, therefore, the lineaments of the whisk I recommend. It is a spoon-shaped utensil whose frame consists of a single piece of heavy wire conformed, roughly, to the outline of an ordinary wooden cooking spoon. The upper end is thus an open wire handle; but the lower, or business, end, has a coil spring of finer wire threaded around the circumference of the "bowl." It is a model of domestic efficiency.

First, its angles and general conformation enable it to touch every inch of saucepan surface. Second, it works well in both small and medium quantities of liquid—which, after all, is what the household cook has to cope with. The typical professional whisk (shaped like an elongated light bulb made of wire loops) is fine for cooking on the grand scale, but unless you own an exceedingly small one, it will not reach into the corners of domestic pots. On the other hand, the usual flat whisk is awkward for tall, narrow pots, and it, too, is weak at scouring into corners. The spiral cream whip (conical wire helix fastened at its narrow end to a vertical handle) is a little better at reaching out of the way spots, but it defies firm handling. If anything ever sticks to the pot, you will feel as if you are working with a wet noodle. Finally, there is the old-fashioned continental whisk, made of a bundle of strawlike twigs. It works exceedingly well, but is hard to keep clean. If, however, you don't mind living a little closer to nature than the chrome and stainless American kitchen normally allows, it makes a good second choice. Only specialty stores carry them, but they are cheap enough to warrant your picking one up if you ever get the chance. (It will work wonders on egg-thickened sauces.)

Along with your whisk, you will also want a supply of wooden spoons. Experiment will have to guide you to the most desirable sizes and shapes. There are pointed ones which will

fit sharp-cornered pans, flat ones which will scrape bottoms to
a fare-thee-well, and there are round ones, doughnut-shaped
ones, oval ones, slotted ones and truncated ones—all waiting
for your fancy to light. Add to that the fact that they can be
had in assorted sizes, up to the length of a man's forearm, and
you have the full picture. The next time you see a display of
them, give in to the temptation you have been fighting since
childhood: Buy yourself one of every shape and size in the
store. There are few indulgences in this life that can match
this one for safety, economy, and long-term supportability.
Besides, you will set your cooking progress ahead by a full
year or two. Your battery of wooden spoons is not only
good for the ego; they are kind to porcelain, gentle with
aluminum, easy on the purse, and, as non-conductors, ideal for
snitching samples from boiling pots. No more blistered lower
lips from accidental contact with the bottom of one of Satan's
stainless steel spoons. True enough, they burn easily and become cracked with age; but then, so do we all. It's nice to have
a few things around that make no pretense of imperishability.

One final word—on pots. Contrary to what most cookbooks
tell you, do not thicken sauces in a double boiler. It can, of
course, be done. But it is about as exciting as watching the
grass grow. It is so unbearably time-consuming that the sensible cook will sooner serve thin broth than put up with the
boredom of waiting for boiling water to boil water. Use your
double boiler as such, therefore, only for its unquestionably
legitimate purposes—chiefly for warming what you do not
wish to watch. For sauces, put the bottom part away.

It is the top part, with its round corners, that is ideally
suited to sauce making. Just put it over direct heat, add fat
and flour, and stir constantly with a whisk. Add the liquid,
crank up the heat as high as you like and, with whisk in one
hand and pot handle in the other, stir vigorously until it comes
to a boil. Then beat as if your life depended on it. In practically no time at all—and with no prescalding of liquids or

dirtying of other pans—you will have thickened the sauce
and be well into the next job. (The double-boiler cook would
still be waiting for things to get hot enough to go to work.)
All it takes is energy, verve, slap, and dash. A good gravy
cannot be made *grave;* great sauces must be executed not
only *con fuoco* but *con brio.*

Let me add a note here on the subject of thickening sauces
with eggs instead of flour. The principle is the same: the free
suspension of finely divided particles in a liquid. Only the
materialities of the situation are different: Instead of expanded
grains of flour, gently cooked particles of egg yolk are used to
achieve the desired result. In this case, however, care must be
taken not to *boil* the sauce once the egg is in: With anything
more than the gentlest cooking, the bits of egg yolk become,
not soft and resilient, but granular, stringy, and tough, like
overcooked scrambled eggs. Forewarned is forearmed. Here
are two methods.

⧲1. In a warm deep bowl, whisk some egg yolks vigorously
  (one yolk per half cup of liquid).

  Bring your pot of unthickened liquid to a rolling
  boil, carry the pot promptly to the bowl, and pour a
  generous one third of the potful on to the yolks, whisking incessantly and vivaciously while you do. As it
  begins to thicken, add the rest, still whisking.

  Reheat again if necessary, but never, repeat *never,*
  boil again.

  (Note: Many cooks fail to achieve thickening by this
  method; the reason being that the egg yolks never
  actually cook. Cold bowls, cold yolks, and small quantities of liquid are the chief causes of failure. If your
  finished product should look thin and frothy, put it
  back over the fire, and, plying your whisk as you have
  never done before—scraping the bottom and corners of

the pan continuously—bring it back to, but not over, the boiling point. If necessary, lift the pan from the fire and stir it in the air for a moment to insure uniform heating. Under no circumstances, however, stop whisking. Nothing is more depressing than a sauce full of cooked egg fragments.)

#2. HOLLANDAISE SAUCE, FAST

In a deep pan, put one egg yolk, one tablespoon cream or top milk, and salt, cayenne, and lemon juice to taste. Whisk well.

Then, pan in one hand and whisk in the other, heat over a medium flame, whisking without let or hindrance. Scour every corner of the pan rapidly, and never take your hand off the handle. Hollandaise made this way happens like lightning. As soon as it begins to reach the consistency of thick custard, back away from the stove, stirring constantly, and walk to the spot where you have set aside a generous two tablespoonfuls of butter. Throw that in and continue whisking. By the time the butter dissolves, you will have perfect and foolproof Hollandaise.

(There is a knack to it, of course, but once it is learned, you will be able to bring off a superb sauce in three minutes. Just remember the basic proportions and multiply accordingly for larger quantities: For every egg yolk, use one tablespoon of cream and two of butter. Salt, pepper and lemon juice are matters of taste, but, for a guide, try starting with a generous teaspoon of lemon juice per yolk.)

If I have now persuaded you of the merits of the whisk, the wooden spoon, and the practice of making all sauces (even egg-thickened ones) over direct heat, let me close with two directions which I deliberately omitted from the several methods I gave you for thickening. They are 1. Check consistency; and 2. Correct seasoning. Without due regard to these, even the best saucier can come to a miserable end.

Take consistency first.

If your sauce is too thin, simply take out some of it, overthicken it by whatever method you started with and return it to the main pot, stirring well. With a little judgment, you should get it right on the second try. If not, take a third; you can't go wrong.

If, on the other hand, your sauce is too thick, a number of remedies are possible. If you are lucky enough to have more of the original stock on hand, simply dilute the sauce with it. Lacking that, add any liquid of complimentary flavor. Here are some possibilities: wine (boil it out, though); vegetable pot liquor; milk; cream; sour cream (it will not thin the texture much, but it will lighten the flavor marvelously; tomato juice; leftover soup (strained); any stock; and (*in articulo mortis*) water.

Remember, however, that consistency in a sauce is a function of two variables, texture and flavor. They are, respectively, the body and the soul of cooking. Sour cream, for example, has a thick texture but a thin flavor. It will provide body where you have plenty of soul (as in Beef Stroganoff); or it will furnish a subtle soul to a dish that is afflicted with a gross and leaden body (undistinguished cream of vegetable soup, for one case in point; lethargic turkey gravy, for another).

Accordingly, you must ask yourself not simply *whether* your sauce is too thick, but also *why*. If the flavor is good, you may choose any diluent that is lean of body; but if it is lumpish and stodgy, you will want something more acid and snappy to do the job: tomato juice or a fairly emphatic thin soup.

After that, you can turn your attention to the seasoning. Salt and pepper (freshly ground) are the most important of all, but since taste and experience count for everything here, no general rules can be given.

With those properly adjusted, however, the acidity of the sauce deserves the most consideration. If it is excessive, you will need something bland to cut it down. Sweet cream, good mellow stock (appropriately thickened), or plain milk come to mind as possibilities. If, however (and more likely), your sauce is too bland, a touch of sharpness is called for. In this case, you might try: lemon juice; dry wine; tomato juice; tomato paste; sour cream; Madeira (Sherry affects the bouquet of a sauce but not its acidity—it is Madeira that has the subtly lemony undertone); or (if you use discretion), vinegar, Worcestershire, mustard, horseradish, or Tabasco.

On the other hand, if the flavor seems a bit weak, though otherwise in balance, something with body and a nose is called for. Enter here, therefore: Sherry, garlic powder; meat extract; Worcestershire; soup; soy sauce; Chinese bead molasses; Chinese oyster sauce; good paprika; grated cheese (Cheddar, Parmesan), or any of the stronger pot liquors: mushroom, onion, or turnip, for example.

There is no substitute, of course, for striking close to the mark the first time around. Beyond a certain fairly minimal level of correction, you run the risk of making your sauce taste as if it had been produced in a correctional institution. Be careful from the first, then. Remember that, provided you have something to say, understatement is better than overstatement nine times out of ten.

One last secret. There is almost no sauce that will not be improved by having a lump of butter whisked into it the moment before it is served. In addition to what it does for the flavor, it provides the sauce itself with a patina, a sheen which delights the eye even before the palate begins to judge. It is an embellishment not lightly to be foregone. Dishes should come to the table vested, robed. *Don Giovanni* is marvelous any way you can get to hear it. But given a choice between seeing it performed full dress, or on a bare stage with the cast in T shirts and sneakers, no rational man would hesitate. A great sauce deserves a great finish. Whatever you do, therefore, don't omit the final grace—the loving pat of butter.

TEN

✤

And She Took Flour...

Having finished thus the main part of the first half of the initial section of my recipe for Lamb for Eight Persons Four Times, I suggest that we now relax in earnest. Well begun is half done. St. Augustine started a commentary on the Bible, but never got past Genesis. It takes me a year to get through the first paragraph of the creed in dogmatic theology. For the task at hand, only the noodles that go with the stew remain to be dealt with, and I shall get to them as directly as I can. You have had, however, the last apology for the pace of this book.

That is not a warning; it is a compliment. If you are still with me at this point, it can only be because you are a serious drinker of being: a man who will walk back ten paces to smell privet in bloom; a woman who loves to rap sound turnips with her knuckles. Let us congratulate one another: The party has taken a distinct turn for the better. The busybodies with late meetings to attend have long since departed. The fidgeters who yawned their way through the evening have flaunted their early rising and vanished mercifully into outer darkness. Rejoice, dear heart; the ribbon clerks are finally out of the game. At last we may speak freely of the things that matter. (Have you ever looked at the thousands of five-pointed stars on the underside of blossoming spirea?) Put away the cooking Sherry, Margaret; only the real ones are left. The good stuff is in the right hand end of the sideboard.

Our progress to noodles must not be hasty.

SCENE I: HELL

There was a day when Satan took counsel with his chief tempters. "What," he asked the assembled Principalities and Powers, "are we doing to hasten the dehumanization of man?"

One by one, they reported. Formidable Senior Vice-Presidents in charge of Envy, Pride, and Avarice gave glowing accounts; the Chiefs of the Bureaus of Lust and Sloth read lengthy bills of particulars. Satan, however, was not pleased. Even the brilliant report of the Head of the War Department failed to satisfy him. He listened restively to the long treatise on nuclear proliferation; he fiddled with pencils during the section on the philosophy of the brushfire war.

Finally, Satan's wrath overcame him. He swept his notes from the table and leapt to his feet. "Self-serving declarations!" he roared. "Am I doomed to sit forever listening to idiots try to hide incompetence behind verbiage? Has no one anything new? Are we to spend the rest of eternity minding the store as we have for a thousand years?"

At that point, the youngest tempter rose. "With your permission, my lord," he said, "I have a program." And as Satan sat down again, he launched into his proposal for an inter-departmental Bureau of Desubstantialization. He claimed that the dehumanization of man was going so slowly because the infernal strategy had failed to cut man off from one of the chief bulwarks of his humanity. In concentrating on offenses against God and neighbor, it had failed to corrupt his relationship to things. *Things*, the tempter declared, by their provision of unique delights and individual astonishments, constituted a continuous refreshment of the very capacities Hell was at pains to abolish. As long as man dealt with real substances, he would himself tend to remain substantial. What was needed, therefore, was a program to deprive man of *things*.

Satan took evident interest. "But," he objected, "how shall we proceed? In an affluent society man has more things than ever. Are you saying that in the midst of such abundance he simply will not notice so bizarre a plot?"

"Not quite, my lord," said the tempter. "I do not mean to take anything from him physically. Instead, we shall encourage him *mentally* to alienate himself from reality. I propose that we contrive a systematic substitution of abstractions, diagrams, and spiritualizations for actual beings. Man must be taught to see things as symbols—must be trained to use them for *effect*, and never for themselves. Above all, the door of delight must remain firmly closed.

"It will not," he continued, "be as difficult as it seems. Men are so firmly convinced that they are materialists that they will believe anything before they suspect us of contriving their destruction by spiritualization. By way of a little insurance, however, I have taken the liberty of arranging for an army of preachers who will continue, as in the past, to thunder against them for being materialists. They will be so busy feeling delightfully wicked that nobody will notice the day when we finally cut them loose from reality altogether."

And at that, Satan smiled, sat back and folded his hands. "Good," he said. "Let the work go forward."

SCENE II: A DINNER PARTY

"What can we give you, Harry? Large helping or small?"
"If it's all the same to you, Martha, just a little of the Chicken Paprikash. No noodles. I'm counting calories."

There are, to be sure, greater blasphemies than that against the goodness of creation; but none illustrates better the fundamental antimaterialism of the age. Harry sits in front of one of the finest and simplest goods in the world, and he begs off, not because he does not like it, but because he has ceased to see it. Noodles, for him, are not unique and delightful beings; they have become an abstract subject called *highly caloric food.* No matter to him that Martha made the noodles herself—that he has before him something he will not meet again for years: He turns them down precisely because they are, to him, no *matter* at all. It is calories, not noodles, that count.

Yet nothing could be further from the truth. A calorie is not a thing; it is a measurement. In itself, it does not exist. It is simply a way of specifying a particular property of things, namely, how much heat they give off when burned. Only *things,* you see, are capable of being eaten or burned, loved or loathed; no one ever yet got his teeth into a calorie. In fact, if you think carefully about it, you will realize that no measurement exists as such. Inches, for example, are not things; they are a way of talking about certain useful marks on sticks. Even the Standard Meter is not *a being:* What really exists is a fancy metal bar with scratches on it.

How sad, then, to see real beings—Harry and all his fellow calorie counters—living their lives in abject terror of things that do not even go bump in the night. What a crime, not only against hospitality, but against being to hear him turn down homemade noodles in favor of idols and abstractions— to watch him prefer nothing to something. And what a disaster to himself! To have capitulated so starchlessly before the devil's policy of desubstantialization! His body may or may not lose weight; his soul, however, is sure to wither.

What shall we say to him? He has strayed, of course, into ways of darkness and error. But it will not do simply to condemn him as a heretic. He does, after all, have a legitimate point: The response to the infernal strategy of desubstantialization must not be a mindless gambit that oversubstantializes him into a monster of twenty stone: His heart and circulatory system are as legitimate a human concern as Martha's noodles. As an attempt to strike a balance, therefore, I give you, and Harry, my own answer to the weight problem—a brief sketch of one man's resolution of the noodle-heart dilemma.

It all began with the realization that by the age of forty, my metabolic rate had retired from the rat race and settled down to a truly dignified and leisurely pace. It seemed, indeed, that three deep breaths early in the morning were more than sufficient to put me over the top as far as intake for the day was concerned.

Coupled with that, was my wife's arrival at ripeness and perfectness of age as a cook. Homemade bread, pastries, and buns proceeded in abundance from her hands. Homemade noodles and ravioli gazed imploringly at me from the table. As a true product of my age, I tried to cut down, but, month by month, the needle on the bathroom scale recorded the increasing gravity of the situation—and of myself. In my alarm, I counted calories: A miserable 900 a day was what it took to get me anywhere at all. The physical results, of course, were satisfactory enough; but the vision of existence without an unstinting abundance of the delectabilities of which flour is capable began to press upon me. A life sentence to one slice of homemade bread or three ounces of noodles per meal is a sad fate for the proud descendant of three generations of legendary eaters.

It was spaetzle that brought me to my senses. Spaetzle, if you do not know, are the very flower of all foods made with flour. They are tiny bits of soft noodle dough, boiled to a light and lovely perfection, and served with butter or gravy. It took only one taste of my wife's first batch to make me realize that I could not go on as a dieter. Spaetzle exude substantiality: A man who takes a small helping is a man without eyes to see what is in front of him. Accordingly, I passed my plate back for seconds and then thirds, and made a vow then and there to walk more, to split logs every day and, above all, to change my religion from the devilish cult of dieting to the godly discipline of fasting.

I have never regretted it. To eat nothing at all is more human than to take a little of what cries out for the appetite of a giant. One servingspoonful of spaetzle is like the opening measures of Vivaldi's *Four Seasons:* Any man who walks out early on either proves he doesn't understand the genre—and he misses the repose of the end. To eat without eating greatly is only to eat by halves. While God gives me meat in due season and the sensibilities with which to relish the gift, I refuse to sit down to eat and rise up only to have picked and fussed my way through the goodness of the earth. My vow, therefore, was beautifully simple: If I ate, I would eat without stint; and if I stinted, I would not eat at all.

I offer it as my prescription for Harry. Let him fast until he is free to eat like a true son of Adam. Let him take but one meal a day (or even one every other day, if he is one of the chosen ones whose metabolism marks him for a special vocation); let him fast in good earnest; nothing but liquids—no nibbles, no snacks. But then let him take meals worthy of the name. (If he needs exercise, let him walk five miles a day—or go in for sit-ups, push-ups, and four-wall handball, if it comes to that; but let him not try to skimp his way to greatness.) It is bread that strengthens man's heart; it is the valleys thick with grain that laugh and sing. It is only when Harry, by feast and fast, lays a firm grip on the fatness of the earth, that he himself will return to sanity and substance.

To begin with, real eating will restore his sense of the festivity of being. Food does not exist merely for the sake of its nutritional value. To see it so is only to knuckle under still further to the desubstantialization of man, to regard not what things are, but what they mean to us—to become, in short, solemn idolaters spiritualizing what should be loved as matter. A man's daily meal ought to be an exultation over the smack of desirability which lies at the roots of creation. To break real bread is to break the loveless hold of hell upon the world, and, by just that much, to set the secular free.

But second, he will, by his fasting, be delivered from the hopelessness of mere gourmandise. The secular, for all its goodness, does not defend itself very well against mindless and perpetual consumption. It cries out to be offered by abstinence as well as use; to be appreciated, not simply absorbed: Hunger remains the best sauce. Beyond that, though, it cries out to be lifted into a higher offering still. The real secret of fasting is not that it is a simple way to keep one's weight down, but that it is a mysterious way of lifting creation into the Supper of the Lamb. It is not a little excursion into fashionable shape, but a major entrance into the fasting, the agony, the passion by which the Incarnate Word restores all things to the goodness God finds in them. It is as much an act of prayer as prayer itself, and, in an affluent society, it may well be the most meaningful of all the practices of religion—the most likely point at which the salt can find its savor once again. Let Harry fast in earnest, therefore. One way or another—here or hereafter—it will give him back his feasts.

With that preface, we are at last ready for the noodles.

If you are disposed to try the experiment of making your own, I have a recipe for you. Theoretically, it is a marvel of simplicity: flour and eggs, period. In practice, however—as with all simplicities—it takes a bit of technique to bring it off. Only the complex and random happens easily; so, good luck—and don't give up too soon.

NOODLE DOUGH

Take three cups of flour, and place it in a heap on your bread board, pastry table, noodle board, or chopping block. Make a well in the center of the flour and break four eggs into it. Mix with your hands until it forms a ball, and then knead and knead until all the scraps have been picked up and the dough itself becomes smooth. It will be alarmingly stiff—in fact, if it seems easy to work, add some more flour to make the riddle harder. You must be remorselessly thorough here. Noodle dough cannot be overkneaded.

When done, wrap in a damp towel and let rest for at least a half hour in a warm place. (The success of all doughs of this sort depends entirely on allowing the glutinous properties of the flour to develop to the fullest extent—hence all the kneading and resting.)

When the dough is ready, divide it into thirds, and, leaving the rest in the damp towel, take one piece and roll it out into a long strip. Fold the piece lengthwise to a width of about three or four inches, and continue rolling. If you use enough main force, you should end up with a piece between two and three feet long, about four inches wide, and very, very thin.

Cut the strip into four or six equal parts, stack the pieces, and cut them into noodles of the width you desire. Repeat the process with the other two lumps of dough still in the towel.

The finished noodles can be dried of course, but if you have gone to all the trouble of making them, it is a shame not to reap the fruit of your labors. Put on a pot of water, and have yourself a real dinner. It might be just what you need to inspire you to tackle homemade ravioli the next time around. No story could have a happier ending.

SPAETZLE

Compared to noodles, spaetzle are as easy as breathing—provided you have a convenient gadget for getting the dough to separate into droplets. In an emergency, you can flick the dough out of the bowl and into the boiling water with the tip of a spoon, but it does take time. If you are a serious spaetzle man, you will no doubt want to acquire one of the many varieties of spaetzle mill. Perhaps the easiest to use is the one which looks like an ordinary rotary food mill, but which has a bottom plate full of ⅜-inch holes. All you do is drop the dough into the gadget, hold it over the boiling pot, and turn the handle—forward only for large spaetzle; forward and backward in short strokes for finer ones.

Here is a recipe, though it makes only a beginner's quantity. If you cook for true men, prepare to multiply the amounts.

2 cups sifted flour	2 eggs, beaten
¾ teaspoon salt	¾ cup (approximately) milk
¼ teaspoon nutmeg	

Mix the first four ingredients in a bowl and add only enough milk to make a stiff batter. Beat well, and let it rest.

Force through the spaetzle mill into a large pot of rapidly boiling salted water and cook until tender. This is a matter of personal preference, of course—at six minutes they will be done *al dente;* at fifteen minutes you will find them as I like them: more on the *saftig* side. Take your pick.)

Drain, rinse, and drain again. Pile in a serving dish and toss with unconscionable amounts of butter. Serve with the pepper mill close at hand. Even without gravy, they will delight the heart of any real eater; with it, they are unutterably good. And who knows; with such a beginning, where may you not end? If noodles can lead a cook to ravioli, spaetzle may well carry him to gnocchi, which, as everyone knows, are noodles risen and glorified: the apotheosis of boiled flour.

The ultimate transfiguration of noodle dough, however—the final revelation of *pasta in excelsis*—comes only when you reach the subject of strudel. It is in strudel dough that the glutinous properties of flour enter the new Jerusalem in a triumph of elasticity. Admittedly, no noodle preparation is more demanding. But the rewards! An end result, of course, like nothing else on earth—and the unparalleled satisfaction of bringing off such a marvelous piece of business with your own hands. The process itself is sheer fascination. Mastery comes slowly, to be sure. You will make untidy strudels before you make magnificent ones. But if you are any beholder of being at all, you will find it one of the great culinary absorptions of your life.

Herewith, then, the whole story.

STRUDEL DOUGH

Take 2½ cups of flour. (There is a special superglutinous strudel flour which is handled by specialty stores: You can make do with ordinary pastry flour, but get the real thing if you can. Just don't try to use cake flour.) Place the flour in a pile on the pastry board, make a well in the center, and in the well, put one egg lightly beaten, three tablespoons of peanut oil, and ½ teaspoon salt. Mix to a crumbly consistency, spread out on the board, and gradually add about ⅔ cup of warm water. (Flours vary not only in their elasticity, but in their ability to absorb water. The right amount is, in the long run, a matter of feel—just as the real cooks have always exasperatingly insisted.) Your goal is a very soft, sticky dough, just barely kneadable. Work it with your hands for a while, and then perfect its elasticity by lifting it in the air and flinging it down on the pastry board 100 times.

This is the step without which nothing, so be violent. It is marvelous therapy. If you are a woman, think of all the intolerable members of the PTA, and give each one a crash. *That* for you, Ethel Smith! Elizabeth Wilkinson, I have had *enough!* If you are a man, you will find it better than using the boss's picture for a dart game. Even before you pass fifty throws, you will be at peace with the world.

The dough will stick to the board rather badly at first, but use as little additional flour as possible. Toward the end it should come away from both hands and table easily. When finished, make a smooth ball of the dough, brush it lightly with oil, put it on a warm plate, cover it with a warm bowl and let it rest in a warm place for half an hour. Fight the temptation to curl up and take a nap in the presence of all this coziness.

STRETCHING

Spread a tablecloth or bed sheet on a table about 3 feet wide and 5 feet long, and sprinkle all over with flour. When the dough is ready, put it in the center and roll it out as thinly as you can with a pastry pin. The larger you get it at this point, the better.

You are ready for the ticklish part of the job. You have had your moment of extreme violence; it is now time for extreme care. Take off all rings and wrist watches, flour the backs of your hands and wrists, reach under the dough, palms down, and begin to lift and stretch it with a hand over hand motion, using only the backs of your hands. Try your very best not to tear the dough—minor lesions can sometimes be worked around or patched, but there is no way of repairing them. You have arrived at the moment of truth. Continue stretching —walking around the table as you do—until the dough is large enough to cover the table completely, and to hang over the edges. It will be incredibly thin, and you will be either wildly elated or horribly depressed—depending. Far be it from me to lure you on with false assurances.

Let the dough dry for a bit before you brush it with melted butter. (In humid weather you can take your time, but in the wintertime, with the heat on, it dries so fast that you will have to work quickly. The butter must go on before the dough gets brittle.) That done, take a pair of scissors and cut off the thick edge of the overhanging parts of the sheet. (Throw the surplus out—or give it to your five-year-old to use for modeling clay. Just don't let him park it on the sofa—it leaves grease spots.)

FILLING AND ROLLING

Melt ¾ cup of butter (nobody in his right mind would go to this much fuss for margarine). Brush the entire surface of the dough, reserving some butter for further brushing. Spread your filling over one end of the sheet—covering not more than ⅓ of the dough. Lift up the overhanging flaps of dough on the long sides of the table, fold them gently over the filling, and brush them with butter.

Then pick up the tablecloth at the filled end of the sheet and flop the dough over on itself. Continue flopping (loosely) until the entire piece has been rolled up like a jelly roll. Pull the cloth toward you as you work, and at the last flip, have a buttered baking sheet ready to receive the finished strudel from the cloth. You may find, at this point, that your strudel is too long to fit in your oven. You have two choices: You can either cut it in half, or else gently bend it into a horseshoe. Both methods work, but if you want to avoid the dilemma altogether, buy a commercial stove the next time around.

(It should be noted that the rolling of a strudel calls for a certain amount of finesse. Violence, of course, is out; but so are faintheartedness and apologetic flipping. Quiet boldness is perhaps the attitude to strive for. Again, I wish you good luck. Whatever you do, though, don't try to make a cheese strudel your first time out. It's like trying to make a jelly roll out of soup. Leave the more liquid fillings alone until you reach the master-class level.)

Finally, brush the strudel with melted butter and bake in a moderate oven (375°) for 45 minutes to 1 hour, or until golden brown, basting occasionally with any remaining butter. When done, sprinkle lavishly with confectioners' sugar and serve warm (not hot) with whipped cream.

Admittedly, it's a lot of work. Not to mention the wear and tear on the nerves. There are at least three points at which you can come a cropper—in the mixing: dough too dry; in the stretching: major and uncircumventible lesions; and in the rolling: general sloppiness, or a bad job of fielding the strudel onto the baking sheet. But then, life is like that: What is good is difficult, and what is difficult is rare. If you have a vocation for strudel, you will, late or soon, come through with flying colors.

ELEVEN

❖

Better a Dinner of Herbs...

Let me anticipate an objection. If, in your youth, you were
put upon by nutritionists—if you are one of those whose
tastes have been terrorized by Home Ec bogeymen—you are
probably, by this time, nursing a bone to pick with me.
"Cookbook author, indeed!" I hear you muttering. "He writes
as if the science of nutrition had not even been discovered.
Does he seriously hope to pass off this rhapsody on meat and
starch as a treatise on cooking? Does he actually think that
anyone who has the least notion of what is involved in a
balanced diet would condescend to settle down in the waist-
land of gravy and spaetzle he praises so extravagantly?"

Well, believe it or not, I am willing to concede you your
point. I have no quarrel with the general validity of nutritional
considerations; any more than I would try to argue you down
on the subject of the germ theory. The only caution I would
insist upon is that, given modern man's tendency to idolatry—
his preference of meaning over matter, his penchant for the
useful rather than the delicious—both of them can, while remaining true as far as they go, be turned into dangerous

con jobs. There are people, you know, who will not kiss you on the lips.

I grant you that my children need their meals balanced. If you like, I shall take the pledge here and now to see to it that they get greens along with their starches. My own feeling, however, is that they need something else even more. They need to have their tastes *un*balanced: to have them skewed, driven off dead center, and fastened firmly on the astonishing oddness of the world. If they get a course from me at all, it should not be a string of lectures on how best to adapt reality to their uses, but a series of laboratory sessions where their senses can be exposed to the delectability of being as such.

True enough, food is only one small corner of the field. They need these experiments even more in music, art and literature, and they need them most of all in their relationships with people—the most startling realities on earth; but for all that, the table is not a bad place to start.

Give or take a few years, we have just been through our first half century of energetic nutrition-mongering. Unless you have a vested interest in it, however, the results are not wildly encouraging. As I write, a child passes my table, armed with the makings of a TV snack. Exhibit A is a two-pound box of something called Pasteurized Process Cheese Food Spread; exhibit B, a plastic bag of supermarket bread; exhibit C, a bottle of soda pop. One way or another, they all pass some kind of abstract nutritional test. The first is full of protein; the second is enriched beyond all imagining (the superconscientious manufacturer seems to add new dietary virtue to his bread every time you turn your back: Its body-building capacities have recently been raised from eight to twelve); the third is guaranteed not to add unnecessary sugar to the diet of affluent teen-agers. The world, in short, assures me and my children that all these things are good for us. What alarms me is that, in themselves, they are not good at all.

Take exhibit A. I have nothing against process cheese: I grew up in the same society you did. But to raise a generation to expect no more than this from cheese is to raise them in fundamental ignorance of the subject. First of all, this is not even process cheese: The vigilance of the Pure Food and Drug authorities assures us of at least a modicum of honesty on the label. It is process cheese *food:* meaning that there is a lot more in it than cheese—defatted milk solids, powdered whey, vegetable gum, and a string of unpronounceable chemicals. More than that, it is process cheese food *spread:* meaning that there is so little cheese in it that it never gets much firmer than cold day-old oatmeal—nor, for that matter, much closer to the taste of cheese. And yet, assured by a whole culture that it is passably nutritious, your children and mine swallow it all uncritically. Swallow it? They wolf it down.

Exhibits B and C are no better. The bread (whose taste and texture every red-blooded American child prefers to anything homemade, or even bakery-baked) has the consistency of quilt stuffing. Hold a wrapped loaf by the ends. Compress it lengthwise; then draw it back to its original shape. Where have you felt that response before? What is the comparison your mind is searching for? Ah yes! It handles exactly like a leaky concertina.

And the soda? I rest my case on a simple transcription of the government-inspired small print: IMITATION CITRUS FLAVORED DIETARY ARTIFICIALLY SWEETENED CARBONATED BEVERAGE. That, I submit, is not a label; it is an incantation. Someday, it should be set to a suitable plainsong tune or Anglican chant. (For an antiphon in Eastertide, the additional words, A NEW TASTE SENSATION, could easily be added.)

We live surrounded by dietary and nutritional pitchmen. I sit down to breakfast, only to be confronted with cereal boxes plastered with tables of vitamin and mineral values.

My attention is riveted, not on what is in the bowl (more often than not, that tastes like old ironing-board covers soaked in milk), but on niacin, thiamine and riboflavin—on wheat gluten, lysine hydrochloride, defatted wheat germ, pyridoxine, and several items referred to, with what I am sure is regrettable familiarity, as BHA and BHT.

The cereal disposed of, however, we move on to the subject of school lunches and the daily debate over who will take and who will buy. The mimeographed biweekly school lunch menu is trotted out. Before getting to the *carte du jour* for Monday, June 5, however, we are forced to wade through a pretentiously literary *mise en scène:* three paragraphs of self-serving prose, courtesy of the dietician's office, on the history and nutritional goals of the school lunch program from the Depression to the present. The business of plunking down thirty cents in a cafeteria is presented as a highfalutin educational experience.

Mercifully, my children are not total losses. Their tastes and sensibilities have not wholly prostrated themselves before the idol of meaningful food. Nor has their sense of humor. The Frosted Orange Juice, I am assured, spends several hours developing full bouquet at room temperature; the Fluffy Buttered Rice (the upper-case letters are not mine) is dished up with an ice cream scoop. Once compacted into a ball, it is apparently pretty hard to unfluff: One boy, they tell me, was hit on the foot by a wild service and spent the afternoon in the nurse's office.

Perhaps you see, therefore, why I think taste must come before nutrition. Our infatuation with the quasi-scientific has left us easy marks for con men and tin-fiddle manufacturers. They are not disinterested parties, you know. The breakfast food business began when the internal combustion engine replaced the horse as the chief locomotive force in American life. The jolly millers hardly missed a stitch. They simply got together with the ad men and arranged to have their products shoveled into human, rather than equine, hay-burners.

Not that I am sanguine about the forming of children's tastes. I have fed too many teen-agers to have illusions. Given a choice between cheeses, for example, they will skirt the Pont l'Evêque, the Reblochon, the Appenzeller and the Triple Crème, and head with unerring aim for the prepackaged process slices or the supermarket Swiss (which has the texture, but nowhere near the flavor, of rubber gloves).

The younger ones, of course, make the heart lift. Until they are standardized out of it by the world, or conned out of it by their older brothers and sisters, their tastes remain catholic. They will eat mushrooms, parsnips, Blütwurst and Liederkranz—and gladly take beer or wine to wash them down. As they grow up, however, they turn inexorably into protestants—little Zwinglis of the dinner table. It is a struggle to find anything they like. Hamburgers? "Well, sure, Mom; but not these. Why can't you make them like Hamburger (200 Billion Sold) Heaven?"

It is a situation which I classify (along with most other aspects of domestic life) as desperate but not serious. It is desperate simply because it involves dealing with other human beings. Their tastes are their own. Apart from a general (and generally frustrating) attempt to keep their minds open, and their palates at least willing to try something new every now and then, we can hardly do more. Someday, we hope, they will fall in love, as we did, with all sorts of things and all kinds of people. But on no realistically foreseeable day will they fall in love with precisely what or whom we took to heart. We live too close to them for that. They have too many other things to prove to allow them ever to let on they have been listening to us.

Perhaps the hardest thing for parents of teen-agers to accept is the fact that, by nature, they are almost the last persons on earth their children will come to grips with as

persons. It takes a bit of swallowing to realize (we ourselves having at last arrived at some roundness and ripeness,
and they just beginning to get worth knowing well) that
to them we are not Harry and Martha, but Mom and Pop.
Not warm, lovable, interestingly youthful characters whose
wit and wisdom gladden their hearts and kindle their minds,
but plump and almost entirely ignorable hierarchs. Parents
are not called by title for nothing. They call me Dad to keep
me humble—and well out of their hair.

On the other hand, this desperate situation is anything but
serious. First of all, every generation has survived it. We did,
and they will. Disaster comes only from taking it seriously—
from playing for keeps what is only a game of tasting and
testing. But second, they continually surprise us. Sometimes
they will wipe out the Triple Crème before their parents have
had even two passes at it. Never count, therefore, on their
not eating what they never eat. The day you and your wife
decide to treat yourselves to creamed sweetbreads while they
eat their beloved macaroni salad will be just the day the
macaroni salad goes begging.

Don't worry then. Their tastes in food are only as important
as their grades in school and their choices in marriage. Under
the Mercy, we shall all live to become friends, provided
we don't set each others' teeth on edge too badly in the
meantime. The best we can do is let them see, between the
bursts of bad temper and the dire warnings of imminent
shipwreck, that we ourselves are still mainly concerned to
be lovers of being, and that we hope they will in due time
manage to be the same.

But, you say, turn about is fair play. If we are called to
so magnanimous and exacting a display of patience, surely
they must owe us something. What is the best they can do?
Are there no goals we can set for them to strive after? Ah!
That is the last and hardest lesson of all: Give them any
goals you like—but don't hold your breath. When all is said

and done, their loves are in their hands, not ours; we went into this business only to go out of business. No matter how sad it makes you feel, everything here remains a game: We have yet to sit down to the really serious Supper of the Lamb. Say Amen, and let them go in peace.

With that all-important working rule out of the way, we may now proceed to the practical resolution of the tensions between nutrition and taste. As the problem commonly appears among the young, it takes the form of an extreme choosiness about vegetables. With great good sense, of course, children refuse to be snowed by talk about nutrition but with equally monumental stupidity, they also refuse to try anything with a distinctive taste. How many housewives have been driven to distraction by the effort to tempt their families' appetites with the new and the unusual? How many rare vegetables have been bought at outlandish prices—how many hours of labor expended on fancy recipes—only to bring forth the word that enters like water into the bowels and like oil into the bones: "Why do we have to have this stuff, Mom? What's the matter with canned corn?"

To that harassed housewife—and to all of us lost with her in the dismal swamp of middle life—I bring a word of hope: It would be utterly unconscionable to join 'em; take heart, therefore—it is time to rise up and lick 'em. The situation may be too much for lesser men, but the old foxes are not dead yet. It may be a young people's world—half the population may well be under twenty-five at this very moment— but that is no reason to bow down before the culinary tyranny of the wasp-waisted and flat-stomached. My figure may be rapidly approaching the shape of a utility pole, and yours may be far closer to 36–36–36 than you care to admit, but there must be no peace with oppression. To arms then! I give you some choice and tested gambits to help you regain the upper hand.

For the first: Feed them lettuce before you feed them anything else. You will have noticed that at the beginning of my recipe, I included four heads of lettuce along with the leg of lamb itself as fundamental ingredients in Lamb for Eight Persons Four Times. Each successive meal, as I have conceived it, begins with an empty plate and one eighth of a head of lettuce for each person. No dressing, no vinegar, no oil—not even salt, if you want to drive home with these bitter herbs how utterly they have committed their sensibilities to an Egyptian bondage of tastelessness.

By a single stroke, you have come out ahead of the game. For one thing, you have satisfied your conscience on the subject of nutrition: They will have had their greens before they have anything else at all. For another, they will be fuller, by just that much, when they get to the main dish. Nothing is more expensive than eating on an empty stomach. As a matter of fact, if you have really hungry children, you might give them a loaf of dry bread to break with their greens, just for a little added insurance against a hurricane attack upon the entrée.

Once the lettuce-and-bread opening has been firmly established—once action has convinced you that the initiative is still in your hands—you will find that you are in a position to put them in check almost at will. Exploit their weaknesses. If they will not taste, so much the better for us. My wife and I spent years trying to urge teen-agers to eat mushrooms, until it suddenly dawned on us that, far from our being defeated, victory had been handed to us on a china platter. Now, if it looks as if the main dish will be in short supply, my wife regularly includes one or two sliced mushrooms. When I serve it, I announce solemnly: "You children really must have a good helping of this; the mushrooms are marvelous."

True to form, they object. Equally true to form, I become incensed at their gastronomic inflexibility. The beginnings of a scene hover for a moment over the table; but then, with a sigh and a not altogether gracious gesture of resignation, I give in and serve them small portions. My wife and I exchange a knowing glance, and feast quietly in triumph. I commend the strategy to you. It is the only way I know of to serve sweetbreads to a large family and still insure that the people who really care get enough.

But perhaps you feel that this itself is unconscionable. You hear echoes of ancient, preaching voices saying, "Children need their food; they must have full and rounded meals." I suggest to you, however, that you know better than that. Unless you have paid no attention to the feeding habits of your domestic fauna, you must be aware of how much they eat without any parental supervision at all. If you were to add up carefully the amounts of soda, ice cream, potato chips, peanut butter, process cheese, corn friskies, and party snackies they put away in a single day, your mind would instantly come to rest. A little meat, lettuce, and bread are more than enough to keep their embarrassingly healthy bodies and frighteningly springy souls together.

I suggest, therefore, that you keep track of the paths they beat to the refrigerated water holes and fertile upland kitchen cupboards. It will quiet your conscience once and for all. All you have to do is keep your senses sharp. My wife and I are well matched in many ways; but the compatibilities for which we are most grateful when it comes to child-rearing are her incredible hearing, and my own more than adequate nose. As we sit of an evening, TV at full volume and electric guitars twanging away in the back room, she will suddenly cry out from her armchair: "Get out of the bread drawer!" The kitchen is two rooms away, but the rustle of cellophane never escapes her.

Similarly, I can, during a commercial break, walk past my two amplified rock-and-roll addicts and, at a distance of ten paces, smell the peanut butter on their breaths. (Needless to say, I can smell tobacco at twice the distance. They are boxed, therefore: My wife hears the cigarettes being lifted from her purse in the kitchen closet, and I detect the residual effects twenty minutes later. *Ante* and *post delictum*, we have them nailed. It doesn't slow them down much, of course; but it makes the two of us feel much better about the whole business.)

Assurances about the size of their food intake, however, are not the only comfort I can give you. My lettuce-and-bread strategy not only leaves them perfectly nourished; more important, it leaves them no way out of their self-imposed dilemma except the avenue of taste. There is always the hope that they will, late or soon (be prepared for it to be late), actually sink their teeth into mushroom, parsnip, Swiss chard, or celeriac. Be bold, therefore. Feed them, yes; but do not cook for them. Cook for yourself. What they need most of all in this vale of sorrows is the sight of men who relish reality. You do them no lasting favor by catering to their undeveloped tastes. We have not acquired our amplitude for nothing. No matter what they *think*, we *know:* We are the ones who have tasted and seen how gracious it all is. What a shame if we were to hide that light under a bushel.

On the subject of vegetables, therefore, I urge you to please yourself first, last and always. Until they awake out of their youthful and dogmatic slumbers, even lettuce is too good for them.

❖

TWELVE

The Mysterious East

At this point, let me clear my decks even further and give you the recipes for meals number two and three—parts II and III of Lamb for Eight Persons Four Times. Since they require cooked lamb, however, I must first give you a brief word about part I (B) of the master recipe: Quite simply, it is a good preparation of braised lamb designed to be cooled and used in its entirety as leftovers.

BRAISED LAMB

Take the remainder of the raw leg of lamb and six cloves of garlic. Peel the cloves and cut them lengthwise into three or four slivers each. Then, with the point of a sharp knife, make gashes all over the surface of the meat and insert the slivers.

Put a little olive oil in a heavy pan or Dutch oven large enough to take the leg, and brown it well on all sides. (Be thorough, of course, but don't make a fetish of it. Unless you sawed off the jutting bone exposed by your amateur butchering for part I (A), you will have a fairly untidy piece of business on your hands.)

Next, take two or three medium onions, peel and slice them, and add them to the pot with the meat. Stir until lightly browned.

Add a cup of dry white wine, a little salt and pepper, and a pinch or so of thyme. (Department of little-known distinctions: When you wish to take a large pinch, separate your thumb and forefinger and plunge them, parted, into the box of thyme; close them, picking up all the herb you can get. For a small pinch, however, insert them into the box already joined and take out only what you can pick up by flexing them without separating them.)

Cover the pot and cook on the stove top or in a moderate oven for two hours.

Cool and divide into three portions: two equal ones of meat only, and one of scrap, bone, and juices. Wrap well and refrigerate or freeze.

Keep this recipe in mind, by the way, the next time you see lamb shanks on sale. Just use orégano instead of thyme, be a little more liberal with it, and thicken the sauce by some appropriate means at the end. Served with a saffron risotto and a bottle of something really robust (red Hermitage, for example), there are few occasions, plain or fancy, on which it will not be meat in due season.

Now we may proceed.

PART II: LAMB AND SPINACH CASSEROLE

1 pound or so of cooked
lamb, cut into bite-size
slices. (Here is where you
use the first package of
deliberate leftovers from
the braised shank end of
the leg)

2 pounds fresh spinach (or
3 or 4 packages frozen
spinach) cooked and
chopped (don't oversalt)

¼ cup butter
4 tablespoons mayonnaise
4 tablespoons grated
Parmesan or Cheddar
cheese
A few drops of Sherry
Salt and freshly ground
black pepper to taste

Add all ingredients to the hot, drained spinach, correct
the seasoning, place in a casserole, cover, and heat thoroughly
in a moderate oven. Serve with plenty of bread and butter—
and with a salad, if it looks as if there won't be enough to
go around.

Actually, this recipe entered my household back in the bad
old days when we were all frantically trying one diet after
another. Any expert on the subject will quickly recognize it
(minus the lamb and, of course, the side order of bread) as
a low-carbohydrate spinach thing straight out of one of those
drinking man's diets. Needless to say, the longing for bread
—the impossibility of life without starch and sugar—effectively
finished off the diet; but the spinach recipe has stayed with
us as a kind of monument to less enlightened days. All we
have done is make it the vehicle for leftovers of various kinds.
You will find it excellent in the case of any relatively dry
meat for which you have run out of gravy. It is just moist
enough and oily enough to take the curse off the hard outer
parts of an old roast of beef (use a little Worcestershire

in place of the Sherry) or for lonesome and crumbly bits of turkey breast.

It makes a good light meal. Those who want to go easy can take only the casserole. Teen-age sons can make up the difference with bread if they have to. They will act as if you are trying to starve them into submission, but, in most cases, they survive quite nicely. It does a family good to see a meal wiped out completely before surfeit has destroyed enthusiasm. One of the commonest graces prays that we may be mindful of the needs of others. But faith without works is dead. An occasional entrée in short supply puts a few more teeth into the prayer.

PART III: LAMB FRIED RICE

Leftover cooked lamb, cut into bite-size slices (package number two)	Peanut oil
	Salt
	3 eggs
2 onions sliced (or a couple of scallions, if you have them)	Drop of Sherry
	Splash of chicken stock
	3–4 cups cooked rice
1 cup shredded cabbage (or a can of bean sprouts)	Imported soy sauce

Put sliced onions and shredded cabbage in cold water until ready to use.

In your favorite deep skillet or, best of all, in a large *wok,* put a little oil, add some salt, turn up the heat, and scramble the 3 eggs until broken into firm but still tender pieces.

Scoop these into a temporary dish, add a little more oil and salt, turn the heat up again and add the drained vege-tables, together with the Sherry and the chicken stock. Stir-fry these for a few minutes, add the lamb and then the rice and eggs.

Mix well and heat through, taking care that it does not stick too badly. Season (lightly) with soy sauce. If it looks a little dry for your taste, add some more stock. The dish, however, should never be wet and sticky. The grains of rice should salute you individually, not simply glare back at you as a single glutinous mass.

This, obviously, is more an exercise in Chinese method than it is real Chinese cooking. Nevertheless, since the method is obviously one of my favorites, let me give you a few additional pointers and recipes.

First, a word about the *wok*. If you have never seen one, it is a shallow, bowl-shaped pan with two handles. Commonly, it is made of sheet iron, and when you buy it (any restaurant supply house can get you one), it will be pleasantly silvery. That, however, is a temporary condition. The first thing you must do with it is coat it well, but not sloppily, with peanut oil and carefully blacken it over your largest top burner. (Several old pot holders or even a pair of large pliers will come in handy here.) The process is long-winded—twenty to thirty minutes to do a good job on a new wok—and things get pretty hot. They also get pretty smelly and smoky, so turn on the exhaust fan.

The purpose of the blackening is to give the pan a better cooking surface than raw iron. Accordingly, you will have to keep wiping the inside with light coats of fresh oil, and to move the pan around on the flame so that it darkens evenly all over the inside surface. The real trick is not to let any one spot get so terribly hot that the coating of oil blisters and burns off. That would only take you down to bare metal again and defeat the purpose of the whole exercise. (Also be careful not to use too much oil. Toward the end, it's very easy to start a fire.)

Well, you say, that seems to be a lot of fuss and feathers for nothing more than a pot.

That is only because you have never owned a wok. It is one of the most intelligently conceived pieces of cooking hardware the race has ever invented. First of all, it comes in many sizes. I, for example, own two: a small one, 12 inches in diameter and 3 inches deep, and a large one, 20 inches across and 6 inches deep. In the case of all except the smallest sizes (which will sit adequately on the stove top), you will need an iron ring stand (homemade or bought) for your wok. Without something of the sort, its round bottom becomes a liability rather than an asset.

It is the round bottom, of course, that is the cleverest thing about the pan. It has the effect of insuring that any liquid invariably runs to the hottest part of all. That, in turn, guarantees that fresh steam proceeds continually upward through your food and, unless you run out of liquid altogether, prevents anything from sticking to the bottom. (If you are a lover of creamy scrambled eggs, you will never use a frying pan again. In a wok, there is always a depth of egg nestling warmly in the center—never a miserable scattering of it all over the searing surface of a flat pan. Furthermore, if you have ever tried to make Egg Foo Yong at home, and wondered why you got thin, tough egg pancakes instead of thick, fluffy, tender, well-browned omelets, it is because you didn't have a wok.)

The fuss and feathers, therefore, turns out to be aimed at something more than a mere pot. The wok is the consummate pot—a whole collection of pots rolled into one. If you are convinced, go out and buy one. If not, buy one anyway. It will convince you, even if I didn't.

In all fairness, however, I owe you a warning. If you have an electric stove, forget about the wok and about the Chinese method generally. Much as I know it will get me into trouble with all kinds of people, I simply cannot see electric stoves at all. They are perhaps the biggest tin fiddle in the American household—the perfect example of a product which no professional ever uses, but which has been neatly fobbed off on the public. (Electric ovens, of course, are not nearly such a bad idea; my condemnation is addressed principally to the use of electrical elements for top burners.)

Go into any restaurant kitchen. You will find a gas stove. It is there because, on the basis of long experience by people who know and care, it is the most flexible and responsive cooking instrument yet developed. A boiling-over pot can be stopped with a flick of the wrist; (with an electric stove, you have to move the pot). Full heat is available instantly. (With electricity you have to tap your foot through the agonizing warmup.) Oh, I know, they make them with "speed" burners. Another con job. All that means is that the speed burners get worked to death and have to be replaced at forty or fifty dollars a throw, while the rest of the stove is still new. Finally, the gas stove gives you the most intelligent means of all of gauging how much heat is being applied to your pan: You can *see* what you're doing. No need to trust blindly in the con men who put little numbers around the rims of the electric stove knobs; you simply look under the pot and, yourself the master, build the flame you know you need. Fire is too old a friend to be forsaken for glowing rods. Perhaps I overstate my case, but it seems to me that cooking with electricity is like trying to play the piano with mittens on. I blame the electric stove for many a woman's insensitivity when it comes to food.

But I do not stop there. I am not even willing to speak kindly of all gas stoves. Except for the fact that they do have the saving grace of tongues of fire, many of them seem to have been designed by the same sheet metal Stradivarius manufacturers. They are frequently too small, they have too few top burners, and they are sadly lacking in oven and broiler space. My advice about stoves, to anyone who will listen, is just what it is about most other kitchen equipment: Stick with items intended for commercial use.

You are afraid of the price? Put your fears aside. A few years ago, we decided that, for a family of eight, a six-burner, two-oven stove was the only answer. Obviously that kind of equipment doesn't come cheap; but what we were amazed to learn was that, for about ten dollars more (at that time) than a fancy-dan pinball machine of a domestic range, we could (and did) buy a first-class small restaurant job: six big burners, two drive-in ovens (22 by 26 inches), a broiler you don't have to lie on the floor to look into, a magnificent (24 by 24 inches) solid iron griddle, and, best of all, a five-foot shelf all along the back for spices and other classics. It was black, of course. But then, white stoves are only for compulsive cleaners and other hapless victims of the con men. If you insist on having something to polish, you can get restaurant equipment in stainless steel; but if you do, you are just asking for trouble. Black is the kindest color of all. (I should know. As a priest, I figure it is good for about twenty pounds of sheer flattery. In civilian clothes I look like a 210-pound flour sack tied in the middle. In clericals, the situation is considerably better.)

Besides, there is something professional and business-like about a big black stove. I will never believe a woman who tells me she is no cook, unless she has given a restaurant range a fair try. It rubs off on you. With five pots, two ovens, and a broiler going at once, you cease to be a piker; you become an operator. If you're going to invest heavily in a stove, then, forget completely about domestic equipment. Visit your restaurant supplier, and take the plunge. (While you're there, confirm your resolution by buying some commercial-weight aluminum pots. Start at six or seven quarts and work your way up by two's till you run out of money. You'll never regret it.)

Since it was the Chinese method of stir-frying that got me off on this tangent, let me now give you something more specific by way of guidance. What follows is not, of course, truly Chinese cooking: That, to be authentic, calls for certain ingredients (mainly vegetables) that are not normally available in most places. Specialty stores in large cities can usually supply you with what you need, but then, they are not too available either.

It would be a shame, however, to miss the excellence, the fascination, and (given a little advance work) the convenience of stir-frying just because exotic ingredients are not at hand. In these recipes, therefore, ordinary American vegetables are used. Fresh ginger root and imported soy sauce are the only two ingredients I really insist on making a fuss about. The ginger is not as hard to come by as it used to be—if worse comes to worst, you can order some by mail. It keeps for weeks, and its flavor and bouquet are worth any trouble you have to go to. Fresh ginger is not only hotter and more gingery than the usual dried item; it also has a beautiful lemon-lime fragrance that enhances almost any dish. If you must substitute, however, use ¼ teaspoon of ground ginger in place of the quarter-size piece of ginger root in the recipes.

As far as the soy sauce is concerned, get yourself a fifth each of the light and dark varieties of the genuine Chinese article, plus a bottle of oyster sauce (a bit smelly by itself, but marvelous in combination). Lacking the Chinese products, use imported Japanese soy sauce, which currently seems to be available at decent stores everywhere. In any case, forget the American varieties. They are only for the utterly desperate: All salt and no finesse makes Jack a dull cook.

To begin with, then, let me set down the Chinese method of *chow*, or stir-frying, in outline form.

(1) *All* ingredients are prepared in advance and placed in covered dishes or bowls of cold water, as appropriate.

(2) A small amount of oil is spread over the inside of the wok, a little salt is added, and the heat is turned up high.

(3) The meat is then stir-fried for a few minutes (until the desired color is reached), and removed to a temporary dish. (Use two wooden spoons to keep things moving.)

(4) Step (2) is repeated, if necessary.

(5) Next, the onion, garlic, and ginger are put into the wok and cooked for a few seconds only, so as not to burn them. (The purpose of this brief preliminary cooking is to take the roughest edges off their several flavors and make them better company for the ingredients to follow.)

(6) The drained vegetables are then added (the water that adheres to them is quite sufficient); they are tossed for a minute or so with two spoons and then covered to steam for three to five minutes more. Once again, it is color, not texture, that is your guide to doneness: When the dish *looks* good, it *is* good. *Question:* Where do you find a cover large enough for a 20-inch wok? *Answer:* You buy an 18-inch aluminum pizza tray, drill a ⅛-inch hole in the middle, and steal the knob off an old pot lid.

(7) At the end, a mixture of cornstarch, stock, and (sometimes) soy sauce is added, and the dish is boiled just enough to thicken it.

Not counting preparation time, it takes ten minutes at the most to put such a dish on the table. It is a blessing not only on ordinary days when you want something quick and easy after an afternoon's shopping, but also at parties when you would like to spend as much time as possible looking coolly relaxed in front of your company. Furthermore, it is perfect if you are plagued with guests who show up late. Nothing need be cooked until the last straggler is firmly in hand. Tardiness will not even call for forgiveness; it will have become ignorable.

Two footnotes.

(1) This stir can be made with a variety of meats and vegetables. Sliced raw beef or chicken are excellent, and raw shrimp or lobster are magnificent. Just remember that, generally speaking, a white-meated dish needs no soy sauce. Simply salt to taste, and you will find delectabilities you never expected. Also, other vegetables may be used. The darker greens (kale, Swiss chard) make a lovely appearance. So does a fresh, peeled tomato, cut in eighths. Your sense of color and shape is the best guide of all.

(2) Besides being delicious, a stir made in the Chinese style is also cheap. No other method of cooking will yield as much flavor from so little meat. Try it, therefore; then pronounce judgment. Unless you are no cook at all, you will be hooked before stir number three.

One warning. Impressive though it is, I advise against carrying the wok to the table for use as a serving bowl. Leaving a moist dish in it for any length of time will strip off the protective coating of baked-on oil as fast as anything. The last few helpings will taste as if they had been made with wet iron filings. You will also have to spend another twenty minutes putting a decent surface back on your wok.

Perhaps this is the place to warn you against an excessive zeal for cleanliness when it comes to ironware. Properly seasoned, iron is one of the greatest cooking materials in the world, but the average American housewife has been so brainwashed that she commonly scours off the cooking surface without thinking. Woks and iron skillets should be rinsed and wiped, never washed. If someone comes along and tells you cleanliness is next to godliness, the proper answer is, "Yes—next. Right now I'm working on godliness."

If, however, your family persists in a compulsive and unreasonable attitude, accustom them to a little harmless but definite untidiness in their food. An occasional burned paper match dropped into the gravy will help them relax a bit. My wife has even managed, mysteriously, to include a cigar band in a casserole of Spanish rice. Once you've seen something like that, it's hard to get upset about the fine points of kitchen cleanliness.

A sense of proportion is a saving grace.

THIRTEEN

✣

Bread to Strengthen Man's Heart

As you have no doubt gathered, the culinary philosophy of this book is heretical, at least as far as the secular orthodoxy of our times is concerned. The world is engaged in a vast missionary effort (spearheaded by zealous Madison Avenue Fathers) to convince us that it is our gastronomic destiny to eat like kings while practicing nothing but the most minimal kind of cooking. We are no longer a boiled-meat-and-potatoes nation. We are rather a Frozen-Peas-with-Tiny-Onions-in-Butter-Sauce people, a ready-to-serve Lobster Newburgh in Cooking Pouch race of men. We have been persuaded that the choice, the rich and the rare, are our rightful province, and we have been led to expect that these treasures will simply defrost themselves into our laps.

Against all that propaganda for fancy eating and plain cooking, I hope to persuade you to cook fancy and just plain eat. First of all, it is better for your soul. Only a daily renewed astonishment at things as they are can save us from the idols;

it is our love of real processes and actual beings that keeps us sane. The little plastic pouches filled with commercial New-burgh sauce are bound, late or soon, to cut the taproot of refreshment. They are designed more for effect than for in-herent goodness, and they are marketed by means of incanta-tions which harp upon the purportedly posh status they confer.

For a second point, fancy cooking and plain eating is as good for your taste as it is for your soul. The elegant con-coctions the world tries to sell us are not all that good. They consist, far too often, of supremely average stuff gussied up by press agentry. Try the Newburgh sauce some day. If you can't do better than that on your own—and in less time than it takes to go to the supermarket to buy it—you are either a rank beginner or a person who needs a better cookbook. In any case, what you *don't* need is another pouch of instant prestige. The plainest things in the world, prepared with care and relished for what they are, are better than all the com-mercial flummery in the dairy case.

Finally, if you cook fancy and eat plain, you move yourself a little closer to that fasting without which our age has little chance of keeping its head threaded on straight. Great cook-ing demands great eating; that is as it should be. But such frank eating, unless we are all to swell up and burst, must be a sometime thing. As I said, I would rather have one magnificent meal followed by a day of no meals at all, than two days full of ambitious mediocrities at close intervals. In this vale of sorrows, we should be careful about allowing abundance to con us out of hunger.

It is not only the best sauce; it is also the choicest daily reminder that the agony of the world is by no means over. As long as the passion goes on, we are called to share it as we can—especially if, by the mere luck of the draw, we have escaped the worst pains of it. Do all you can to help, of course; but don't, for all that, forget that you are also called simply to bear. In the end, the agony lies too deep for any cure except the cross. Fast, therefore, until His Passion brings the world home free. He works through any crosses He can find. In a time of affluence, fasting may well be the simplest one of all.

But, you say, not all men are ready for such heroic discipline. Even supposing that they were willing to fast, they are too far gone in the ways of the world to leave it flat. Is there no middle way, no intermediate course of eating through which they might approach perfection by degrees?

Of course there is. If you do not feel up to a single meal a day, begin by reducing all meals but one to the starkest possible simplicity. Take breakfast, for example. Americans already have one leg on fasting as far as their morning meal is concerned. If it were not for the propaganda of the horse-feed barons, most of us would probably be more than content with fruit and coffee. Anyone who finds he really needs more can always take bread and butter—or cheese. How much better it would be than the daily self-deception that 240 calories' worth of rolled wheat chaff or powdered protein will make a man healthy, wealthy, and wise. That kind of thinking only makes him a setup for another day of idolatry.

To begin with, breakfast is an unmerciful meal. Unless you live in a house full of larks, you know perfectly well that few people are fit company at that hour. Accordingly, a completely routine meal, unvarying from day to day, is a blessing to everyone. The mistress of the house is responsible for nothing more than brewing decent coffee and keeping fruit juice and bread on hand. Moreover, the rest of the family is freed from the burden of decision. Breakfast is a time to be left alone with one's thoughts. To have to face an array of boxes and a barrage of arguments about whose favorite style of eggs will be forced on everybody is simply too much.

Secondly, except for men who have already worked hard for hours, an ordinary weekday breakfast is no time for a feast. When we go to work, we go forth, by obedience to vocation, to draw the world into the Passion. Of all meals it is the one that most plainly has Stranger and Pilgrim stamped upon it. What a shame to bury all that under pseudogastronomic frou-frou.

Nothing I say in favor of the plain breakfast, however, should be construed as prohibiting the really festal late-morning spread. I am as partial to eggs, sausages, hash browned potatoes (with a scraping of onion), wheatcakes, bacon, kippered herrings, and left over *kartoffelklösse* sliced and fried in butter as any man on earth. Sane men, when they take such a meal at ten on Saturday morning, do not eat again until eight at night. But we have given ourselves a bad conscience because of the idol of three square meals a day. We will not eat little normally; accordingly, we feel guilty about eating much occasionally. It is the old fate of the narrow-gauge epicure: If you take all your meals seriously, none of them gets a chance to matter.

On the other hand, consider lunch. Once again, it need be nothing more than a crust, a leaf, and a glass of wine. I have long been convinced (since college, in fact, when I had a two-hour lecture at 1:00 P.M.) that man needs sleep more than food in the middle of the day. A piece of cheese, a bottle of beer, and a twenty-minute nap would solve more of the problems of industry, politics, and the church than all the pretentious martini-logged luncheon meetings in the world.

Almost as clearly as breakfast, lunch is a meal *in via*, on the run. To sit down as if the world were our oyster at 12:30 is to face the second half of our daily obedience pretending that the agony of the world is over already. It is only at night, *in gremio familiae*, in the lap of that questionable luxury by which God takes the sharpness off our solitude, that we can properly rejoice and eat like men. Many women are poor cooks only because their native greatness has been beaten down by ingratitude. A husband's hunger is one of the principal ornaments of his household. How sad, then, when he spends his day blunting the edge of the easiest, truest compliment he can pay his wife.

Light meals, therefore—or none at all—until we can use our appetites for their true and human end: not simply to satisfy ourselves, but to confer greatness on what we love.

If you are persuaded of any of this, pave the way for reform by providing honest bread, butter, and cheese for your family. Let me take them up in reverse order.

Cheese is at once a testament to the Creator's ingenuity in providing enzymes and bacteria that will do fearful and wonderful things for milk and to man's audacity in the face of some pretty forbidding stuff. The blander varieties, of course, are hardly more alarming than milk itself; but the farther reaches of the subject put even brave men to the test. There are cow's-milk cheeses which will convince you that someone has dragged a whole barnyard indoors, and goat's milk cheeses which taste as if the goat sat in them. There is something grandly faithful to the real being of creation about strong cheese. Good Limburger (with onions and rye bread, by all means), noble Liederkranz (America's greatest cheese), French Münster, ripe Reblochon, vile Livarot, and all the deceptively pretty, shockingly flavorsome goat cheeses recall man to the humbleness of his grandeur and the greatness of his low estate. The first man is of the earth, earthy. If I had only a single temporal blessing to wish you, I would not hesitate a moment: May you be spared long enough to know at least one long evening of old friends, dark bread, good wine, and strong cheese. If even exile be so full, what must not our fullness be?

As is to be expected, however, the cheeses which are the stuff of such epic evenings are like great wines: rare, expensive, and hard to come by. What I have in mind for routine family sustenance are two less exalted items. The first is cottage cheese. I can see no reason why a house should ever be without two containers of it—one open and one in reserve. You will, of course, have to pick the type you like, and you will have to avoid the poor excuses for the subject that seem to abound from time to time. For the record, let me put down my own preference: Large curd, creamed. I fail to grasp the point of trying to make smooth that which nature has gone to considerable lengths to make lumpy.

With your ice box thus perpetually stocked, even the most timorous taster has a lunch or breakfast that will speed him on his way. Taken with salt and plenty of freshly ground black pepper—and, if you like, with bread, butter, and beer— it is a meal that can become an old friend: solid, unpretentious, and good. Don't forget, however, that it is just as good sweetened as salted. Someday, when it takes your fancy, sprinkle your bowlful with sugar and a little plain ground fresh coffee. (If you live in an Italian neighborhood, try keeping *ricotta* on hand. It is another cheese, to be sure, but it has a finesse which cottage cheese lacks, and it takes to sweetening better than anything.)

For a more robust cheese, I suggest plain old American Cheddar in the largest pieces you can afford—even in whole wheels, if you are a real plunger. We make excellent rat cheese in this country. The great Cheddars of Vermont, Wisconsin, and New York State (I am no mere rebel, you see—I may be governor of New York after all) can hold their heads high in any company, however exotic. They are good plain, or with any kind of bread, and they are, to my mind, the greatest toasting cheeses in the world. I remember one long Sunday morning on vacation. We held Mass on the cottage porch by the lake, and then settled down with good company and a gallon of Sicilian red to grilled Vermont Cheddar and homemade bread from 9:30 to 1:00 P.M. Talk about days of wine and roses.

Having given my native land her due, though, let me make two additional suggestions on the subject of robust cheeses to be kept in quantity. The first is Appenzeller—one of the most emphatically delightful of all the Swisses. At its best, it is pungent, firm, and utterly satisfying. Unfortunately, it is usually handled only by the more ambitious cheese stores, and I imagine it is hard to find in most parts of the country. It is also expensive; but if you have the money, you could hardly spend it more wisely.

My second recommendation is a little easier to buy, particularly if you are near Italian specialty stores. It is *Ricotta Pecorina*. Not to be confused with mere ricotta, this is a sheep cheese which comes in small, high, round wheels of four to six pounds each. It is white, fairly firm (though it should not be hard or dry) and, like many of the great sheep cheeses, it has a distinct flavor of lamb about it. To some degree (or at least for some people), it is an acquired taste; but the labor of acquisition is light and rewarding. Try it.

With a considerable wedge of any of these on hand, you are ready to provide plain but exquisite eating for all comers. By one stroke, breakfast and lunch will have been lifted from the category of fuss and nonsense, and put back in the mainstream of true humanity. Your family will be men *in via* once again, and, because of that, all the more grateful when, night by night, you light the lamps of home.

Cheese done, however, we come to butter. I shall be brief. First, as to what it is not. It is not, in any except the merely technical sense of the word, grease. It melts at the temperature of the tongue, and consequently goes down as easily as cream. (You do not like to drink cream? I am sorry. Let us agree to disagree and get on with it.) Any man who cannot tell the difference between butter and margarine has callouses on the inside of his mouth. Margarine *is* grease. It never achieves real liquidity upon the tongue; accordingly, it leaves a coating where butter leaves none, and betrays itself every time.

Second, butter is not properly a spread. To be sure, it can *be* spread, and delightfully so; but then, so can *pâté de foie gras,* and anyone who calls that a spread is out of his mind. Butter is a substance in its own right, justified by its own delectability, not by its contributory services. It is a unique and solid sauce; it is apt to more dishes than anything in the world, and it is, like all the greatest sauces, worthy of being eaten plain. It is probably possible to divide the human race into butter-eaters and non-butter-eaters. I am not sure what the division really says about us (and no wise man should go around looking for more divisions than we already have), but I am sure where my sympathies lie. I find cold butter simply irresistible.

From that, you can anticipate the conclusion of my argument. Since butter is not grease and not a spread, it is not replaceable by anything that is simply a greasy spread. Exit here, therefore, into outer darkness and weeping and gnashing of teeth, margarine and all its works. And enter good butter. If you care about taste at all, use the best: AA only. The realm of the irreplaceable is no place to count cost.

Above all, be liberal with it. My grandmother was a great cook and always insisted on quality ingredients when she could get them. My taste for fine butter derives from her house, I am sure. I fault her for only one thing. She made me use warm butter on my *knackerbröd*—and she made me put it on the flat side. The side with the little holes in it held too much butter for her old Swedish sense of frugality. I am all in favor of fasting; but as long as God is not frugal about being, I see no point in eating stingily. In my house, hard tack gets cold butter, and on the right side.

Last and plainest, though—and best of all—comes bread. I shall not give you a recipe. It would be merely burdensome to supply you with what any decent cookbook will provide. What I shall give you, however, are a few pointers about the making of bread which may help take away some of the awe which cookbooks often inspire. I have never quite understood possessions is a little handwritten book of recipes from my why, but far too many authors make the process more complex than it really is. Herewith, then, the householder's guide to fast bread. With my strictures, and your favorite cookbook's recipe, you should be able to keep your family in real bread with your back turned.

First. Use baker's yeast. Find a bakery that will sell it to you by the pound or half pound, and forget about the little packages of granulated dry yeast. For one thing, baker's yeast works faster. For another, you will use more; any blow against mere thrift is on the side of the angels. Finally, you can eat it. Once again, just as with butter, the world divides itself between eaters and non-eaters of yeast. One of my priceless grandfather. It contains menus for elegant luncheons, several punches for fifty persons, his own recipes for the sweet martini (yes, Virginia, there was once a sweet martini, why do you think the dry one is called dry?), the dry manhattan (men were freer in those days), and assorted clippings from New York *Sun* food columns *circa* 1920. The cover of the notebook is blank except for a small word from the furniture store which gave it away free: Compliments of Cowperthwait's (Park Row at Chatham Square); but it is the cryptic inscription on the initial page which I love best of all. My grandfather's first word to the world on the subject of gastronomy was: *I prescribe fresh yeast to strengthen a weak stomach.*

I join him in the prescription. Besides being delicious, it is one of the best morning-after remedies I know. A tablespoon of yeast, taken with a tablespoon of sugar and washed down with lukewarm water, will fill your lethargic stomach with fresh life. It will also liberate enough CO_2 to provide you with the greatest relief of all: a good, healthy belch. Admittedly, it gives you the air of a walking brewery; but then, the first man *is* of the earth, earthy. Why deny it? (By way of additional testimony, my wife holds it as an article of faith that yeast is also good for cesspools. When, by mismanagement or inactivity, she happens to have a large amount of super-annuated baker's yeast on hand, she simply puts it down the sink while the washing machine is pouring warm water into the septic tank. I will admit that I approach the household drains with a little trepidation afterward, but there is at least a skin of reason on her ritual, so who am I to doubt?)

For the second point on breadmaking, however: Work with only one pot. Scald your liquids in a six- or seven-quart pan, let it cool, and add your flour directly to it. (The yeast, sugar, and water solution can be stirred up in an idle coffee cup: Bread needs no array of pots and bowls.)

For the third: If you want your bread to keep, use extra butter and creamy milk—and an egg, if you have one to spare. (Just break it into the pot when the mixture is still more a batter than a dough. The subsequent kneading will mix it in quite nicely—no need to dirty another bowl and beater.)

For the fourth: Knead well. It perfects the texture of the bread, and, more important, it is good for your soul. There are few actions you will ever take that have more of the stuff of history in them. A woman with her sleeves rolled up and flour on her hands is one of the most gorgeous stabilities in the world. Don't let your family miss the sight.

Finally: Don't let your bread rise too long the last time. Its final fullness should come only in the baking. Bread that rises too high in the pan shrinks in the oven: Sharp edges on the finished loaves are the telltale sign. Don't be fussy, however, about finding the perfect warm place for the dough to rise in. Most cookbooks give you the impression that you can hardly succeed without rigorous climate control, but with baker's yeast, your bread will rise nicely almost anywhere in the house.

On second thought, I think I shall give you a recipe. It

makes beautifully crusty loaves, and while it is not designed to keep long, it is seldom called upon to do so. It disappears even faster than it is made.

CUBAN BREAD

4 tablespoons yeast	2 cups lukewarm water
1 tablespoon salt	6 cups flour (approximately)
2 tablespoons sugar	

Dissolve the yeast, salt, and sugar in a coffee cup with some of the water. With a wooden spoon, beat enough of the flour into the rest of the water until you have a batter. Stir in the contents of the coffee cup, and continue adding flour till you have a manageable dough. Turn it out onto a board and knead well, adding flour till you arrive at a fairly stiff dough. Then knead some more.

Place the dough in a greased bowl, cover with a damp towel, and let rise until doubled in bulk. When risen, turn out on the board and cut it in two. Shape it (squeezing out the yeasty gasses as you do) into two plump, round loaves.

Sprinkle some cornmeal on a greased baking sheet big enough for both loaves, place the loaves on the sheet, and let them rise for five (only five) minutes.

Gently cut a generous cross in the top of each with a sharp knife, and place them in a cold oven. Set the temperature control at hot (400°), place a large pan of boiling water on the bottom of the oven, and turn on the heat. In forty-five minutes or so, you will have the crustiest homemade bread of your career.

Unless I miss my guess, though, you won't have it for long.

❖

One Good Turn
Deserves Another

If I have persuaded you of the merits of that plain eating to which bread, in its earthy unfussiness, is the greatest single invitation, let me now reverse engines and insist once more on the rightful place of the fussy, the fancy, and the fantastic. Paradox is the only basket large enough to hold truth: It is the very simplicity of bread which provides the foundation for all the complexities that man has wrought with flour. The violin is an astonishingly plain piece of business, carried beyond itself by craftsmanship: Stradivarius, Guarnerius, and Amati have gone down in history because they went to the inordinate bother of perfecting the ordinary. Unfortunately, we do not know the names of the first cooks who fiddled with the elastic properties of flour long enough to invent pastry, but their care is just as much a monument to the true work of man. We were meant to lift the world with loving eyes and hands; pastry is bread transfigured by concern.

By why pastry? you ask. Does he plan to do a whole chapter on the upper reaches of baking without so much as a kind word for cake?

The answer, I am afraid, is yes. If it will make you any happier, I shall record here my genuine but limited enthusiasm for a very few cakes (chiefly ones with at least five mercifully thin layers separated by shamelessly moist filling), and return straightway to pastry. If that does not satisfy you, I am sorry. I suppose I am just not a cake eater. In spite of forty years of looking at magazine illustrations, the sight of a giant wedge of high, dry cake, whether it can be sliced with a feather or not, simply appalls me. One bite and I revert instantly to my childhood vices of stirring crumbs into melted ice cream, and dunking when nobody is looking.

But I have a better reason than mere prejudice for choosing pastry as the epitome of baking: It illustrates one of the chief paradoxes of life. If you were to poll the man in the street on the question: Which is harder to accomplish—something simple or something complex? you would no doubt find that most people take it for granted that simple things are easy and complex ones difficult. Yet if you were to ask the question of knowledgeable men in respect of their own trades, you would find that the reverse is true. The writer would tell you that he wrote 5000 words because he didn't have the time to write 1500. The decorator would inform you that she worked longer and harder to produce her dramatically simple window treatment than the dabbler in the next apartment who spent one hour and produced a splendid complexity of chintz and gingerbread. The monk might tell you that he had a simple life, and the married man that he had a complex one; but the married man has bought cheap what the monk has sold dear —he proves the point as well as anyone.

It is simplicity, therefore, that takes the most doing, even though complexity has more going on. Take cake as opposed to pastry, for example. Pastry is simplicity itself: a rough-and-ready paste separated by rough-and-ready layers of butter.

Cake, on the other hand, is complex. It is a veritable chemical formula, requiring the utmost precision of weight and measure. But when all is said and done, cake is easy and pastry is hard—or at least fussy. To make a cake, all you have to be able to do is follow directions and stir. But to make pastry? Ah! Without technique, competence, hands, *feel*, you get nowhere.

Accordingly, I take pastry as the crown of baking. Nowhere is process more essential to success; in no other act of cooking is the cook more an agent and less a spectator. I have made this point before, of course, in the discourse I gave you on strudel, but it remains to be borne out specifically here. Consider, therefore, precisely what is involved in the high art of the *pâtissier*.

First, however, a procedural note. I shall not treat of what is commonly referred to as plain, or common-garden-American-piecrust pastry. For one thing, you are probably up to that already. For another, and more important, it is a compromise with the real thing. As you know, the recipes for it are set up on the analogy of cake recipes, with precise measurements. If you fail to be exact, you lose the essence of what you are after. True pastry—puff paste, that is—is much less fussy as far as the basic mixture is concerned. On the other hand, the paradox of complex-easy/simple-hard comes into full play. Plain pastry requires only a minimum of technique; puff pastry is *all* technique.

The pastry cook is concerned with two basic simplicities which have already appeared several times in this book: the elastic properties of flour-and-water paste, and the separating properties of layers or coats of butter. He is at pains to manufacture the thinnest possible sheets of paste and to guarantee equally thin layers of butter between them. Let me illustrate it for you on the grand scale.

Imagine a *chef pâtissier* of heroic proportions. Make him a giant a mile tall. Having mixed flour, salt, and water into a dough on his stadium-size pastry table, he rolls it out with a rolling pin the diameter of a submarine until it covers the area of two square eight-room houses and stands one story high upon the board. Next, he takes a weight of butter equal to half the weight of his dough and kneads it under cold water to the size and shape of the entire first floor of one of those houses. This billet of butter he places in the center of his dough and folds the paste over to encapsulate the butter completely. He now has a three-layered envelope (dough, butter, dough) which lies upon his board like a three-story, eight-room house. He is ready to roll.

With his pin, he flattens the structure into a strip as long as several football fields. But as he does, each of the three layers become progressively thinner. His entire elongated house is now hardly half a story high and each of his layers is slightly less than two feet thick. Next, he folds both ends of his strip to the middle, and then folds one end over the other, so that he has a four-layered square, two stories high.

Before we allow him to repeat the process, however, consider this latest structure. Each of those four layers consists of two layers of paste and one of butter. When rolled out once more, it will produce a strip consisting of five layers of paste and four of butter. By that time, though, each layer of butter will be only one fourth as thick as it was after the first rolling: not two feet, but six inches.

Now he may go on. We shall keep track of his progress mathematically. He gives the dough a total of four "turns" or rollings. At the end of the second turn, he produces a square of 16 layers of butter and 17 layers of paste (the butter is now a mere $1\frac{2}{3}$ inches thick). At the end of the third turn, he has 4×16 or 64 layers of butter and 65 layers of paste; and (to spare you the suspense), at the end of the fourth turn (and after a final chilling and rolling before baking), he has brought forth a magnificent creation of 64×4 or 256 layers of butter and 257 layers of paste, with the butter (and, of course, the paste) now only .08333 of an inch thick. Rough that out at $\frac{1}{12}$ of an inch. You are at last in a position to understand what makes puff paste puff.

Imagine a single round of this pastry the size of a giant's cookie (as large, let us say, as the circular track of the Synchrotron at the Brookhaven National Laboratory) and sprinkled with sugar grains the size of medicine balls. He pops it into a 450° oven and closes the door. Consider carefully now. There are 257 layers of paste in that cookie, separated by 256 layers of butter. Each layer is $\frac{1}{12}$ of an inch thick, making the entire confection 43 inches in height. But every one of the thin sheets of paste is full of water. Consequently, when, after eight minutes or so, the heat of the oven raises the temperature of the layers above 212°, the water expands violently into steam. Since, however, this steam is entrapped, it forces the layers apart to make a way of escape—a task made easy now, for the butter has melted and each layer of paste is nicely free of the others. With even moderate success, the giant's pastry cookie will rise to a height of 16 to 18 feet.

At this point, he turns his oven down slightly and waits until all the steam is driven out and all the layers have been frenchfried by the intervening butter. The triumph of puff paste is complete. He removes it from the oven, and, if he is half the giant we think he is, gobbles it down immediately, giving himself great satisfaction and, in all likelihood, a gigantic burn on the tongue. 'Twas ever thus.

With that as your introduction to the theory of pastry, I propose to pass on to the actual details of making puff paste. Perhaps, though, it would be just as well if I took advantage of your new enlightenment and explained right here just why plain pastry is a compromise and, above all, why pastry made with oil is not pastry at all.

Take plain pastry first. As you know, it is made most successfully by cutting butter into salted flour until it has been reduced to lumps smaller than small peas. To this mixture (most conveniently produced by using a wire pastry blender), water is added discreetly, and the resultant dough is then immediately rolled out for use. Note the differences between this and puff paste. First of all, the paste itself comes into being only just before the rolling; it is not worked extensively to exploit its elastic properties. Second, the butter is not worked down to incredible thinness in vast, continuous sheets; it is rather divided minutely and left to form whatever haphazard flakes it can manage. Third, plain pastry is given no turns, only one rolling out. This means that if either paste or butter was less than perfect the first time, it will remain so for good.

All of which demonstrates clearly that plain pastry is quite a different breed of cat from puff paste. It is shorter, crumblier, and less flaky. I do not say that pejoratively. It has its uses. By reason of its very shortness, it makes a more pleasant bottom crust for a wet pie. Damp puff paste can be unyielding indeed. As a matter of fact, I would prescribe plain pastry for any condition where your crust will not have ample opportunity to arrive at a dry and crisp maturity.

Plain pastry also has its abuses, however. Chief among them is its employment as an analogy for the production of something that is not pastry at all, namely, piecrust made with oil. By now it should be obvious that mixing flour with oil does precisely what blending flour with melted butter does in sauce making: It produces, not a true paste, but a *roux*—a mixture in which the separate grains of flour never become an elastic mass. By the time the water enters the picture, each grain has acquired a greasy and non-adhesive surface. Oil pastry is, in fact, more a cookie dough than a pastry and should be thought of accordingly. Once again, that is not necessarily an insult. It has its uses too. At the end of this chapter, I shall give you a recipe which uses a Swedish short crust, similar to but vastly better than any oil pastry you ever tasted. As in all things, it is just a matter of knowing what you really want and paying attention long enough to find out how to get it.

PUFF PASTE

2 cups pastry or bread flour (put away the cake flour; it's not glutinous enough)	½ teaspoon salt Cold water sufficient Butter sufficient (as indicated later)

You have arrived at the point where you will have to trust me. I am a teacher. Every time I start a class in elementary Greek, I tell the members that I can teach Greek to anyone, provided he will do exactly what I tell him and nothing else. The ones who believe me go fast; the others give themselves a hard time. I say the same thing to you about pastry. You are not the first member of the race to travel this road. Listen carefully to what the old travelers have to say and you will be surprised at your own speed. Just do what you are told.

(1) Work on a large pastry board or on a large chopping block or, best of all, on a wooden pastry table. Don't use any bowls.

(2) Sift the 2 cups of flour onto the middle of the board, and add the salt.

(3) Scatter the flour about the board and begin dripping small amounts of cold water onto it while you keep the flour itself moving about with a spatula, a broad-bladed knife, a pastry scraper, or, most logically of all, your fingertips.

(4) Add only enough water to make a reasonably moist dough that will gather easily into one piece. *Do not work the dough any more than is absolutely necessary.* It will develop its full elasticity later, during the rolling. If it is massaged and kneaded now, it simply becomes intractable after the first turn.

(5) Step 4 is obviously a matter of feel. Be patient with yourself. If your dough is too crumbly, rescatter it and sprinkle on a little more water. If it is too slimy, throw it out and start over. Flour isn't that expensive. Better to waste that than butter. Just keep at it till you get it right. With a little talent, three or four tries should put you securely in the pastry business.

(6) Next, take your gently gathered lump of dough and weigh it. Yes, I know; I can hear the anguished cries of the American cookbook reviewers now. "The man is mad! Why does he insist on European-style measurements by weight, when all loyal Americans go by volume?" Well, for their information, volume measurement is irrelevant, incompetent, and immaterial here. Even in America, professional bakers work by weight. Flours absorb water at different rates. It is much easier to find out how much butter you need by weighing the dough after it is already in being.

But, you say, what if there is no small scale in the house?

I give you two alternatives. For one, take a yardstick and tape two equal plates to its flat upper surface, one with its center over the 36-inch mark and the other with its center over the 9-inch mark. Put the dough on the plate at 9 inches, guess at an amount of cold butter equal to half the weight of the dough, and put that on the outermost plate. Then take a broad-bladed knife, place its edge under the 18-inch mark to serve as a fulcrum, and add or subtract butter until the whole thing balances. (For the other alternative: If you are a good guesser, just guess.)

(7) You now have the required amount of butter: a piece equal to half the weight of your dough. Fill a bowl with cold water and work this lump of butter under water with your hands until it becomes reasonably elastic. Then form it into an oblong billet and leave it in the water. (The purpose of this kneading is to insure that the butter will stretch properly under the pressure of rolling and not simply crumble and

break. Butter as it comes from the store has the characteristics of a casting: It is coarse-grained and easily broken. Butter which is to be used for puff paste, however, needs the qualities of a *forged* substance: elasticity and tensile strength. Hence the kneading under water.)

(8) Return to your dough, which has been resting comfortably while the butter was being attended to. Get out the rolling pin (a plain pie pin, if at all possible—one, say, 20 inches long and 1⅜ inches in diameter, with tapered ends; the common American rolling pin—fat and handled—is a tin fiddle as far as puff paste is concerned: Actually it is good only for noodles). With this pin, roll the dough into a square large enough to receive the prepared piece of butter, with enough left over around the sides to fold over the top and enclose the butter. Place the butter in the center, bring up the flaps and seal the butter into the envelope of dough. You are now ready to go.

(9) Gently but firmly (again it is a matter of knack and feel—keep at it) roll this envelope out into a strip at least 24 inches long (width doesn't matter here). Keep your board nicely but lightly floured during all of the rolling. Don't let the pastry stick to the table.

(10) Fold the ends of this strip to the center, and then fold again, making four layers. Pat this piece gently into a square shape, give it a quarter turn, and roll out as before.

(11) Fold again into four layers, wrap in plastic foil, and put it in the refrigerator for at least three quarters of an hour. The purpose of this step is twofold. First, it allows the butter to cool after its exertion. The cold, kneaded butter you began with is a perfect partner to the flour and water paste: They are both of approximately the same elasticity, and proceed through the stretching in an equality. As it warms, however, butter becomes runny and tends to squirt out all over the pastry table. Light flouring of the bread board keeps things under control for a while, but by the end of the second turn,

refrigeration is the only answer, unless you are an expert indeed and work like lightning. Second, however, this rest cure in the ice box not only restores the butter; it also has a tranquilizing and relaxing effect on the paste. Much working makes it tense and resistive; when you come back to your dough after three quarters of an hour, you will find that it is in a more co-operative frame of mind.

(12) After the dough has chilled, give it two additional turns; that is, roll it out and fold it up four times more. Then put it back in the refrigerator for several hours (or better, overnight) until you are ready to use it. For this long storage, be sure it is well wrapped to prevent surface drying. Plastic wrap followed by neatly sealed aluminum foil does nicely.

Well! There you are. If nothing else, I trust you will admit that puff pastry makes an excellent paradigm of the paradoxicality of being: stark ordinariness intimately conjoined with incredible complexity; the simple and the difficult rolled into one; plainness transfigured by care.

I have, I admit, devoted an inordinate amount of space to it. But I make no apology. You have just heard the words of a man who learned to make puff paste the hard way. Even good cookbooks are full of false starts and blind alleys when it comes to pastry. I have one before me which recommends kneading the dough before adding the butter. It makes me wonder whether the author ever made puff paste at all. Kneaded dough is an out-and-out liability. By the second turn, it feels as if you're working with rubber sheeting. I have another book which carries on at length about the necessity of trapping as much air as possible in the carapace of paste which first encloses the butter. More nonsense! It is not air which puffs the paste, but steam. Besides, after four turns, there is precious little air left anywhere in the dough.

And so it goes. I have heard people recommend using frozen butter, warm butter, and, horror of horrors, margarine.

What can such people have in mind? *In true puff paste, the single most important consideration is to be sure that the paste and the butter are of about the same consistency.* If you strive for that, success will not be far off. With the advice I have given you, and with the recipes on pages 253–55 for finger exercises, all you need is practice.

Having come this far, however, I find it impossible to end without giving you a similar inside track to the subject of true Danish pastry. Contrary to anything you have ever heard, seen, tasted, or read, real Danish is simply puff paste made with sugar, eggs, milk, and yeast, instead of plain water. Pay no attention to the books which tell you to make up a batch of kneaded, raised dough and then work in butter. Just follow the instructions I have already given you and you will do beautifully. Danish and puff paste are two species of the same genus of beast; if you can tame one, you can manage the other. Herewith, then, a short recipe.

DANISH PASTRY

(I have never made a small batch in my life. I apologize for the size of the recipe.)

4 cups flour (approximately)
4 tablespoons baker's yeast
2 eggs
½ cup sugar
1 teaspoon salt
¾ teaspoon ground
  cardamom

1 cup top milk
Butter sufficient (Half the
  weight of the finished
  paste. This recipe will
  take 1½ to 2 pounds)

Sift the flour onto the pastry table and scatter it about. Dissolve the yeast with a little warm water in a large bowl (or, better yet, in a one-quart measuring cup).

To this add the eggs, sugar, salt and cardamom and whisk well. Last of all add the milk.

Sprinkle the liquid mixture over the flour until you have produced (as for puff paste) a suitably moist, but not sticky dough. *Do not handle it any more than is absolutely necessary.* The light touch is everything.

Weigh the dough, take a piece of butter equal to half its weight, knead this into a workable billet, and proceed as before for puff paste, right through all the turns. The technique is exactly the same.

At the end, however, there are a few notable differences. First, I would suggest that you always make the dough for your Danish the night before you plan to use it. That way, it can spend hours in the refrigerator and be thoroughly workable before the final rolling. (Don't forget, though, when you wrap it up, to leave room for expansion. Remember the old affair of yeast and sugar? Even in the ice box, they have their love to keep them warm. What you put away at night as a flat, aluminum foil slab will, in the morning, be a gorgeous silver pillow. Romance is everywhere.

Second, don't forget that, as a yeast dough, Danish must be allowed to rise before baking. After you have made it up into ready-to-bake pastries, allow them to rise until nearly doubled in bulk. Without this step, you will never achieve perfect lightness. Remember, though, that your dough was cold to begin with. The rising will take longer than you expect: usually well over an hour.

Lastly, bake your Danish at one temperature, not two; 375° will do for a start, provided you keep an eye on things so that you don't go beyond the limits of good color in the finished pastry.

With that, all you need are a few suggestions as to suitable presentations. They are found on pages 257–60. If you love good things, go to them. Remember, calories are only demons to be exorcized.

FIFTEEN

�֍

The Long Session

According to my wife's sensibilities at least, it is only a short step from pastry to parties. For her, tiny crescents of puff paste—or *bouchées,* or a *vol au vent*—constitute the sine qua non of a festal occasion. I agree with her; but as an unreconstructed olfactory type, I find that there are certain smells which put me in the party spirit even faster than pastry. All my wife needs to do to brighten my spirits is add an onion, a clove and a splash of Madeira to a cup of stock and boil it. The minute I come in the door, the smell says, loud and clear, Guests! (Court bouillon is equally effective; so are about a dozen other soups and sauces. I need only minimal prompting to incline me to the pleasure of company.)

I have firm convictions on the subject, however, and I simply cannot resist giving you a chapterful of prejudices, reflections, and free advice on the subject of entertaining in the grand style. I make but one disclaimer: Nothing I say here about formal dining should be taken as in any way disparaging the thousand lesser devices by which man puts himself at home with his fellows. I have already praised evenings of wine and cheese. If I had the space, I would similarly glorify late mornings of *wurst* and beer, ordinary suppers with another family taken in, and, out of respect to my Swedish heritage, the *smörgåsbord cum* idiotic games, Greek dancing, and all the ribaldry the gathering can afford.

Here, however, I shall confine myself to what I take to be the most elegant and considerable of all forms of entertaining: the sit-down dinner. But me no buts, if you please. I know we are told by the culture in which we live that dinnering is passé. I am as aware as you are that the large cocktail party is the accepted American style of having company. Nevertheless, I choose to swim against the current. I find hard liquor and goodies from 5 to 8 P.M. to be inhuman, unmerciful, and frustrating.

It is inhuman because, as commonly practiced, it is impersonal. The only time a man's *name* counts at a cocktail party is three weeks before the event when it is scrawled on an envelope containing (usually) a coy commercial invitation. From the moment he enters the door, however, he is reduced to a mere member of the crowd. True, a zealous host and hostess, working themselves into a fit of omnipresence to their guests, may manage to take some of the sting out of the spectacle; but even such heroic efforts are seldom more than slightly successful. The entire function is designed to frustrate any real meeting of all concerned.

To begin with, most people are continually on the move at such affairs. You know the experience well: You are constantly under the impression that the interesting conversations are going on somewhere else, and you spend three hours trying vainly to get where the action is. The secret, of course, is that there usually isn't any; when there is, it is entirely accidental to the occasion: Somebody just happened to bring it in with him. Furthermore, the perpetual motion at cocktail parties— their failure to provide each person with an assigned and proper place—effectively prevents the company from becoming *a company* at all. Indeed, it would seem that the large cocktail hour is deliberately designed to avoid the result altogether. "Well, Helen, if we don't have a bunch of people in one of these days, we're going to be written off as deadbeats. Let's throw a cocktail party."

Oh, the facelessness of it all! No solicitous phone calls to line up just the right guests for true conversation. No anguish over the possible absence of Harry, or the indisposition of Martha. Just a clutter of messages in bottles, and a trusting to luck that any beachcombers who show up will have the sense to make later appointments and clear out by 8:30.

Besides being inhuman, however, the exercise is unmerciful. Too much liquor too fast is only the half of it. What is just as bad is having to wander around like a lost soul while people spill drinks down your back and wipe dips on your front. We are homeless enough, without having to come in out of the cold to nothing better than a warm exile, followed by a cleaner's bill.

Finally, cocktail parties are frustrating. Not because fascinating conversations are impossible—fortunately a few still happen in spite of it all. Rather, they are frustrating because they promise so much and deliver so little. The spectacle of a houseful of apparently convivial people is one of the most inviting sights on earth. It makes the heart leap to poetry—to apostrophes of *Quis rex, quae curia, quale palatium!*—and to a passionate longing to seize this whole splendid company in one vast embrace for the expounding of their glory. But alas, they are ungraspable except as individuals. They have all the trappings of a fellowship, but none of the substance.

I used to come away from cocktail parties with a vague sense of guilt at having somehow missed what others apparently found. But I do so no more. Nobody finds it. The fault here, dear Brutus, is not in ourselves, but in the system. I go to them now for two reasons only: altruistically, out of loyalty to my friends; or selfishly, for whichever of my own purposes I think they will serve. From the party, as such, I expect nothing. Never is a long time, I know; but I have taken a vow, for as long as I am in possession of my faculties, to throw no cocktail parties at all. If you ever get an invitation from me, simply drop it into the wastebasket. You may safely assume that I have been certified and committed.

From all these strictures, I imagine you can write my justification of the dinner party for me.

First, it is an honest attempt to create a company, not a crowd. Persons matter at the table. We sit in real and estimable places marked with the most precious and intimate device we have: our names. Harry sits next to Martha not because he wandered to her side out of whim or loneliness but because, in his host's loving regard, he is Harry and she is Martha, and that is where they belong. Place cards may well be pretentious (they are, in any case, a dispensable formality); but assignment to place by name is the host's announcement that he cares. I always take it as a compliment when a good man tells me where he wants me to sit.

He has, you see, been willing to take me on as God takes me—as a risk. He pays me the supreme tribute of putting himself in my power. The giver of a cocktail party is a man who hedges his bets and cops out of the dangers of entertaining. He requires nothing of his guests but their physical presence. If they turn out to be untempered duds or ill-tempered boors, it is no skin off his nose: They can simply find their own corner of outer darkness and fall apart any way they like. But when he sits me down at his table, he declares himself willing to let me into his own life. He puts me into my place; but he also puts me in a position to make or break his party as I will. It is no small boldness; if you have such friends, treasure them.

Next, the sit-down dinner is merciful where the cocktail party is not. It provides us with better food, more attractive service, and, beneath it all, a seat to sit on. But it provides more than that. Early in this book, I defined *place* as a Session, a meeting, a confrontation—of real beings. The old descriptions of heaven as the celestial banquet, the supper of eternal life, the endless *convivium,* hit close to the truth. Nowhere more than in good and formal company do we catch the *praegustatum,* the foretaste of what is in store for us.

Last, the dinner party is a true proclamation of the abundance of being—a rebuke to the thrifty little idolatries by which we lose sight of the lavish hand that made us. It is precisely because no one needs soup, fish, meat, salad, cheese, and dessert at one meal that we so badly need to sit down to them from time to time. It was *largesse* that made us all; we were not created to fast forever. The unnecessary is the taproot of our being and the last key to the door of delight. Enter here, therefore, as a sovereign remedy for the narrowness of our minds and the stinginess of our souls, the formal dinner for six, eight or ten chosen guests, the true *convivium*—the long Session that brings us nearly home.

Quite obviously, any subject which lies as close as dinnering does to the center of human nature, is bound to have had endless attention lavished upon it—and by better men than you or me. This is no place—and I am not the man—to give you an exhaustive treatise on how to give a formal dinner. Instead, therefore, permit me once more, as I have done so often before, to play not *on,* but *between* the keys of the instrument: to give you a series of reflections, aphorisms and paradoxes which will, I hope, strengthen your heart and hands to recapture a territory we have all but lost. I articulate my notes in the simple order of their occurrence.

THE GUESTS

This, clearly, is the first of all considerations; most dinner parties are made or broken within five minutes of the time they are first thought of. It is impossible to take too much care with your guest list. I cannot, of course, give you any specific advice: In so deep a matter, each man has to fashion his triumphs and shipwrecks boldly, with his own two hands. I can, however, make a few suggestions as to basic principles and procedures.

For the first, have at least one solidly personal reason for inviting whomever you call to your table, and be sure that that reason looks chiefly outward at your guest and not inward at yourself. To ask a man to break bread with you is to extend friendship, to proclaim in love that you want not his, but *him*. The dinner table is no place for the canvassing of advantage. If you want to *use* people, feed them restaurant food, invite them to cocktail parties—or hire hatchet men and do the job up brown; but do not lie to them under the guise of love. To invite guests is a courtesy, a *courtly* act: It confers greatness on all concerned, and therefore must never be done for mean reasons.

Second, since people are the ultimate reason for having a dinner at all, try your best to summon guests who will enhance each other as persons. A courtly host invites, as much as he can, courtly people. His table is no mere feed trough; it is one of the heights of the world and only those who can breathe freely and graciously at such altitudes should be there. He cannot, to be sure, plan their conversation, and if he is wise, he will not even occupy himself much with it in advance. He simply does the best he can in his own judgment, and then graciously commits his party into their hands.

Next, as you come to firm conclusions about your guests, assign them to their seats at the table immediately. See them, for all the days or weeks before the party, in the places of their names. You have called them, not to sit solitary, but to become a company, a *convivium*. Feel free to move them about a bit mentally as your estimation of their coinherences and reciprocities ripens, but as soon as convenient, settle the seating plan. It is an unexpressed and subtle honor that you thus pay them, and it makes for great strength in the foundations of your dinner.

Finally, remember that, like all created things, a dinner party must reckon with the real limitations of physical reality. You cannot make dinner company of just any number of people. Accordingly, in your planning, put down eight as the optimum number and vary from it only for good reasons. Four persons, if they are all unmarried, is a possibility; but two couples is not, save under unusual circumstances such as first friendship or reunion after long separation. Six is better, especially with couples who see each other occasionally, since it provides not only variety, but also a physical arrangement by which no one, except the host, sits either next to, or across from his own wife. Eight, as I said, is ideal. It is large enough to allow for considerable interplay between personalities, yet it is still small enough to permit the service of some of the most elegant dishes of all. With more than eight, a soufflé is impossible; and that, as the Duchess of Windsor once said, is always a lamentable omission. Admittedly, a dinner for eight does not seat itself as symmetrically as one for six, but no subject is without its intractabilities. To get around the problem, the host and hostess should sit, Continental style, opposite each other in the middle of the long sides of the table, with the other couples disposed diagonally on axes drawn through the center.

Larger groupings are sometimes desirable, but they become difficult for various reasons. Ten is gala, but it rules out not only the soufflé, but almost anything from the broiler. Twelve is sumptuous, but it tends to breed isolated conversations at opposite ends of the table and so imperils the very company it sets out to form. After that, however, any greater number has so many drawbacks that it precludes a true dinner altogether. For such a crowd, it would be better to plan a completely different party: a splendid buffet, for example, with guests imaginatively assigned to tables of four each, and with provision for dancing and general clowning afterward. As with all things, it is a matter of paying attention to what you have in hand.

THE MENU

First things having thus been attended to first, the next most important consideration is the food. This is, after all, a dinner. For the devoted cook, and especially for the true host, few pleasures can compare with the intellectual satisfaction of planning a notable meal. During all the time before the event itself—over nondescript breakfasts, minor lunches of beer and cheese, and late-night cups of tea, husband and wife can return gladly to the task of putting together the best dinner they can manage.

Here, more than anywhere else, however, you will have to be governed by your talents, your tastes and your resources. I give you only aphorisms, therefore, not a treatise.

(1) The greatest meals, like the greatest musical performances, must always seem simple, no matter how complex the execution of them really is. Strive for the good rather than the fancy; mere clutter, however expensive or recherché, is no virtue at all.

(2) Never cook anything for a formal dinner that you have not cooked before. No matter how good you are, it is an insult to your guests to sight read your way through something when they have given you the honor of their undivided attention. The Lord takes care of children, drunks, and fools. I am not so sure He is equally provident with cooks who fake out formal dinners. Don't take any chances.

(3) Within reasonable limits, cook to *please* your guests, not to edify or amaze them. Your dinner party is an act of love, not a lecture on gourmandise. They will thank you for a little uplift, but not for a vast effort at improving their sensibilities.

(4) Choose the number of courses intelligently. Consider the appetites of your guests, the capacities of your kitchen, and

above all, the stamina of the cook. To do less is to court a fiasco, if not a disaster.

(5) Bear in mind the simple mechanics of producing and serving the meal. In the ordinary household (even with restaurant equipment), you must plan your courses so that they do not all end up in the same facility at once. A first course from the refrigerator, a second from the stove top, and a third from the oven is reasonable. Three courses involving frying pans will drive anyone straight out of his mind.

(6) Select your wines with the best care and/or advice you can manage. Two good wines—or even a single great wine for the main course and a fine dry Sherry with everything before that—are vastly better than a procession of mediocrities, however numerous and pretentious. Be sure, however, that you provide more than enough wine. To run out of wine is less excusable than to run short of food. For a true dinner party, the absolute minimum is ¾ bottle per person, not counting the apéritif. Eight completely moderate souls will, over three hours, easily wipe out three bottles of white and three bottles of red without batting an eye. If you have friends of any magnitude at all, therefore, play safe and figure one bottle apiece.

(7) Last of all, serve wine and not liquor before dinner— and serve no food at all. A good fino, a rainwater or sercial Madeira—or, if you have guests who are absolutely convinced they will die before they get to the table, Cinzano and peanuts—is all anybody really needs before dinner. If, however, you have unregenerate American hard-liquor drinkers for your friends, let me suggest the first course of a Swedish formal dinner as an elegant compromise. Nothing at all is served away from the table. The guests simply arrive on time (no mean feat, I grant you) and sit down after a minimum of aimless wandering to the following: a small plate containing three modest but tastefully prepared open sandwiches—one of meat, one of fish and one *ad lib;* a pipestem sherry glass full of

freezing cold akvavit (schnapps—caraway flavored Scandinavian firewater); and a six-ounce glass of first-class beer. Even
the gruffest of loyal Americans will hardly fault you for giving
him such an apéritif: no pantywaist spiced wine, but an honest
old-fashioned boilermaker and a free lunch to boot.

THE VESTING OF THE TABLE

Since all my taste is in my mouth, I shall not presume to
lecture you on any of the more artistic matters involved here.
There are very few people in the whole U. S. of A. who have
less talent for such things than I. Instead I shall confine myself
to bits of advice which lie strictly within my competence.

(1) Don't crowd the table. Provide your guests with elbow
room, even if it means faking out a larger board by putting
two tables together.

(2) Don't clutter it either. It should be spread as handsomely as possible, but knickknacks, geegaws, and other odd-
ments in the wedding present category should be left in the
china closet. Keep things fairly open and business-like. A floral
piece in the center, if you like flowers, is always pleasant,
but keep it low. Your guests should not have to talk around it.
The full array of silverware and glassware required for several
courses is usually quite enough decoration for any table. Remember, though, to keep the colors under control. Plain
glassware is essential for good wines, and I even go so far as
to forbid anything but white tablecloths and napkins. You
may not approve of such austerity, but if you are wise, you
will still use restraint.

(3) By all means, set out service plates at each place, even
if you have to use the main course plates for the purpose.
They can always be cleared away with the first course, wiped
and brought back when needed. Also, be resourceful about
bread and butter plates. You may not have to put them out at
the start if you can figure a way of leaving behind one of the
small plates from the early courses. About glasses, I ask only

that they be large and reasonably correct in shape. Nothing is worse than trying to drink greatly from a four-ounce restaurant burgundy glass. If you look, you can find excellent glassware for under ten dollars a dozen. Just keep trying.

(4) Consider the smells at your table. Here I am in my rightful province. Don't wax your furniture the day of the meal; any one with a good nose will pick it up. Don't use room air freshener either, unless the smell of the outside air is so bad that you have no choice; even then, use only the mildest one you can find. Select flowers which have gentle and fresh scents, not overpowering ones. Finally, if at all possible, air your napkins before the meal and put them on the table as late as possible. There is no more delightful small touch than this, especially in the colder seasons when the house is closed up. To unfold a napkin and smell the marvelous odor of clean linen and fresh air is to know that one's hostess has thought of everything.

(5) Set out place cards if you like. I never use them myself, because I find them stuffy; but tastes differ. In any case, you will have already settled on the seating plan long before.

(6) Get out the ash trays, but don't put them on the table. Smokers should be accommodated, but not encouraged. It is a losing fight, I know, but I have never given up and probably never will.

(7) Last of all, survey your finished table and be sure *you* find it delightful. Spend the extra resourceful minute discovering the touch you didn't think of. It is one more tribute to your guests.

THE VESTING FOR THE TABLE

The great astronomer Tycho Brahe never went into his observatory to study the heavens without first putting on his court robes. We should make ourselves as splendid as we can when we sit down to a great dinner.

(1) First of all then, don't write off the possibility of asking

your guests to come in evening clothes. We live, in spite of our affluence, like pikers and slobs. Any blow struck against coolness and the cult of the impromptu is worth the effort it takes. Man is the lord of this world. What a shame if he dresses like a king only for boring public performances and never for his friends. No single detail will lift your dinner as high as the spectacle of women in long dresses and men in tuxedos, at least. If you think that is silly, think again. Swallow your embarrassment at acting out your own greatness and try eating your soup and fish in soup-and-fish. You'll never forget it.

(2) Failing that, however, dress as splendidly as possible in whatever style you choose. Silks, satins, and brocades belong to the formal dinner. People who wear dotted swiss dresses think dotted swiss thoughts; tweedy women make tweedy conversation.

(3) Above all, consider your cologne. Nothing overpowering, please. It is the meal and the company that are to be remembered, not some *femme fatale* redolent of *Mille Nuits d'Amour* or *Toujours Whatever-You-Had-in-Mind.* (Men, of course, are often the worst offenders. A little Bay Rum or 4711 should be considered the upper limit. I spent a whole dinner once next to a fellow who was wearing one of those after-shave colognes which promise to turn women into quivering suppliants. I don't know what it did to the women, but by the end of the meal, the smell was so firmly entrenched in the back of my nasal cavities that I was sure the sherbet had been prepared with Tiger, or Loincloth, or whatever it was. I could still taste it the next day in my noontime Cinzano.)

(4) Along the same line, set out good cigars. Cigarettes are a burden we simply have to put up with; but the sensible host will always try to head off the men who bring with them aromatic pipe tobaccos and outdoor cigars. I remember one guest who insisted on smoking pipeful after pipeful of a Dutch

specialty that smelled as if it had been prepared with old maraschino cherries and mashed Christmas cookies. By the end of the meal, even the salad dressing tasted of it.

THE DINNER ITSELF

(1) As much as possible, urge your guests to arrive on time. Provided it is honest, a little note along with the invitation explaining just what dish it is that demands their punctuality may be just the thing to catch them where they live and inspire them to better things.

(2) If you serve an apéritif away from the table, keep it mercifully brief. Your guests have been invited to form a company in the places of their names, not across one end of the piano or out on the patio. You have done your best to arrange a Session. Don't delay putting the arrangement into effect.

(3) If it is your custom to say grace, recite it standing; if your guests are up to it, use something a bit special and apposite to a great occasion. Your company is an earthly image of the Divine Sociality of the Godhead. Convene it then in the Name of the Father and of the Son and of the Holy Ghost. A host is the priest of his own house. Even if there is an ordained priest at the table, it is the householder himself who should say the blessing. No one else has proper jurisdiction.

(4) Finally, as you sit down, have in mind one or two conversational gambits, but use them only if necessary. This is the moment of truth—the agonizing minute after the champagne when the ship starts slowly down the ways and slips into its proper element. No true host ever gets through it without holding his breath; but if his guests have been well chosen, and if his other preparations have been what they ought to be, he will be rewarded inwardly with the shout of joy that accompanies every successful launching. As the con-

versation quickens and the company begins to form in earnest, he will survey the work of his hands and, over soup or fish, catch his wife's eye to give her the old triumphant word: She floats! By George, she swims!

With that, I leave you. From this point on, a well-made dinner party is on its own. With only minor nudging from time to time to prevent its running aground in the shoal waters of disagreement or bad taste, it should come, with flags flying and bands playing, to a happy berth. I wish you well. May your table be graced with lovely women and good men. May you drink well enough to drown the envy of youth in the satisfactions of maturity. May your men wear their weight with pride, secure in the knowledge that they have at last become considerable. May they rejoice that they will never again be taken for callow, black-haired boys. And your women? Ah! Women are like cheese strudels. When first baked, they are crisp and fresh on the outside, but the filling is unsettled and indigestible; in age, the crust may not be so lovely, but the filling comes at last into its own. May you relish them indeed. May we all sit long enough for reserve to give way to ribaldry and for gallantry to grow upon us. May there be singing at our table before the night is done, and old, broad jokes to fling at the stars and tell them we are men.

We are great, my friend; we shall not be saved for trampling that greatness under foot. *Ecce tu pulcher es, dilecte mi, et decorus. Lectulus noster floridus. Tigna domorum nostrarum cedrina, laquearia nostra cypressina. Ecce iste venit, saliens in montibus, transilens colles.* Come then; leap upon these mountains, skip upon these hills and heights of earth. The road to Heaven does not run *from* the world but *through* it. The longest Session of all is no discontinuation of these sessions here, but a lifting of them all by priestly love. It is a place for *men,* not ghosts—for the risen gorgeousness of the

New Earth and for the glorious earthiness of the True Jerusalem.

Eat well then. Between our love and His Priesthood, He makes all things new. Our Last Home will be home indeed.

SIXTEEN

The Burning Heart

That is not quite the place to end, however. For one thing, I still owe you the last part of my Lamb for Eight Persons Four Times. For another, such companying as befits the formal table—such a lifting of the world as is wrought by love in long sessions—will, one way or another, leave a true man with heartburn. I consider it my duty, therefore, before letting you depart with a final sheaf of recipes, to give you one last word on the cause and cure of man's oldest disquietude: the lump in the throat and the fire in the bosom which are the aftermath of inconvenient love.

I distinguish two kinds of heartburn. The first, or lower, is the one that comes to mind in the normal use of the word: the pain caused by the rising of digestive juices into the esophagus. That, in turn, can be caused by excessive fullness—or by excessive emptiness—and by tobacco, tension, or ten thousand other things, most of which are either useful, salutary, or delightful. In any case, the discomfort is acute indeed: The healthy stomach is equipped to withstand the ravages of its own juices, but the rest of the anatomy sends out violent alarms when they make excursions.

The second kind of heartburn is what I choose to call the Major or Higher Heartburn. It is, however, far too profound a malady to take up at the moment. Accordingly, I introduce it here by title only and return to the possible cures of the lower variety.

There are, of course, plenty of people who stand ready to give you advice about what to do for simple indigestion: Most of them are no help at all. They have a blind and unshakable faith that logic will take the full measure of life under any and all circumstances, and they counsel you, with pitiless rectitude, that the best way to avoid difficulty is to keep away from the things that cause it. Accordingly, they will advise you to stop eating greatly, or to quit fasting, or to give up tobacco, whiskey, and hot sausages. In other words, they tell you to abandon all those extremes and counterpoisings by which you have so far kept your balance on the high wire of existence, and sit down quietly on the ground where you won't get hurt. They invite you to join them in a condition of philosophical indifference—in a state of *ataraxia,* where you will never again give an emphatic damn about anything, nor ever, under any circumstances, allow yourself to get worked up.

Such remedies are fanatical. They have about them the monomaniacal logic of schemes to eliminate inconvenient thoughts by chopping off the heads that think them. The world is a tissue of involvements inseparably interwoven with bothers. It is no solution to get rid of the second by abolishing the first. If the only way around distress is to stop loving, well, then, let us be men about it and settle for distress.

Furthermore, when my gorge rises violently, I thank no man for self-righteous lectures on preventive medicine. I do not want to be told what will help me next time; what I need is something that will work this time—something that will meet me where I am, here in the thick of my inconvenient loves, and not in some cautious never-never land of pure thoughts and wheat germ bread.

Accordingly, as far as I am concerned, the only sane answer to the lower heartburn is a remedy that can be taken after the fact to bring the fire under control. Fortunately, there are literally hundreds of them. Indeed, standing in front of the usual drugstore counter display, it is hard to make up one's mind just which of the little wonder-working rolls of pills to settle on. At that level, therefore, I leave you to your own devices. My real purpose here is to persuade you of the merits of a better remedy than all the pills in the world: baking soda.

Well! you say. I thought *that* went out with gas lights. Why should I forsake my laboratory-tested, ultra-scientific array of pills for something my wife keeps in the kitchen closet with the detergents?

I shall tell you why. To begin with, you want two kinds of relief from heartburn. The first is the extinguishing of the fire by the simple device of neutralizing the acid that threatens to burn its way straight out of the front of your chest. Any alkalizing agent, of course, will cut the acid in your stomach; but only one that is swallowed *in solution* will be effective in the esophagus. Pills will prevent further heartburn; but half a teaspoon of bicarbonate of soda in half a glass of water is present help all the way down: It deals with the heartburn you have. Furthermore, as everyone should know, baking soda is one of the greatest sweetening and deodorizing agents in the world. It renders the added service of killing odor as well as flame. Almost instantly it makes a man bearable again, not only to himself, but to others.

The second kind of relief for which heartburn cries out is the restoration of the ability to belch satisfactorily. As a matter of fact, the most characteristic torment of the whole situation lies in the tension between a growing certainty that one good belch would set things right and a gnawing suspicion that you may never in this world belch again at all. A pill sent down to remedy *that* distress is worse than useless. It goes quietly, as an undercover agent; it does its work and is never heard from again. All that you, as its principal, know is that at some unspecified point, things imperceptibly begin to get better. You are denied the satisfaction of dramatic changes joyfully proclaimed.

With baking soda, however, a mere one minute's wait rewards you with a glowing, not to say resounding *report*. The relief, so long awaited, comes in force: not little by little like spies in the night, but all at once, like an army with banners and shouting. Add to that the fact that bicarbonate of soda has no particular flavor other than a bland saltiness—and that it is cheaper than any pill you can buy—and you have more than enough reasons for preferring it to pills right now. It has no delicious mintiness to stick in the back of your throat for hours and remind you of indigestion the next time you eat candy. It just works *fortiter suaviterque*, mightily and sweetly, like the Wisdom of God; and like the same Wisdom, it courteously lets us get about our business without backward looks or second thoughts. It is hard to ask for more.

Nevertheless, you get it without asking. Baking soda is so much more than a digestive that the mind boggles. Your roll of pills will do one thing and one only; your box of sodium bicarbonate will do a hundred and still have talents left to spare. Since this book is above all a celebration of the material and the common, I would like at this point to enter baking soda as a candidate for the title of Most Extraordinary Ordinary Thing in the World. Firmly convinced that it will win hands down over all comers, I take the liberty of composing the citation to be read in the ceremony at which the title is bestowed.

SODIUM BICARBONATE, NAHCO₃, BAKING SODA, BICARBONATE OF SODA:
Longtime and steadfast retainer of the human race, your many names betokening not only varied talents, but also innumerable kindnesses for which men hold you dear: Friend of the flatulent, Soother of the savage, scotch-soaked breast,

and blessed Bestower of peaceful sleep after four beers, two heroes, and a sausage pizza;

Sweetener of life in general and of organic disagreeabilities in particular: Cleanser of vile coffeepots and putrid refrigerators, Tamer of gamy bones, Purifier of school lunch vacuum bottles whose milk has turned to cheese, Polisher of teeth, Gracer of breath, Remover of smells from diapers, nursing bottles, smoking pipes and old hair brushes, Deodorizer of floors made foul by messing cats, Sweetener of urine-soaked mattresses, and Restorer of freshness to automotive interiors rendered uninhabitable by retching children;

Leavener, and nearly omnicompetent Lifter of the otherwise forlorn flatness of our lives: Raiser of biscuits, muffins, cookies, cake, and bread, and faithful member, in this capacity, of many committees—notably of Baking Powder- and Self-Rising Cake Flour;

Last, but far from least, sovereign Extinguisher of conflagrations of all sorts, from the metaphorical burning in the stomach to the literal flaming of the fat that falls in the fire: Soother of sore throats and bee stings, Cooler of prickly heat and sunburn, Smotherer of grease fires, Protector of the home and Very Present Help in all our troubles;

We who stand so deep in your debt praise your generosity; we who play not more than two instruments, who understand only four languages and can hardly express ourselves in any of them, salute the range of your abilities; we who require praise and publicity for what little we do stand in awe of your humility;

ACCEPT, THEREFORE, at our hands, this ORDER OF MERIT which we, though unworthy, bestow: If we were half as faithful as you have been, we would be twice as good as we are. May God hasten the day.

One more word of counsel on the subject of the lower heartburn before we move on to higher things: Eat lightly and simply the day after your great feast. Your stomach, so lately and sorely tried, needs time to recover its cast-iron properties.

With or without indigestion, however, you will probably choose such a course quite on your own. On the one hand, your intuitive perception of the fitness of certain alternations and rhythms in eating will incline you to a plain meal. On the other, no matter what your inclinations, your wife will probably refuse to stand in front of the stove any longer than she has to. I suggest, therefore, (not entirely without ulterior motive—it enables me to discharge my last stated obligation to you) that she simply thaw out Part IV of Lamb for Eight Persons Four Times, bring it to a boil and set it out with bread, butter, greens, and beer.

As I see it, this fourth meal is one which is prepared in advance and served on short notice. The soup can be made any time you like and frozen until needed. The bread, too, is nothing more than a spare loaf from last week's homemade batch which has been living in the freezer. The rest is just as obvious: greens with salt only, to underscore simplicity; and beer rather than wine, because it sits better on a tender stomach. All you need now are the directions for the soup.

LAMB AND BARLEY SOUP

2 medium onions, cut up
2 carrots, sliced
2 stalks celery, sliced
Several thick slices of turnip, cubed
4 tablespoons butter
All of the bones and scraps from the leg of lamb
3 quarts water

½ cup barley
1 bay leaf
Pinch of rosemary and thyme
Salt and freshly ground pepper to taste (but make allowances for reduction)
Chopped parsley, added just before serving

Cook the vegetables in butter until the onion is transparent, but not brown. Add the bones, the scraps, the water, the barley, and the herbs. Season preliminarily and boil for 2 hours.

Cool quickly, remove the bones, pick off any available meat, and add it to the soup. Skim and freeze—or serve immediately if the cupboard is bare.

Making allowances for the shortage of meat—and for the use of cooked rather than raw lamb—this is nothing more or less than Scotch Broth. Remember, though, that it can easily be nudged in the direction of minestrone. By cooking a couple of crushed cloves of garlic with the vegetables, by substituting chick-peas, fava beans and macaroni for the barley, and by adding some shredded cabbage and a few peeled fresh tomatoes for the last hour, you can become the first Italian Scotsman in your neighborhood. Homemade soup is no place for narrow dogmatism. Do anything that comes into your head except oversalt. It is impossible to go wrong.

That much done, however—having provided baking soda for your solace and soup for your sustenance, I press on to the last consideration of all: the higher distress for which earth has no cure—that major, vaster burning by which the heart looks out astonished at the world and, in its loving, wakes and breaks at once.

For all its greatness (trust me—I am the last man on earth to sell it short), the created order cries out for further greatness still. The most splendid dinner, the most exquisite food, the most gratifying company, arouse more appetites than they satisfy. They do not slake man's thirst for being; they whet it beyond all bounds. Dogs eat to give their bodies rest; man dines and sets his heart in motion. All tastes fade, of course, but not the taste for greatness they inspire; each love escapes us, but not the longing it provokes for a better *convivium*, a higher session. We embrace the world in all its glorious solidity, yet it struggles in our very arms, declares itself a pilgrim world, and, through the lattices and windows of its nature, discloses cities more desirable still.

You indict me, no doubt, as an incurable romantic. I plead guilty without contest. I see no other explanation of what we are about. Why do we marry, why take friends and lovers, why give ourselves to music, painting, chemistry, or cooking? Out of simple delight in the resident goodness of creation, of course; but out of more than that, too. Half of earth's gorgeousness lies hidden in the glimpsed city it longs to become. For all its rooted loveliness, the world has no continuing city here; it is an *outlandish* place, a foreign home, a session *in via* to a better version of itself—and it is our glory to see it so and thirst until Jerusalem comes home at last. We were given appetites, not to consume the world and forget it, but to taste its goodness and hunger to make it great.

That is the unconsolable heartburn, the lifelong disquietude of having been made in the image of God. All man's love is vast and inconvenient. It is tempting, of course, to blunt its edge by caution. It is so much easier not to get involved—to thirst for nothing and no one, to deny that matter matters and, if you have the stomach for it, to make your bed with meanings which cannot break your heart. But that, it seems to me, is neither human nor Divine. If we are to put up with all other bothers out of love, then no doubt we must put up with the bother of love itself and not just cut and run for cover when it comes.

First of all, such faintness is unworthy of true men. We are the lords, the priests, and the lovers of the world: It is by our hands that its cities will be built if they are built at all. But anything to which we lie so close cannot be a matter of cool detachment and scientific indifference. If I am to lift music, I must lay such hands upon it as not only give me power over it, but also give it power over me. If I am to be the priestly agent by which some girl with high cheekbones enters the exchanges of the city, I must be prepared for the possibility that she may wind my clock beyond all mortal hope of repair. Love is as strong as death. Man was made to lead with his chin; he is worth knowing only with his guard down, his head up and his heart rampant on his sleeve.

But second, last and most important, playing it safe is not Divine. We have come to the end. I tell you simply what I believe. Love is the widest, choicest door into the Passion. God saved the world not by sitting up in heaven and issuing antiseptic directives, but by becoming man, and vulnerable, in Jesus. He died, not because He despised the earth, but because He loved it as a man loves it—out of all proportion and sense. And when He rose again, He stood up like a man indeed: with glorious scars—and with flesh, bones, and all things appertaining to the perfection of man's nature.

It is through that Sacred Humanity—and through the mighty working whereby He is able to subdue all things to Himself—that He will, at the last day, change these corruptible bodies of ours, make them like His own glorious Body and, *through them,* draw all things into the last City of their being. The world will be lifted, as it was always meant to be lifted, by the priestly love of man. What Christ has done is to take our broken priesthood into His and make it strong again. We *can,* you see, take it with us. It will be precisely because we loved Jerusalem enough to bear it in our bones that its textures will ascend when we rise; it will be because our eyes have relished the earth that the color of its countries will compel our hearts forever. The bread and the pastry, the cheeses, the wine, and the songs go into the Supper of the Lamb because we do: It is our love that brings the City home.

It is, I grant you, an incautious and extravagant hope. But in such a place as this—in a world that so regularly winds our clocks and breaks our hearts, that laughs at caution and cries from every corner for extravagation—only outlandish hopes can make themselves at home. Spare me, therefore, the sanity of more modest expectations and less loving looks. *If I forget thee O Jerusalem, let my right hand forget her cunning. If I do not remember thee, let my tongue cleave to the roof of my mouth; yea, if I prefer not Jerusalem above my chief joy.*

And I saw the holy City, New Jerusalem coming down from God out of Heaven prepared as a bride adorned for her husband.

> Raise her not for what she is not;
> But lift her up herself
> To grace the Supper of the Lamb,
> The unimaginable Session
> In which the Lion lifts Himself Lamb Slain
> And, Priest and Victim
> Brings
> The City
> Home.

❖

SEVENTEEN

Recipes

I *BREADS, FLOUR MIXTURES, AND RICE*

PLAIN BREAD WITH SEVERAL VARIATIONS

2 cups milk (or part water)
1 tablespoon butter
2 teaspoons salt
2 tablespoons sugar
4 tablespoons yeast

¼ cup lukewarm water
1 teaspoon sugar
6 cups sifted flour
  (approximately)

Scald the milk in a large (6 quarts) pan. Add the next 3 ingredients. Cool to lukewarm.

Combine the yeast, water, and 1 teaspoon of sugar in a small bowl and let stand while the milk mixture is cooling.

Sift ⅓ of the flour into the cooled milk mixture. Beat well. Pour in stirred yeast mixture, and continue beating in flour until you have a moderately stiff dough. Turn this out onto a floured board and knead for 5 minutes until glossy.

Return the dough to the same pot you scalded the milk

in (but washed, dried, and buttered), cover with a damp towel, and let rise until doubled in bulk.

Turn out on board, cut in two, punch down well, and shape into 2 loaves. Place these in buttered loaf pans and let rise 15–30 minutes, or until they hold a depression made by the gentle pressure of two fingers.

Bake at 350–370° for 50–60 minutes.

VARIATION I: CHEESE BREAD

While the first liquid is still hot, add ½ to 1 pound grated Cheddar cheese and ¼ cup of grated Parmesan cheese.

After adding yeast mixture, add 1 egg. Continue as above.

VARIATION II: ONION BREAD

Scald 1 cup minced onion with milk.

After adding yeast mixture, beat in 1 egg. Continue as above.

When you come to shape these, however, braid them. Divide the dough in half, and divide each half in 3. Shape each piece into a long rope, and make 2 braided loaves. Put these in buttered loaf pans, let rise, brush with milk or beaten egg white, and sprinkle with some chopped onion. Bake at 350°.

VARIATION III: RAISIN BREAD

Increase sugar to ¼ cup. Add 1 egg and 1 pound of raisins. When dough is risen, roll out into a large rectangle. Sprinkle with cinnamon and sugar. Roll up, seal edge, divide into 2 or 3 sections. Place in loaf pans, let rise, and bake.

CUBAN BREAD

(See above, page 154)

IRISH BREAD

Good (with plenty of butter) for a plain dessert—or for something to go with coffee and guests at short notice.

1 recipe of baking-powder-biscuit dough (homemade or packaged, but increase butter and sugar by 1 tablespoon each)

½ cup raisins
½ cup currants
1 tablespoon caraway seeds

Add last 3 ingredients to baking-powder-biscuit dough. Turn onto floured board and knead 10 times. Shape into a flat ball.

Bake in a well-buttered iron frying pan for 30 minutes at 350°. Increase heat to 400° the last 5 minutes.

Serve in wedge-shaped pieces.

CROISSANTS

As far as technique is concerned, follow the instructions for puff paste, pages 161–64. This is simply a richer dough with yeast added.

2 cups pastry or bread flour
½ teaspoon salt
2 tablespoons sugar
2 tablespoons yeast, dissolved in a little warm water

1 egg
Milk sufficient
Butter sufficient

Sift the flour and salt onto a pastry board and scatter it about. Put sugar, yeast, and warm water in a bowl and mix well. Add the egg and whisk well. Pour this over the flour, and add enough milk to make a dough suitable for puff paste (see directions pages 161–64).

Weigh the dough, knead a piece of butter equal to half its weight, and proceed as for puff paste, making 4 turns in all.

Chill dough for at least 3 hours (or overnight). When ready, roll it out into a large rectangle ⅛-inch–³⁄₁₆-inch thick. With a knife or pastry wheel, cut this into isosceles triangles measuring 4½ inches along the base and 6 inches in altitude. Roll each of these jelly-roll fashion, beginning at the base and ending at the point.

Shape into crescents and place on a baking sheet (no greasing is necessary with puff paste).

Let rise well, brush with beaten egg, sprinkle lightly with coarse salt if you like, and bake to a good color. (Start at 450° and come down to 350°, or lower, after 8–10 minutes.

STOLLEN

This is a fairly orthodox recipe as far as the dough is concerned, but the final shape of this holiday bread is a bit out of the ordinary. Sprinkled with powdered sugar and surrounded with holly or sprigs of green, it makes a handsome (and edible) centerpiece for the Christmas table.

1 teaspoon salt	1 cup raisins
½ teaspoon nutmeg	1 cup currants
2 cups milk	½ cup chopped, blanched
1 cup butter	almonds
1¼ cups sugar	½ cup citron, chopped
4 tablespoons yeast	1½ teaspoons lemon extract,
1 teaspoon sugar	or 1 tablespoon lemon
¼ cup lukewarm water	rind plus ½ teaspoon
6 cups flour	lemon juice
2 eggs	

In a large pot (8 quarts) place first 5 ingredients. Scald and let cool to lukewarm. Combine yeast, sugar, and water, and let stand.

Sift ⅓ of the flour into the milk mixture. Beat well. Add yeast mixture and continue beating. Add remaining ingredients, together with enough flour to make a soft dough. Turn out on floured board, and knead 5 minutes until glossy. Place in original scalding pot (washed, dried, and buttered), cover with a damp towel, and let rise until doubled (about 40 minutes).

Turn out on a floured board and shape.* Let rise. Bake at 350° until done, about 1½ hours. Lower oven if it starts to brown too much.

Then take the next largest piece of dough, shape it into 3 ropes and make a braid of three. Pound a modest depression into the braid of four with the edge of your hand and place the new braid on top of it. (It should be, of course, slightly narrower and shorter than the bottom one.)

Finally, take the smallest piece of dough, shape it into 1 long rope and make a twist of two out of it. Place this on top of the rest, and pat the whole into a nice shape by hand. It's supposed to represent the Christ child (the braids stand for the swaddling bands). Nevertheless, if you aim at making it look like a large model of the *Merrimac*, you are on the right track.

When baked, sprinkle immediately, and liberally, with powdered sugar.

PANETONE

2 cups milk	6 cups flour (approximate)
½ cup butter	2 eggs
½ cup sugar	3 egg yolks
2 teaspoons salt	1 cup white raisins
4 tablespoons yeast	¾ cup pignoli (pine nuts)
1 teaspoon sugar	1 cup mixed candied fruit
½ cup lukewarm water	2 teaspoons anise extract

* To shape this monster, divide the dough into 3 pieces, respectively, ⅚, ⅔ and ⅙ the size of the original lump. Take the largest piece, shape it into 4 long ropes and make a braid of four. (Practice with clothesline if you're not sure how.) Place this on a buttered baking sheet.

Scald milk in a large pot. Add next 3 ingredients. Let cool to lukewarm. Combine yeast, sugar, and water, and let stand. Sift 2 cups of the flour into milk mixture. Beat well. Add yeast mixture, eggs, egg yolks, and remaining ingredients. Beat. Add remaining flour and mix thoroughly. Dough should be soft but manageable. Knead on floured board 5 minutes. Return to original scalding pot (washed, dried, and buttered). Cover with a damp towel and let rise until doubled in bulk.

Turn out on floured board. Punch down and divide dough into thirds. Shape into 3 balls. Place in buttered tins. (Three-pound shortening tins are perfect: They are cheap—and they give you loaves of the traditional shape.) When well risen, cut a cross in the top of each loaf and brush with melted butter. Bake at 375° until brown (about 40 minutes). Remove from pans, place on rack, and glaze well with confectioners'-sugar icing made with water and a little lemon juice.

VÖRTLIMPA

A deluxe holiday version of Swedish rye bread. Serve it sliced thin with cold butter.

3 cups stout or dark beer
1 teaspoon salt
¼ cup butter
1 cup molasses
6 tablespoons yeast
1 teaspoon sugar
¼ cup lukewarm water
6 cups rye flour

3 cups white flour
Peel of 4 whole oranges, finely chopped (remove any white pulp before chopping)
2 tablespoons fennel seed, well pounded (or 2 tablespoons ground fennel)

Heat stout, salt, and butter in a large pot. Add molasses, and cool to lukewarm. Mix yeast, sugar, and water and let stand.

Sift 3 cups of the rye and 1 cup of the white flour into stout mixture. Beat well. Add yeast mixture, orange peel, fennel, and remaining flour, turn out on floured board, and knead well. Put back in pot which has been washed, dried, and buttered, cover with damp towel, and let rise until doubled.

Turn out on a floured board and divide in 3 parts. Shape into long loaves. Place on buttered baking sheet and let rise. Prick all over with a toothpick and bake in a slow oven (300°) 30–40 minutes. When half done, brush with water to which a little molasses has been added; brush again when done. When cool, wrap in foil or plastic wrap to keep crust soft.

SAFFRANSBRÖD

My own holiday favorite. The dough can be shaped any way you like, but the huge pretzel is especially festive.

2 cups milk
⅔ cup butter
¾ cup sugar
2 teaspoons salt
4 tablespoons yeast
1 teaspoon sugar
¼ cup lukewarm water
1 teaspoon saffron
Sugar

Milk
7 cups flour (approximately)
1 egg
½ cup finely chopped almonds
1 teaspoon almond extract
⅔ cup seeded muscat raisins

COATING

1 egg, beaten
2 tablespoons sugar

2 tablespoons chopped almonds

Bring the first 4 ingredients to a boil in a large pot. Let cool to lukewarm. Combine yeast, sugar, and water, and let stand.

Pound the saffron in a mortar with a little sugar and stir in a small amount of milk. (A heavy-bottomed Old Fashioned glass will serve nicely as a light-duty mortar; the wrong end of a wooden spoon will do for a pestle.)

Sift 2 cups of flour into the milk mixture. Beat well. Add yeast mixture and saffron mixture, beating well after each. Add other ingredients and the rest of the flour. Keep dough as soft as possible.

Turn out on floured board and knead. Place in original pot (washed, dried, and buttered), cover with a damp towel and let rise until doubled in bulk. Turn out on floured board. Shape into braided loaves or into a large pretzel (see below). Let rise once again. Brush with beaten egg and sprinkle with sugar and chopped almonds. Bake at 375° about 35 minutes, or until done: Keep it golden brown, not dark; turn oven down if necessary.

SHAPING

To make a large pretzel, divide the dough in 3 pieces and squeeze each into a rope at least 6 feet long. Lay these out side by side and make a long braid of three. Then form this braid into one huge pretzel. Place this on a buttered baking sheet and, if you like, place 4 small shot-glasses at convenient and symmetrical locations. When the pretzel rises and cooks, it will pretty much run together, and the spaces left by the shot-glasses will form excellent candle holders—thus turning your saffransbröd into another edible centerpiece.

NOODLES

(See above, page 116)

SPAETZLE

(See above, page 117)

Don't forget that leftover spaetzle, if you ever have any, are delicious fried in butter. An egg scrambled in with them at the very end is also good.

PARSLEY DUMPLINGS

An elegant and slightly different topping for a chicken stew. Also good made small and dropped into boiling chicken soup.

1½ cups sifted flour
2 teaspoons baking powder
¾ teaspoon salt
2 tablespoons chopped
   fresh parsley

½ teaspoon crushed rosemary
3 tablespoons butter
¾ cup milk (approximately)

Sift together flour, baking powder, and salt. Add parsley and rosemary, and mix well.

Cut in the butter (as you would for plain pastry) until the mixture looks like coarse corn meal. Add enough milk to make a thick batter that can be mounded on a spoon and dropped into the stew or soup. Cook 15 minutes.

These are also very good *steamed*. As a matter of fact, I like dumplings best when they have never actually touched the liquid at all. That way they are the soul of lightness.

WILD RICE

Wild rice can be "cooked" to perfection without actually boiling it. This method takes time, but it involves very little work, and it is practically foolproof.

Put 1 cup of wild rice in a large pot or bowl and cover well with boiling water. Let stand about 3 hours. Drain, and repeat twice more at 3 hour intervals, adding salt to the last water. Let it stand for 3 hours more. Drain (saving the last water for gravy, if you like). Next, sauté 2 medium onions, chopped fine, in 4 tablespoons butter until transparent. Add the "opened" rice and heat.

The first beauty of this method is that the rice may be prepared the day before. Or, if convenient to do so, the third water may be put on just before going to bed. In the morning, drain and add to the sautéed onions. When completed, the rice can be reheated many times.

The second beauty is that it really opens the rice, giving you maximum volume. At the wild price of wild rice, anything that stretches it is on the side of the angels.

TWO RISOTTOS

SAFFRON RISOTTO

¼ cup chopped onions	½ teaspoon pounded saffron
2 tablespoons butter	soaked in 1 tablespoon
2 cups raw rice	milk
4 cups beef broth	1 tablespoon tomato paste
2 teaspoons salt	

Sauté onions in butter 3 minutes. Add rice, and stir with a fork. Add stock and all other ingredients. Cover and bring to a boil over medium heat. Reduce heat and continue to simmer 12–15 minutes, stirring 2 or 3 times. Remove from fire, keep covered and let stand at least 20 minutes. At the back of the stove, this will stay hot enough for 1 hour without reheating. To serve, pack it firmly into a 2-quart ring or melon mold, unmold it smartly onto a platter or plate, and garnish with a vegetable.

RISOTTO WITH GREEN PEPPERS AND PIMIENTOS

2 tablespoons butter
¼ cup chopped onions
½ cup chopped green pepper
¼ cup pimientos, cut in
  strips

2 cups raw rice
4 cups chicken stock
2 teaspoons salt
4 tablespoons chopped fresh
  parsley

Sauté vegetables in butter 3 minutes. Add rice, and continue to cook for 1 minute more. Add other ingredients. Cover and bring to a boil. Reduce heat as above, and continue cooking. Before serving, stir in chopped parsley.

II EGGS, CHEESE, AND SOUPS

ASPARAGUS CHEESE OMELETTE

Two of these, served with bread, a generous salad and some red wine, make a perfect simple supper for a large family.

6 eggs	12 spears cooked asparagus,
6 teaspoons water	fresh or canned
Salt and freshly ground	½ pound sharp Cheddar
black pepper to taste	cheese, sliced
2 tablespoons olive oil	1 or 2 pinches orégano

Break eggs into a bowl. Add water, salt, and pepper and beat lightly.

Heat the oil in a 9-inch iron frying pan and add the egg mixture. Cook without disturbing until it sets at the edges and begins to shrink away from the sides of the pan. The center should still be liquid. Remove from heat.

Arrange asparagus on top of the eggs and cover with cheese slices. Sprinkle delicately with orégano, and brown quickly under the broiler.

Serve from the pan immediately, or turn out onto a platter. In any case, cut it into wedge-shaped pieces.

EGGS BENEDICT

Production Line Method

12 thin circles of lean ham	6 English muffins
2 cups Hollandaise sauce	12 poached eggs

HAM

Frizzle ham in iron pan and keep warm.

HOLLANDAISE SAUCE

Prepare (see above, page 105), and set aside.

ENGLISH MUFFINS

Split, toast under the broiler, and spread with butter. Place a circle of ham on each half and arrange all on a large platter. Keep warm.

POACHED EGGS

Break eggs carefully (don't break the yolks) into a shallow bowl with sloping sides. (A large vegetable dish from your good china will do nicely.)

Fill a large (12–14 inches) frying pan ⅔ full of water and bring to a boil. Slip eggs all at once into the water and lower the heat to avoid violent boiling. When whites have set nicely, remove from fire.

With a slotted spoon, separate the eggs from each other, trim off trailing pieces of white and place each egg on top of one of the waiting muffin halves.

Without reheating the Hollandaise, mask each of the egg-ham-and-muffin constructions with a cookingspoonful of sauce.

Serve immediately. Pass any remaining sauce in a boat with a plate of extra muffins.

OLD MAN'S HASH

A quick and delicious addition to the Smörgåsbord—or to any impromptu meal. Be sure to use Swedish anchovies (sprats) and not the Italian variety.

3 large onions, chopped	6 hard boiled eggs, chopped
3 tablespoons butter	Few drops anchovy liquid
12 Swedish anchovy fillets, chopped fine	3 tablespoons heavy cream

Sauté onions in butter until transparent. Add chopped anchovies. Remove from fire and add remaining ingredients. Mix well and serve warm.

(This dish is, obviously, a prime candidate for the office of late-night chafing-dish snack. Serve it with brown bread, butter, Danish beer, and endless conversation about why the play you just saw was inexcusable and/or unforgettable.)

FINNAN HADDIE RABBIT

My Swedish ancestry dictates some kind of codfish on Christmas Eve. I draw the line, however, at Lutfisk, the traditional lye-soaked codfish (it tastes exactly like lye-soaked codfish). This recipe represents a reasonable—and merciful—compromise.

½ pound finnan haddie or smoked cod fillet
½ cup water
4 tablespoons butter
4 tablespoons flour
½ teaspoon English mustard
2 cups milk
¼ teaspoon Worcestershire sauce
1½ pounds sharp Cheddar cheese, sliced
Freshly ground black pepper to taste

Cook finnan haddie with water in a shallow pan until it flakes with a fork. Remove from water and flake completely.

Melt butter in a saucepan, add flour and mustard, and mix thoroughly. Add milk, stir briskly, and cook until it thickens. Add Worcestershire sauce, cheese, fish, and pepper. Cook over low heat, or in a double boiler, until the cheese melts. Serve with toast points or unsalted crackers—and plenty of beer.

GRILLED CHEESE SANDWICHES

I am sure half the people in the United States have already stumbled upon this method, but here it is anyway, along with a recipe for an Italian-style indigestion bomb which you can try when you feel healthy enough to eat nails.

8 slices white bread
Sharp Cheddar cheese
Butter for cooking

Make 4 sandwiches using a generous amount of cheese. Melt butter in a large iron frying pan. (In a 9-inch pan, you can make 2 or 3 sandwiches at a time, depending on the size of the bread.) Add sandwiches and weight them down with a matching iron pan of the same size. When nicely browned, turn the sandwiches and cook the other side. Add more butter as needed. Keep from burning.

PSEUDO-ITALIAN VARIATION

Rye bread
Swiss cheese, sliced
Genoa salami, thinly sliced
Olive oil for cooking
Tabasco (a few drops—or
  more if you like)

Garlic powder
Orégano
Salt and freshly ground
  black pepper

Make your sandwiches with the first 3 ingredients only. Heat oil in skillet. Add all other ingredients to pan and grill the sandwiches. Use 2 iron frying pans, as above. Serve with plenty of beer and paper napkins. Do not attempt to lie down for at least 2 hours. Locate the baking soda before retiring.

BROWN STOCK

(See above, pages 76–78)

WHITE STOCK

(See above, pages 80–81)

MEAT EXTRACT

(See above, pages 78–79)

COURT BOUILLON AND FISH STOCK

(See above, page 82)

SCRAP SOUPS

Delicious off-the-cuff soups can be made from vegetable and meat leavings that would ordinarily be thrown away. Just keep your eyes open for opportunities.

Vegetable trimmings (see specific recipes below)	Butter
Small amount of minced onion	Weak stock, or water plus chicken-wing tips or necks
	Sherry or Madeira

MUSHROOM SOUP

Sauté chopped mushroom stems, skins, or trimmings in butter with a little minced onion until the onion is transparent.

Add a modest amount of stock (or water plus chicken parts) and boil for twenty minutes. Add a few drops of Sherry or Madeira at the end.

You now have an infusion. Remove chicken parts, if any, and put the rest through the blender. Alternatively, simply strain out all the solids.

Make a roux of flour and butter and thicken this infusion judiciously. Taste it, and add as much cream or top milk as you like, just so you do not wash out the flavor. Correct seasoning.

ASPARAGUS SOUP

Save the tough, lower ends of the asparagus spears. Chop them into small pieces and sauté in butter with a little minced onion until the onion is transparent.

Proceed as above, but omit the Sherry. If you blend, strain out the fibers afterward.

Garnish the finished soup with leftover cooked asparagus tips, if you have any.

CELERY SOUP

Proceed as before, using celery ends, light leaves, and odd stalks, but keep the quantity of onion very discreet and omit the Sherry. Don't bother to blend at all.

Garnish the finished soup with finely diced raw celery.

POTATO SOUP

The perfect noontime soup to take the curse off a cold, rainy day. Particularly good with grilled cheese sandwiches.

4 medium potatoes, sliced	1 teaspoon salt
1 medium onion, coarsely chopped	Freshly ground black pepper
1 quart water, or chicken stock	2 bay leaves
2 teaspoons curry powder (or turmeric or cumin)	2 tablespoons butter
	2 tablespoons flour
	½ to 1 quart milk

Put first 7 ingredients into a pot. Bring to a boil and cook for 20 minutes. Put through food mill, strainer, or blender.

Melt butter, stir in flour, add puréed mixture, and cook until thickened. Add milk to bring soup to desired consistency, correct seasoning, bring to boiling point, and serve.

LOBSTER OR CRAB SOUP

Once again, another old classic (Lobster Cantonese) in modified form. Made with live lobster, it takes a little doing; made with fresh or frozen crab meat, it is as easy as crab soup.

1 2-pound live lobster, cut up but left in shell; or 1 pound crab meat	2 large tomatoes, peeled and quartered
Peanut oil	1 quart chicken stock
Salt	1 tablespoon Sherry
1 onion, minced	2 teaspoons light soy sauce
3 cloves garlic, crushed	1 teaspoon oyster sauce
1 slice fresh ginger, crushed	2 tablespoons cornstarch, stirred in a little cold water
1 stalk celery, slivered	
1½ cups shredded cabbage	2 eggs, lightly beaten

In a wok or pot, heat oil and a little salt, add cut-up lobster, and cook for a few minutes until it is red. Remove lobster and set aside.

Add a little more oil and salt, if necessary, and stir-fry the next 3 ingredients for a few seconds.

Add remaining vegetables and stir-fry for a few minutes. Return lobster to the pot and add all other ingredients except eggs. Bring to a boil, and cook for a few minutes.

Beat eggs lightly (just enough to mix yolk and white without foaming). Pour boiling soup into tureen. Then, taking 1 teaspoonful of egg at a time, gently and slowly stir the spoon in the soup so that the egg cooks in graceful ribbons and streamers. Continue working gently but insistently until all the egg has been used. Correct the seasoning and serve.

EMPEROR SOUP

This is the party soup par excellence. Elegant, unusual, and easy.

1 tablespoon butter	Freshly ground black pepper
3 tablespoons flour	4 tablespoons Madeira
7 cups rich beef stock,	2 egg yolks
or canned beef bouillon	4 tablespoons cream
Salt	

Melt butter, add flour, and cook for 2 minutes. Add boiling stock gradually, stirring. Add Madeira, and boil for 5 minutes.

Put yolks and cream in tureen and beat well. Pour boiling soup over them, beating constantly with a whisk. Correct seasoning and serve.

KNACKWURST SOUP

Slice 2 onions, ¼ head of cabbage, 2 stalks of celery, and a little turnip and fry in butter and oil to a good color. Add these to 2 quarts of brown stock (see page 76), throw in as much meat glaze, if any, as you want to get rid of, and cook 6 or so whole knackwurst in the mixture. Near the end, add a splash of Madeira and serve in soup plates (broth plus 1 sausage per person—this is a knife-and-fork soup). With dark bread and butter, and the best beer you can get your hands on, it makes a memorable lunch.

LAMB AND BARLEY SOUP

(See above, pages 187–88)

III *FISH AND SHELLFISH*

BROILED BLUEFISH

Nothing special here; just the best of all possible prepara-tions for fresh-caught blues.

Scale fish, dehead it, gut it, and bone it. Alternatively (if you are no good at filleting), have the fish man clean and split it for you.

Place the pieces on a baking sheet skin side up, and broil them for 5 minutes. (If your fish weighed under 1½ pounds, however, do not bother to broil the skin side at all. Cooking both sides of thin fillets make them too dry.)

Turn the fillets skin side down, sprinkle with salt and freshly ground black pepper and brush with butter plus a little lemon juice or leftover white wine. (Colbert Butter [pp 79–80] is particularly nice. Mayonnaise is good, too.)

Cook until a good color on top, but not dry in the center.

Remove to a warm platter, dot with fresh butter (or Colbert Butter), sprinkle with lemon juice, and serve promptly.

BLUEFISH WITH SHRIMP SAUCE

This recipe works well with moderately oily-meated fish, too (striped bass, for example). If you have fishermen friends who give you free fish, it will provide you with an elegant meal for little more than the price of mushrooms and shrimp.

Take a large bluefish (5–6 pounds), scale it, dehead it, gut it, and bone it.

Make Mushroom Stuffing or Oyster Stuffing (below).

Lay one half of the fish (skin side down) on a buttered ovenproof platter or baking pan, spread with stuffing and cover with the other half of the fish (skin side up).

Cut into serving-size pieces, but leave in the shape of a whole fish and cover the cuts with strips of bacon or salt pork.

Bake 40 minutes or so at 375° (do not dry it out). Baste occasionally with a little white wine and some of the pork dripping.

Serve with Shrimp Sauce (below).

MUSHROOM STUFFING

¾ cup finely chopped mushrooms, sautéed in butter

Few drops onion juice

1 cup stale bread crumbs

¾ teaspoon salt

⅛ teaspoon celery salt

⅛ teaspoon freshly ground black pepper

Few grains cayenne

Few grains nutmeg

½ tablespoon chopped fresh parsley

½ teaspoon chopped chives

2 tablespoons melted butter

½ cup stock, wine or water

Mix all together.

OYSTER STUFFING

Add ½ dozen large, coarsely chopped oysters, or 1 dozen small whole oysters to mushroom stuffing recipe. Omit mushrooms or not, as you like.

SHRIMP SAUCE

Add ½ cup cooked shrimp cut in pieces to a recipe of Drawn Butter Sauce (see below, page 217), bring to a boil, and pour over 1 or 2 beaten egg yolks, whisking vigorously. Pass with the fish.

BRESLIN BAKED BLUEFISH

Excellent at any time, but particularly good for fish that has lain a little longer than it should in the freezer.

2 bluefish, 2 pounds or so each

BRESLIN SAUCE

¼ cup butter, creamed
2 egg yolks
2 tablespoons onion, minced
2 tablespoons dill pickles, chopped

2 tablespoons fresh parsley, chopped
2 tablespoons capers
2 tablespoons lemon juice
1 tablespoon caper liquid
½ teaspoon salt

Dehead, gut, bone, and skin fish.

Place fillets outside down on a buttered baking sheet or ovenproof platter.

Cook fish 10 minutes in a hot oven (400°).

Combine all other ingredients and spread over fish. Continue baking until the finish is a good color.

BLUEFISH PROVENÇALE

Another variation—this time strictly home-brew.

2 bluefish, 2 pounds or so each
2 tablespoons olive oil
2 tablespoons butter
2 fresh tomatoes, peeled and chopped
2 cloves garlic, crushed
2 tablespoons minced onion

½ cup dry white wine
¼ teaspoon Worcestershire sauce
Dash Tabasco sauce
Salt and freshly ground black pepper
Pinch of orégano

Dehead, bone, and skin fish; cut into 3-inch pieces. Salt and pepper fish. Heat oil and butter in an iron frying pan, and fry fish on both sides until a good color. Keep the pan as hot as possible without letting anything burn.

At the end, add all remaining ingredients, reduce for a few minutes, and turn out onto a warm platter. Garnish with 2 tablespoons chopped fresh parsley and serve immediately.

STEAMED FISH PLATTER

The best fish presentation I ever invented. Handsome, easy to serve, and delectable.

8 fillets of flounder
8 very thin 1-inch-wide strips of prosciutto, Smithfield, or Westphalian ham
16 tiny potato balls (cut with melon cutter)
8 tiny onions
12 small hard clams
12 small mussels
8 large or 16 small shucked oysters
A few thin carrot slices (cut with a vegetable parer)
2 tablespoons butter
Salt and freshly ground black pepper
Oyster liquor
A little dry white wine

A serviceable steamer can be made from a large-size covered turkey roaster. Simply lay 2 bricks flat on the bottom, stand the rack on the bricks, and fill with water until it is just below the rack.

Select a platter that will fit inside the steamer. Arrange fish in the center; place 1 strip of ham on each fillet; arrange potato balls and onions around these; surround all with a border of tiny clams and mussels, alternated; scatter oysters and carrots slices over the fish; dot with butter; and sprinkle with salt, pepper, oyster liquor, and dry white wine.

Cover and steam for 15 minutes; serve right from the platter. An excellent snack or first course.

(The platter can be prepared hours ahead of time, covered with plastic wrap, and kept in the refrigerator till needed.)

PAN-FRIED FISH

No recipe; just a couple of hints.

(1) When coating fish, dip the fillets (or whatever) first in flour or cornstarch, then in egg, then in crumbs.

(2) Save left-over almond gratings and mix these with your bread crumbs.

(3) Always coat fish a good hour or so before cooking and return to the ice box. That way, the coating has a chance to set up before cooking, and will not easily fall off the fish when it hits the pan.

(4) Always use butter to pan-fry fish, but do not let it burn while the fish is cooking. Beurre Noir or browned butter is a good sauce for fish, but it should be made after the fish has been removed from the skillet. In any case, when making pan sauce, always start with a splash of water to loosen the goodness that might otherwise stick to the bottom of the pan.

(5) A little lemon juice and a few drops of Tabasco never hurt any fish.

STUFFED TURBANS OF FLOUNDER

Another good first course.

Cut fillets of flounder in half lengthwise, and line buttered muffin tins with the strips. In the center of each, place a little Mushroom Stuffing (see above, page 212), add a raw oyster with a drop of Tabasco, and fill with additional stuffing.

Cover tins with aluminum foil, and bake 20 minutes at 375°. Unmold smartly onto a board, transfer to a hot platter, or to individual plates, mask with Normandy Sauce (see below, page 216) or Shrimp Sauce (see above, page 212) and garnish with lemon wedges, sprigs of fresh parsley, and small boiled potatoes.

Serve promptly.

SOME FISH SAUCES

HOLLANDAISE

Hard to beat for almost any kind of fish. The perfect answer when all other answers fail. (See above, page 105.)

COLBERT BUTTER

Excellent spread on broiled fish before, during, and after cooking. (See above, pages 79–80.)

SAUCES MADE WITH FISH STOCK

These sauces depend heavily on the quality of the fish stock used. When you boil up bones and trimmings, therefore, be sure to include a nice bouquet garni and a generous splash of good dry white wine.

NORMANDY SAUCE

2 tablespoons butter
2 tablespoons flour
1 cup fish stock (see above, page 82)
¼ cup mushroom liquor

2 large egg yolks
⅓ cup heavy cream
Dash cayenne
Salt and freshly ground black pepper

Make a roux of flour and butter. Add stocks, whisk well, and boil. Simmer for a few minutes. Put egg yolks and cream in a warm bowl, whisk well, and pour the boiling sauce on them, whisking constantly. Season to taste with cayenne, salt, and pepper.

DRAWN BUTTER SAUCE

3 tablespoons butter
3 tablespoons flour
1½ cups fish stock
  (see above, page 82)
½ teaspoon salt

⅛ teaspoon freshly ground
  black pepper
1 teaspoon lemon juice
Extra butter (3 tablespoons,
  at least)

Make a roux of flour and butter, salt, and pepper. Add stock, whisk well, and boil for 5 minutes. Add lemon juice to taste and whisk in remaining butter in small pieces.

SEAFOOD STRUDEL

FILLING:

6 medium mushrooms, sliced
Meat from one good-sized
  cooked lobster, diced

1 cup crab meat, in chunks
1 cup cooked and peeled
  shrimp, in pieces

Sauté mushrooms in a little butter for 5 minutes. Put a generous splash of Sherry in the pan; reduce slightly, and add the seafood.

Make a thick white sauce (4 tablespoons butter, 3 tablespoons flour, 1 cup top milk) and stir that, too, into the pan.

Perfect the seasoning. A little lemon juice? A drop of Worcestershire? A few tablespoons of grated Gruyère or Parmesan? A pinch of cayenne? Decide for yourself. Be discreet but firm; it is, after all, your strudel.

Allow the mixture to cool while you make and stretch the strudel dough. Follow the directions (page 120) for filling, rolling, and baking—but, for heaven's sake, stop short of the confectioners' sugar and sweet whipped cream at the end. Serve piping hot.

Well made, it is a handsome dish. With a generous salad, four or five bottles of Muscadet or Pouilly Fuissé, bread, cheese, and some nice fruit, it makes a perfect way for eight people to pass the time from noon till two. For a formal dinner, it will easily serve ten or twelve as a first course.

LOBSTER, SHRIMP, OR CRAB STIR

Follow the general directions for a Chinese stir (see above, pages 140–42), but tilt the list of ingredients in this direction: Use rather more oyster sauce and rather less soy sauce (or none at all); be a little more generous with the garlic and fresh ginger; and finally, omit the cabbage and turnip and substitute mustard cabbage or young Swiss chard, and a peeled, quartered fresh tomato.

SEAFOOD IN AU GRATIN DISHES

Once again, nothing out of the ordinary. Just one way of doing a common job well. (Add some sautéed mushrooms, if you like.)

2 pounds of cooked shellfish (shrimp, crab, and lobster make a good combination)
2 tablespoons butter
2 tablespoons flour
1½ cups liquid: chicken stock, dry white wine (or dry Vermouth), and heavy cream in equal parts
1 teaspoon Worcestershire sauce

Dash Tabasco
Hint of scraped onion
Salt, freshly ground black pepper, and lemon juice to taste
For the gratin: bread crumbs, grated Gruyère or Parmesan cheese and butter

Cut shellfish into bite-size pieces.

Make a sauce of the next 6 ingredients, and season to taste with salt, pepper, and lemon juice.

Add shellfish to sauce.

Put mixture in buttered au gratin dishes or very large clam or scallop shells. Sprinkle with crumbs, cheese, and melted butter, and bake in a hot oven (425°) until brown (about 20 minutes).

SHRIMP WITH WILD RICE

More home-brew. A good way to stretch a little leftover wild rice into a first course or a late night snack. It can be prepared well in advance and baked at the last minute.

2 cups cooked Wild Rice
  (see above, pages 200–1)
1 pound raw, peeled shrimp,
  cut in ½-inch pieces

1 recipe Breslin Sauce
  (see above, page 213)
½ cup dry white wine

Combine rice, shrimp, Breslin Sauce, and wine, and mix well. Fill buttered au gratin dishes or large shells with the mixture and bake at 400° for 20 minutes.

MUSSELS MARINIERE

Mussels are the most neglected shellfish in America. Acquire a taste for them before they become popular and price themselves out of sight.

3 dozen mussels, well
  scrubbed
6 tablespoons butter
1 clove garlic, crushed
2 leeks, chopped
1 small onion, minced

1 small bay leaf
¾ cup dry white wine
½ cup cream
Salt and freshly ground
  black pepper to taste
Chopped fresh parsley

In a deep pan, melt butter. Add garlic, leeks, onion, and bay leaf, and cook for a few minutes.

Add wine and mussels, cover the pot, and steam until the mussels are well opened (5 minutes or so).

Remove mussels, discard top shells, but leave the mussels themselves in the lower shells. Arrange on a warm platter.

Boil liquid hard until reduced by half. Add cream and salt and pepper to taste. Pour over mussels and sprinkle with chopped parsley. Serve immediately.

PICKLED MUSSELS

Another domestic recipe. Good eaten cold; even better heated in butter with a little of the reduced pickle. A first-class hors d'oeuvre.

48 small mussels, scrubbed
½ cup white wine (or water)
½ cup wine vinegar
1 teaspoon orégano
2 teaspoons salt

½ medium onion, sliced
2 cloves garlic, crushed
1 bay leaf
1 tablespoon fresh chopped parsley
Pepper to taste

In a large pot place mussels, wine, vinegar, orégano, and salt. Cover. Place over high flame and steam for 5 minutes. Remove from fire. Take mussels out of shells and pack into jar. Add hot liquid from pan together with the onion, garlic, bay leaf, parsley, and pepper.

If there is not enough liquid to cover, add equal parts of vinegar and wine and extra salt. Seal jar, and store in refrigerator. May be used when cold, but flavor is improved by standing a few days. (Raw carrot strips may be added to give variety and color.)

STUFFED CLAMS

An authentic local recipe from an old-timer on the North Shore of Long Island. Clams for people who hate clams. Food for the fainthearted at clambakes. Also, just plain good.

2 dozen large hard clams
¼ pound salt pork
4 medium potatoes, peeled
4 medium onions
8 slices white bread

Poultry seasoning to taste
Extra pinch thyme
Salt and freshly ground
  black pepper to taste
(Don't overdo.)

Open clams, saving shells. (The purists in the neighborhood open them by hand with a clam knife. If you are lazy or unskilled, steam them in a large covered pot with ½ cup water for 5 minutes.) The liquor or broth, in any case, is not used in this recipe.

Remove rind from salt pork, dice it, and try it out in a frying pan till it is brown. Save the grease.

Put pork, clams, potatoes, and onions through the meat grinder.

Tear the bread into small pieces and add it to the mixture. Pour in the melted pork fat, add the seasonings, and work all together well with the hands.

Fill half the shells generously and cover them with shells of equal size.

Put the stuffed clams in a large baking pan, cover the pan with foil, and bake 1 hour in a moderate oven (350°).

Serve with butter, lemon wedges, and Tabasco. Each mouthful should have the benefit of all three: butter in abundance; the other two with discretion.

(For an outdoor affair, each stuffed clam can be wrapped in aluminum foil. In that condition, they can be thrown directly into the fire and retrieved when nicely heated.)

WASH-BOILER CLAMBAKE

Traditionally an outdoor dish; but if you don't mind a messy dining room, it makes a great indoor party for a relaxed crowd.

Cover the bottom of an old-fashioned wash boiler with large stones 4 or 5 inches in diameter. Add some water, up to ⅔ the depth of the stones. Cover the stones with good seaweed to a depth of 3 or 4 inches.

On the seaweed, place a layer of small, unpeeled, washed potatoes. On the potatoes, arrange 2 or 3 split chickens. On the chickens, place half a dozen small, lively lobsters. Steam vigorously for 30 minutes, well covered.

Open the boiler and place a layer of shucked corn on the cob on top of the lobsters. On top of the corn, put several flat pans of washed live soft clams. (Disposable aluminum baking pans will do nicely: Their purpose is to catch the clam broth, so that it does not lose itself in the bottom of the boiler.)

Cover the boiler again and steam for 10 minutes more—or until the clams are well opened.

Serve with dishes of drawn butter at each place and with nutcrackers, picks, and hatchets to enable guests to cope with the lobsters.

The clam broth should be passed in small cups.

Two tips:

(1) The butter can be drawn nicely by standing a panful of it on top of the steamer during the cooking.

(2) If you like Worcestershire sauce with your lobster, put a teaspoonful in your dish of drawn butter (where it will sink to the bottom). Accordingly, if you want butter only, you dip lightly; if you want butter plus, you dip deep.

DEEP-FAT FISH FRY

As before, no recipe, only pointers.

(1) Flour, egg, and crumb everything well in advance and return to refrigerator until needed.

(2) Have the fat hot enough. Use a fat thermometer unless you are an old hand and know exactly what you are doing.

(3) If possible, avoid using teeny-weeny home-style french-frying equipment. Go buy yourself something more adequate at a restaurant supply store.

(4) Don't use ancient grease.

(5) If you invite me, include a couple of soft-shell crabs, no matter what else you serve.

IV *MEAT AND POULTRY*

STEAMED GROUND BEEF

An excellent Chinese-style presentation which makes a welcome change from meat loaf.

6 scallions or 2 small onions, minced

2 large cloves garlic, crushed

2 pounds ground beef

2 eggs

4 tablespoons cornstarch

1 teaspoon peanut oil

1 tablespoon Sherry

1½ teaspoons salt

4 teaspoons dark soy sauce

1 teaspoon sugar

½ teaspoon freshly ground black pepper

Combine all ingredients and mix well with the hands. Mold on a platter or baking dish and steam* (15 minutes or so for rare beef; 20 minutes or more for well done). Pour off excess fat and serve immediately.

GROUND BEEF AND VEGETABLES

PREPARATION:

(A)

2 pounds ground beef

1 tablespoon cornstarch

1½ tablespoons light soy sauce

3 tablespoons Sherry

1 teaspoon sugar

1 teaspoon peanut oil

Mix all together with your hands. Set aside.

* Use a large covered roasting pan to make a steamer (see above, page 214).

(B)

1 small onion, minced	1 piece fresh ginger root,
2 cloves garlic, crushed	(the size of a quarter),
	crushed

Prepare and set aside.

(C)

Shred, slice, and shave a batch of good-looking vegetables, and set aside in a bowl of cold water. Here is a suggestion:

2 cups shredded cabbage	¼ of a green pepper,
1 stalk celery, sliced thin	sliced thin
crosswise	4 sliced mushrooms
1 1-inch-thick slice of	4 water chestnuts, sliced thin
turnip, peeled and shaved	
into thin strips	

(D)

1 cup chicken stock	Dash of light soy sauce
1½ tablespoons cornstarch	Dash of oyster sauce

Mix well and set aside.

(E)

Cooked rice, timed for the dinner hour.

(F)

Hot mustard and chutney to pass with the dish.

COOKING:

(A)

Oil and salt a large wok lightly. Heat well, and brown the meat, working it with 2 wooden spoons until it separates into bite-size cooked chunks. Remove and set aside.

(B)

Oil and salt again, if necessary, add the onion, garlic and ginger, and cook for a few seconds only.

(C)

Add the drained vegetables, stir-fry with the spoons for a minute and cook, covered, over high heat until a good color (4–5 minutes).

(D)

Return the cooked beef, stir up the cornstarch solution, add it to the whole, and boil briefly to thicken.

Serve promptly with rice and garnishes.

ROYAL POT ROAST

Pot roast with a Swedish touch.

3 to 3½ pounds round or rump	¼ teaspoon white pepper
2 tablespoons oil	1 small red onion, diced
2 tablespoons butter	1 bay leaf
½ tablespoon salt	6 Swedish anchovy fillets
3½ cups brown stock (or milk!)	½ tablespoon light Karo syrup
8 black peppercorns	3 tablespoons Cognac
	1 tablespoon vinegar

Wipe meat with a cloth wrung out of hot water. Brown in oil in an iron Dutch oven. Pour off oil and replace with butter. Add all other ingredients and cook covered for about 3 hours. Turn meat a few times during cooking. When cooked, remove roast to platter, and strain gravy.

SAUCE

| 1 tablespoon butter | Gravy |
| 1½ tablespoons flour | 2 tablespoons cream |

Make a roux of the butter and flour. Add gravy gradually. Cook for 10 minutes. Add cream.

SAUERBRATEN AND KARTOFFELKLÖSSE

Good any time you can get it, but best of all reheated the second day with the leftover kartoffelklösse sliced and fried in butter.

SAUERBRATEN

7- to 8-pound piece of top round, bottom round or crossrib of beef

6 strips of fat pork ¼×¼×4 for larding

FOR THE MARINADE

(Increase the ingredients proportionately if you need more liquid to cover the beef)
2 cups cider vinegar
2 cups water
1 tablespoon salt

1 teaspoon freshly ground black pepper
1 onion, sliced
2 tablespoons pickling spice
1 bay leaf
1 clove garlic

FOR THE COOKING

3 tablespoons oil
2 tablespoons flour
3 cups marinade

10 gingersnaps, crushed
1 cup red wine

Lard the beef (or have your butcher do it for you).

Mix the pickling liquid and marinate the beef in it for 48 hours at least. Keep in a cool place. Turn meat twice daily.

Remove meat from marinade, and brown well in the oil in a large skillet. Transfer meat to a roasting pan. Add flour to skillet, blend with grease, add 3 cups marinade, and boil. Add crushed gingersnaps, whisk well, and pour over meat in roasting pan. Roast at 375°, 20–25 minutes per pound. Baste often, add more marinade if necessary, and ½ hour from the end, add a cup of red wine.

Remove meat to a serving platter, and taste sauce in pan. If too sour, cut with weak stock or cream. If too bland, add a little more marinade. If too thick, dilute with equal parts wine, marinade, and cream. Boil and whisk well and serve.

KARTOFFELKLÖSSE

6 cups seasoned mashed
   potatoes (leave out the
   milk, but don't forget the
   nutmeg)
2 cups flour (or more, if
   needed)

2 large eggs beaten
Croutons (3 slices bread,
   cubed and fried in plenty
   of butter until brown)

Cool potatoes, add flour and eggs, and beat well.

Bring a large pot of water to a boil. Form the potato mixture into balls the size of small oranges. (Drop the first one into the boiling water to test: If it falls apart, add more flour to the mixture before forming the rest of the dumplings.) Poke 4 or 5 croutons into each ball and reshape nicely. (If the mixture is sticky and hard to handle, coat your hands frequently with flour.)

Cook dumplings until the centers are just done (5 minutes or so after they come to the surface). Remove with a skimmer and serve with gravy or browned butter.

ZWIEBELFLEISCH

Something to do with leftover sauerbraten when there are no kartoffelklösse left to reckon with. (Also good for any kind of leftover pot roast.)

Arrange slices of sauerbraten in a baking dish. Cover generously with sliced onions which have been well fried in butter. Top the onions with spoonfuls of leftover sauerbraten gravy and grated cheese (sharp Cheddar is particularly good). Bake in a hot oven (400°) for 20 minutes, or until the topping browns nicely.

SOME BEEF POINTERS

(1) RAW BEEF

Admittedly, it is a matter of taste; but few things are as simply delicious as good ground round steak seasoned with salt, freshly ground black pepper and some onion scrapings.

For the smörgåsbord, put a thick circle of seasoned ground beef on a plate; then put a thin circle of minced raw onion inside that; lastly, put a raw egg yolk in the center of it all. The first guest stirs it up before helping himself. (You can make the same "eye" presentation with chopped Swedish anchovies instead of ground beef. Not for the squeamish, of course, but awfully good nonetheless.)

(2) ROAST BEEF

Roast your beef in a 500° oven for 5 minutes per pound. At the end of that time, turn the oven off and leave the door closed for 2 hours. That's all there is to it. Your beef will be beautifully pink all the way through, and not overdone anywhere. It will also have a lovely dark finish and will make great gravy—if you follow the right procedure (see above, pages 70–72).

SALISBURY STEAK

With a minimum of handling, shape good, fresh ground beef into attractive steaks 1 inch thick and about the size of a compact rib lamb chop. Sprinkle with salt and freshly ground black pepper, and place in a hot, lightly greased pan. Brown one side and turn.

With a knife, make a cut (1 inch long and ½ inch deep) in the center of the top of each steak. When the juices of the meat begin to flow freely out of the cut, the steaks are done. (As the center of each steak begins to cook, it contracts. The slit you made simply gives the expressed juices an avenue of escape, thus providing you with a visible record of what is going on out of sight.) If you like your steaks very rare, remove them from the pan when the juices first begin to flow. If you like them cooked to death, wait until the flowing stops entirely. If you like them somewhere in between, use your judgment.

SWEDISH MEAT BALLS

The real thing, at least as far as I am concerned.

3 tablespoons minced onion
2 tablespoons butter
1 pound each of beef, veal, pork, ground together
1 tablespoon allspice
1 tablespoon salt
¼ teaspoon ground ginger
¼ teaspoon ground cloves
¼ teaspoon ground nutmeg

½ teaspoon freshly ground black pepper
1 cup fine dry bread crumbs
½ cup chicken or beef stock (approximately)
2 eggs
1 quart beef bouillon, broth, or stock

Sauté onion in butter until golden. Combine all ingredients except the last, and mix well by hand. Shape into balls and fry until nicely browned in a little butter or oil. Put in a large pot with the bouillon and simmer for 45 minutes.

This dish is better made one day in advance and refrigerated. The hardened fat on top can then be removed easily and used in place of butter to thicken the gravy.

4 tablespoons fat or butter
4 tablespoons flour
Gravy from pan

Make a roux of fat and flour, add gravy, bring to a boil, whisking well, and simmer for 5 minutes. Add meat balls, reheat and serve.

RULLEPØLSE

Fussy, but very good. Sliced thin, as it should be, it goes a long way. A great smörgåsbord item. (Don't send teen-agers to buy the saltpeter, however; someone is bound to accuse them of trying to manufacture fuses or explosives.) Also be prepared for a rash of old seminary and men's dormitory jokes when you tell your more knowledgeable friends that the dish is prepared with saltpeter. I knew a man once who refused to eat rullepølse on the grounds that it might impair his prowess. The Danes who invented it, however, seem little troubled by such worries. Have no fear then; its function is simply to make the meat pink.

1 large breast of veal, boned, skinned and trimmed
1 pound salt pork, rind removed, and sliced thin, like bacon
1 tablespoon freshly ground black pepper
2 tablespoons salt
1 tablespoon saltpeter (from the drugstore)
1 tablespoon ground allspice
1 cup chopped onion
5 tablespoons finely chopped fresh dill (or parsley)— or 2½ tablespoons dried dill weed

Arrange the breast of veal in a neat, large, flat square.

Lay the sliced salt pork all over the surface of the veal. Sprinkle all other ingredients over the pork, roll up the veal, jelly-roll fashion, encase it firmly in a white cloth (a clean diaper does nicely), and tie the whole sausage at both ends as well as at several points in between.

Make a brine of salt and water. Select a jar or crock that will accommodate your veal, put in sufficient water and stir in salt until a potato will just float in the brine. Add 1 teaspoon of saltpeter, and marinate the rullepølse for 5 or 6 days in a cool place. (Weight down the sausage with a stone so that it will remain covered by the brine.)

When ready, remove, place in a large kettle, cover with water, add salt to taste, and boil gently for 1½ hours.

Drain, cool under a heavy weight, and refrigerate for at least 24 hours. Unwrap from the cloth and serve in very thin slices.

SOME VEAL POINTERS

(1) If you buy a whole leg of veal, be sure to butcher off your own choice cutlets from the upper end before roasting or stewing the rest.

(2) If you pound cutlets very thin, just salt and pepper them—don't get involved with flour. In any case, fry your cutlets in butter only. Don't, however, let them burn.

(3) Don't forget that veal chops are one of the choicest cuts available. Rib chops can be trimmed, pounded a bit, and treated pretty much like cutlets. Loin chops are very good seasoned, floured, and egged and then coated with bread crumbs; or with bread crumbs and grated almonds; or with coarse oatmeal. Once again, though, cook carefully *in butter*.

(4) After the cutlets or chops come out of the pan, make a

decent pan gravy. Here are some suggestions. (Correct the seasoning in each case before pouring the sauce out of the pan. Also, if there is a lot of loose coating in the pan, strain the sauce onto the meat.)

(a) Add equal parts Marsala and chicken stock, reduce well, and pour over meat.

(b) Add cream and meat glaze, boil, and pour over meat.

(c) Add chicken stock, reduce well, add cream, boil, and pour over meat.

(d) Add a little good Half-Glaze (see below) and a splash of Madeira, reduce slightly and pour over meat. Or add Madeira Sauce (see below) and do likewise.

(e) Sautéed mushrooms never hurt any veal dish. Neither did chopped fresh parsley sprinkled over the platter just before bringing it to the table.

HALF-GLAZE, QUICK AND GOOD

1 can Campbell's beef broth	3 tablespoons butter
⅔ can of water	3 tablespoons flour

Make a roux of flour and butter. Brown slightly. Add broth and water, and bring to a boil, whisking well. Simmer for 5 minutes.

MADEIRA SAUCE, JUST AS QUICK—AND EVEN BETTER

1 can Campbell's beef broth	3 tablespoons flour
½ can rainwater Madeira, plus a splash of water	A little freshly ground black pepper
3 tablespoons butter	

Proceed as above for half-glaze.

LAMB CHOPS

(1) Don't forget the virtues of pan frying. You have more control over the process—especially if you put a knife cut in the top of the chops after you have turned them (see above under Salisbury Steak, page 230). When the blood begins to flow, the chops will be just approaching rareness in the center. Govern your cooking accordingly.

(2) Buy lamb chops half as often and order them twice as thick. Who wants lamb *chips* when he ordered lamb chops?

(3) Pan gravies are possible here, of course, but nothing can be better than fresh butter, salt, freshly ground black pepper, lemon juice, and a drop of Tabasco scored into the surface of the finished chops after they are on the platter.

BOILED LAMB WITH DILL

3-pound shoulder of lamb   1 tablespoon salt
   (or a half or whole leg)   A few sprigs fresh dill
7 cups water   (or 1 tablespoon dill weed)

Wipe meat with a cloth wrung out of hot water. Put in a pot with boiling water; add salt and dill. Simmer, covered, about 2 hours. Remove meat, and cut into serving pieces.

Arrange on platter, mask with sauce, and serve. Pass additional sauce in a boat.

SAUCE

4 tablespoons butter   2 tablespoons finely chopped
4 tablespoons flour   dill
3 cups broth from lamb   4 egg yolks
2 teaspoons sugar   1 tablespoon butter
1½ tablespoons vinegar

Heat butter; add flour, whisking. Add stock gradually, whisking well. Cook for 8 minutes. Add sugar, vinegar, and dill.

Put yolks in warm bowl, beat with whisk, and gradually add boiling gravy, whisking constantly. Whisk in last tablespoon of butter and serve immediately.

INDIAN LAMB CURRY

Hot, pungent, and marvelous.

2 pounds boneless leg of
   lamb
1 cup yogurt
2½ teaspoons salt
1 teaspoon ground cumin
1½ teaspoons ground turmeric
½ teaspoon ground cardamom
¼ cup peanut oil, or clarified
   butter
1½ cups chopped onion
1 clove garlic, crushed
1 teaspoon powdered
   mustard

1 teaspoon ground ginger
½ teaspoon ground cinnamon
½ teaspoon ground black
   pepper
¼ to ½ teaspoon cayenne
⅛ teaspoon ground cloves
1 cup water
1 teaspoon lemon juice
2 tablespoons grated fresh
   or packaged flaked
   coconut

Cut meat into 1-inch pieces. Mix with the next 5 ingredients and marinate for 2 hours.

Brown meat in 1 tablespoon peanut oil and pour off excess fat.

In another skillet, cook onion and garlic in remaining oil until golden. Add next 6 ingredients. Stir and cook 2 minutes. Add lamb, cover, and cook 20 minutes. Pour in water, and mix. Cover and simmer 30 minutes, adding water only to keep from burning.

Stir in lemon juice and coconut just before serving. Serve

with plain rice and extra coconut—and with all the other bland curry garnishes you can muster. (If you are ashamed to have a glass of milk at your place, steal some from the child next to you. It is perfect with curry.)

LAMB FRIED RICE

(See above, pages 135–36)

LAMB AND SPINACH CASSEROLE

(See above, pages 134–35)

BRAISED LAMB OR LAMB SHANKS

(See above, pages 132 ff.)

CHINESE STIR

(General Method)

(See above, pages 140 ff.)

TRIPE NICOISE

A dish to destroy all your prejudices against tripe.

2 pounds fresh tripe
Water or chicken stock
A bouquet garni
Bay leaf
Olive oil
6 medium onions
2 cloves garlic
1 cup chicken stock

1 cup white wine
2 fresh tomatoes (peeled and crushed)—or the equivalent from a can
Salt, freshly ground black pepper
Basil, marjoram, rosemary, thyme

Boil the tripe for 1 hour in a little water and/or chicken stock, together with a bouquet garni and a bay leaf. Drain, saving ½ cup of liquid for this recipe, and freezing the rest for an eventual pepper pot soup. Cool and cut the meat into strips as long as your little finger, and half as wide.

Put a little olive oil in an iron skillet, heat to smoking, and add the cut tripe. Use no flour. Brown well. You will find, of course, that tripe, even after 15 minutes over strong heat is only tan—it never does brown like other meat. It also sticks to the pan, crackles noisily, and spits back at you. Ignore it all and plow ahead. Add more oil, if needed. Keep the tripe moving with a vigorously wielded pancake turner, but get it well tanned and slightly crisp before you stop. At the end there should be practically nothing stuck to the skillet.

Next, melt a little butter in the bottom of your stew pot and add the onions (sliced) and the garlic (crushed). Allow these to brown only slightly and then add the chicken stock, tripe stock, and wine (having first rinsed the skillet with them), the tomatoes, salt and pepper. (Remember, easy on the salt. This stew will not be thickened, but only *reduced* to a proper consistency. Enough salt now will be too much later.) Finally (and this is the soul of the recipe), add a generous pinch each of basil, marjoram, and rosemary, and a less generous one of thyme. Cover, simmer for 1½ hours, and reduce if the sauce looks too thin.

Serve on rice, with chopped fresh parsley and a pepper mill close at hand.

SWEETBREADS

One of the loveliest of all meats; no longer cheap, but still, as always, good. Just a few hints.

(1) Soak sweetbreads in salted ice water (1 teaspoon to a

quart) for 1 hour. (If frozen, let them thaw out in cold water.)
Trim away tubes and odd membranes.

(2) Parboil them by dropping them into rapidly boiling
salted (1 teaspoon to a quart) water, to which 1 tablespoon
lemon juice has been added. Ten minutes is enough.

(3) Cool them quickly under weights (between 2 plates,
for example, with a flatiron on top).

(4) Salt, pepper, and flour them lightly (if very thick,
split them), fry delicately in butter, and finish in any of the
ways suggested under Veal (see above, page 232). Madeira
Sauce is especially choice: bathed in that and surrounded by
tiny peas, they greet you as Sweetbreads Clamart.

(5) Don't forget too: Sweetbreads Country Style—baked
quickly under thin strips of salt pork; and Sweetbreads Colbert—broiled or pan fried in Colbert Butter (see above, pages
79–80).

SWEETBREADS GRAZIELLA

On second thought, I cannot resist a whole recipe.

6 fairly thick rounds of fried bread (use butter or beef dripping)	3 pairs sweetbreads, parboiled
	Salt and freshly ground black pepper
3 ripe fresh tomatoes	Flour
Minced onion	5 tablespoons butter
Trace of minced garlic	1 cup Madeira Sauce (see above, page 233)
6 teaspoons melted butter	
Salt, pepper, and bread crumbs	6 sautéed mushroom caps

Fry bread to a good color and keep warm.
Cut each tomato in half horizontally and sprinkle the cut

surface with chopped onion and garlic. Put 1 teaspoon melted butter on each and sprinkle with salt, pepper and bread crumbs. Broil until a good color.

Split sweetbreads, dredge with salt, pepper, and flour, and fry in butter on both sides until a good color.

Place the rounds of bread on a warmed platter, put the sweetbreads on the bread, rinse the pan with the Madeira Sauce, strain a discreet quantity of it over the sweetbreads (pass the rest in a boat), arrange the broiled tomatoes tastefully around the sweetbreads, cap each with a mushroom, and serve—with tiny potatoes roasted in butter.

CHICKEN LIVER PÂTÉ

1 teaspoon rendered
   chicken or pork fat
2 pounds chicken livers
3 eggs
⅓ cup Cognac
1½ cups heavy cream
⅔ cup diced *fresh* pork fat
1 onion, coarsely chopped

2 cloves garlic, crushed
½ cup flour
4 teaspoons salt
1 piece fresh ginger root,
   chopped
2 teaspoons white pepper
1 teaspoon allspice

Grease a 3-quart casserole with rendered fat.

Make a fine purée of all ingredients. (If you use an electric blender, it will be necessary to do it in 3 or 4 installments.)

Mix well, pour into casserole, and cover with a double thickness of aluminum foil.

Place casserole in a pan of water and bake at 325° for 2 to 2½ hours. Cool and then store in the refrigerator.

(Like most pâtés, this is better after it has aged 2 or 3 days. It will keep up to 2 weeks.)

CHICKEN PAPRIKASH

6 leg-thigh pieces of chicken

5 scallions, minced

1 teaspoon salt

5 cloves garlic, crushed

1 tablespoon dried dill weed

2 cups chicken stock

1 cup dry white wine

4 tablespoons Hungarian paprika

¼ cup tomato sauce

¾ cup sour cream

Separate legs and second joints. Cut off the small end of the leg bone with a cleaver. Skin all pieces.

Place chicken in a low, wide saucepan which can be covered. Add next 6 ingredients. Bring to a fast boil. Reduce heat, cover, and simmer 20 minutes. Remove chicken and put in a baking pan or dish in a 300° oven while preparing sauce.

Reduce liquid by half over high heat. Stir in paprika and tomato sauce. If still too thin, reduce to desired thickness. Remove from stove, add sour cream, correct seasoning, pour over chicken and serve—with spaetzle, of course.

FONG WONG GAI

4 whole chicken breasts

8 thin slices prosciutto, Smithfield, or Westphalian ham

FOR THE COATING

Cornstarch and flour, mixed

2 beaten eggs, as needed

FOR EACH EGG USED, ADD

1 teaspoon light soy sauce

1 teaspoon Sherry

Pinch ground ginger

Pinch salt

Dash Worcestershire sauce

Fine dry bread crumbs

Fat for deep frying

Cut chicken breasts in half. Bone and skin them. With a sharp knife, cut a pocket in each breast. Insert 1 piece of ham in each chicken breast. Press together to seal.

Roll in cornstarch and flour mixture to dry. Dip in eggs mixed with soy sauce, Sherry, ginger, salt and Worcestershire sauce. Roll in bread crumbs. Put in refrigerator for at least 1 hour.

Heat fat to correct temperature, and fry breasts until a good color (not more than 3–4 minutes).

Serve on a bed of Chinese vegetables with rice. The beauty of this dish is the fact that the breast meat is cooked so rapidly that it remains light and moist. Good ham, of course, is always a compliment to chicken.

CHICKEN CUTLETS

Just a reminder that boned and skinned breasts of chicken, cut in two and pounded a little between sheets of waxed paper are the full equal of any veal cutlets. Fry them lightly and, above all, quickly, in butter, and finish in any of the ways suggested under Veal (see above, page 232) or Sweetbreads (see above, pages 237–39).

V VEGETABLES

GERMAN FRIED POTATOES WITH ONIONS

Great ordinary eating.

8 potatoes, peeled, sliced
    paper-thin, and soaked in
    cold water

2 onions, cut in rings
Fat or oil for deep frying
Salt

Heat fat to correct temperature for french frying.

Drain potatoes. Pat dry with towel. Put half of the potatoes in fryer basket and fry until golden. Remove from fat and drain on brown paper. Repeat with the rest of the potatoes. When they start to brown, add onion. Continue frying to a good color. At the last minute, put the first batch back into the pot to reheat. Drain it all on brown paper. Salt lightly.

GERMAN POTATO SALAD

Don't be cowed by the word salad. Serve this in place of regular potatoes with any smoked or corned meat—and never omit it from a meal of wurst, beer, and cheese.

2 cans potatoes, sliced
6 strips bacon, diced
1 large onion, chopped
4 tablespoons vinegar
Freshly ground black
    pepper

Salt to taste
Pinch of sugar
Chopped parsley

Brown bacon in pot. Add onion and continue cooking until onions are transparent. Add other ingredients. Serve warm.

POTATO AND ANCHOVY SAVORY

Scalloped potatoes, Swedish style. A must for the smörgås-bord. It goes by the name of Janssons Frestelse—Jansson's Temptation. It's good, but, in all honesty, not as overpowering as the name implies. Whoever Jansson was, he apparently had a different set of susceptibilities than you or I.

10 potatoes, peeled and
  sliced
10 Swedish anchovy fillets
2 onions, finely chopped
6 tablespoons butter

Salt
Freshly ground black pepper
3 tablespoons flour
1½ cups cream or top milk

In a buttered casserole, sprinkle layers of potatoes with anchovies, onions, butter, salt, pepper, and flour. End with a layer of potatoes. Pour cream on top; add a little anchovy juice and salt and pepper. Bake covered at 375° for 1 hour. Uncover, and continue to bake until brown on top.

NEW POTATOES AND BACON

Hearty, good—and a little different.

18 small white onions, peeled
2 tablespoons butter
2 slices lean bacon
1 cup beef broth or
  bouillon
2 tablespoons tomato purée

18 small new potatoes,
  peeled
½ teaspoon salt
⅛ teaspoon freshly ground
  black pepper
Chopped parsley

Cook onions in butter until lightly browned. Add bacon, and brown. Add bouillon and tomato purée. Cook 3–4 minutes. Add potatoes and salt. Cover and cook until vegetables are tender (about 20 minutes). Add pepper.
Sprinkle with parsley and serve.

CELERY KNOBS

Even less recherché, but practically unbeatable for flavor: They taste more like artichoke hearts than celery.

Peel and slice some celery knobs. Cook them, covered, in a very little water (there should be next to no liquid left). Drain, season, and drown in butter.

PEAS BONNE FEMME

Throw some fresh peas and some broken lettuce into a large bowl of cold water.

Cut a few strips of bacon (or lean salt pork) into squares, and fry them briefly in the skillet (they should not become crisp).

Drain the peas and lettuce and drop them into the pan. Toss briefly, cover, and cook only until the lettuce is wilted. If you like, add a little chicken stock and thicken slightly with a small lump of *beurre manie* (1 tablespoon each of flour and butter, kneaded to a paste). Correct the seasoning, if necessary.

SPINACH CASSEROLE WITH MAYONNAISE

Simply leave the lamb out of Part II of Lamb for Eight Persons Four Times, and you have a very good vegetable for both ordinary and extraordinary use. (See above, pages 134 ff.)

RED CABBAGE

¼ cup salt pork, diced
3 tablespoons sugar
2 medium onions, sliced
1 large head of red
   cabbage, shredded and
   soaked in cold water
2 tart apples, pared, cored
   and diced

½ teaspoon caraway seeds
1 cup liquid (stock, wine,
   or equal parts of each)
¼ cup vinegar
½ teaspoon salt

Fry the salt pork in your skillet. As it begins to melt, add the sugar and bring to a deep golden brown. Add the onions, and cook until likewise golden. This gentle process of caramelization is the secret of the recipe. Do it well.

Drain the cabbage, add it to the pot with the remaining ingredients, toss well for a minute, and cover tightly. Simmer for 1½ hours. If necessary, add a little liquid from time to time to prevent sticking. The dish should be moist at the end, but it should not require draining. Correct the seasoning, and get out the rye bread and beer.

SAUERKRAUT

There is no reason for putting up with poor commercial sauerkraut in nasty-tasting plastic pouches. Make your own. Here's how.

Shred finely several heads of cabbage.

Take a crock or large jar and rinse it out. (A 1-gallon mayonnaise jar will make a nice quantity of sauerkraut. Just be careful when you pour in the boiling water; better rinse it out with hot water to start with.)

Put a layer of shredded cabbage in the bottom and sprinkle on some salt. Don't overdo it, however. You can always taste the brine the second day and add a little more salt if needed.

Continue layering the cabbage and salting the layers until the crock is nearly full. Put a stone on top of the exposed cabbage.

Boil a kettleful of water and pour it into the crock until it covers all of the cabbage and the stone as well.

Leave it alone for 3 days. The cabbage does all the work. In 24 hours, you will have strong cabbage water; in 48, young sauerkraut; and in 72, the real thing.

(Don't forget to drink the juice for breakfast.)

STEAMED VEGETABLES

One of the most neglected cooking methods in America— but one of the most appreciated, once it's given a try. (See above, page 214 for instructions on how to make a steamer out of a covered roasting pan.)

Prepare raw vegetables in any combination you like. (Use your head about sizes: Huge potatoes and tiny onions will not cook equally in the same time.)

Arrange the vegetables on the rack in the steamer. Salt and pepper them, close the steamer, and let it go until they are tender (½ to 1½ hours, depending on sizes).

Needless to say, it is always appropriate to park a slab of corned beef or a smoked tongue in the middle of the vegetables. Just start the meat earlier, if it's a large piece. (Don't forget too, that it is quite possible to steam biscuits or dumplings in place of the potatoes.)

Serve steamed vegetables with plenty of butter. It's all they need.

EGGPLANT PROVENÇALE

Attractive and good—but then, so is anything provençale.

4 small eggplants, halved lengthwise, with meat removed and cut in large cubes (save shells)
Salt
Flour
½ cup olive oil

6 fresh tomatoes, peeled and quartered
Freshly ground black pepper
3 cloves garlic, crushed
Chopped parsley

Sprinkle eggplant cubes with ½ teaspoon salt. Let stand 20 minutes. Dredge in flour and brown quickly in ¼ cup olive oil.

In another skillet, heat the remaining oil and quickly sauté the tomatoes.

Combine vegetables and season with salt, pepper, and garlic. Cook 5 minutes. Fill eggplant shells with mixture, sprinkle with parsley and bake at 375° until lightly browned (10 minutes).

RATATOUILLE NIÇOISE

Another one of those Franco-Italian dishes representative of the cradle of great Western cooking. Learn this, and you will never be without a casserole to take to friends who insist on their guests bringing food.

1 large eggplant, peeled and cubed
3–4 small summer squash and/or zucchini (cubed)
4 fresh tomatoes, peeled and chopped
1 large onion, sliced

2–3 cloves garlic, crushed
2 tablespoons olive oil
Salt
Freshly ground black pepper
1 bay leaf
Grated Parmesan cheese

In as little water as possible, boil eggplant, squash, and/or zucchini for 10 minutes. Sauté onion and garlic in oil until golden. Add to eggplant mixture. Add all ingredients except cheese, and simmer ½ hour, covered.

Put in a large casserole (if there is too much liquid, pour some off). Cover generously with cheese. Bake at 350° until nicely browned.

SWEDISH BROWN BEANS

Easy, delicious, and well-received. A smörgåsbord staple.

2 cups Swedish brown
  beans
5 cups water

3–4 tablespoons light Karo
  syrup
3–4 tablespoons vinegar

Rinse beans and put in pot with water. Bring to a boil and simmer about 3 hours. Add water if necessary to keep from burning.

When cooked, add syrup, vinegar, and a pinch of salt.

PICKLED BEETS

Obvious, but once again, necessary to my view of the scheme of things. For the smörgåsbord—or any time.

2 cans sliced beets, or equal
  quantity sliced cooked
  beets
1⅓ cups sugar
⅔ cup cider vinegar
½ cup beef juice

Pickling spice
4 cloves
2 bay leaves
2 medium onions, sliced
  into rings

Boil the sugar, vinegar, beef juice, spices, cloves, and bay leaves. Pour over beets and let cool in a covered jar or bowl. One hour before serving, add onions.

HERRING SALAD

If you own a fish mold, this is the dish to use it for.

2 large cans Swedish
  herring fillets in dill
  sauce, diced
4 tablespoons vinegar
½ teaspoon white pepper
1½ tablespoons sugar
1⅓ cups cooked meat
1⅓ cups cooked beets ⎫ *Cut in*
1⅔ cups cooked potatoes ⎬ *small*
1 pickled gherkin ⎪ *cubes*
2 raw apples ⎭

GARNISH

Unsweetened whipped
  cream, or
Mayonnaise colored with
  beet juice
1 hard boiled egg

Mix all ingredients thoroughly. Pack into mold which has been rinsed in cold water. Chill. Unmold onto a large platter. Mask with cream or mayonnaise. Garnish with egg yolk and white, cut or chopped separately. Decorate border of platter with parsley and stuffed tomatoes, or stuffed eggs—or both, alternated.

(The meat in the recipe surprises most people. Leftover roast beef is very good; so is pork or veal or chicken. Keep an open mind.)

VI *DESSERTS*

STRUDEL DOUGH

(See above, pages 118–21)

STRUDEL FILLINGS

Just three. The Tyrolese filling is particularly useful when (a) there is no decent fruit to be had, and (b) you don't want to be bothered with cheese filling.

APPLE STRUDEL

Make and stretch the strudel dough. Brush the dough with melted butter and sprinkle the dough with ½ cup of fine dry bread crumbs.

Over ⅓ of the length of the dough, spread 8 tart apples, peeled, cored, and finely sliced. Sprinkle apples with 1 cup sugar and 1 teaspoon cinnamon; add 1 cup each of raisins and chopped almonds or walnuts. Roll the strudel, brush it generously with melted butter, and bake until golden brown, basting frequently with butter. Sliced peaches or sweet cherries can be substituted for the apples. Sprinkle with powdered sugar when finished, and serve warm with plenty of whipped cream.

CHEESE STRUDEL

Make and stretch the strudel dough, brush it with melted butter, and sprinkle with ½ cup sugar mixed with ½ teaspoon cinnamon and the grated rind of 1 lemon.

Cream together 2 tablespoons butter and ¼ cup sugar until the mixture is light and fluffy. Stir in 6 egg yolks, well beaten, and 1 pound of cottage cheese forced through a fine sieve. Stir in 1 cup thick sour cream and fold in 6 egg whites, stiffly beaten. Spread the filling over ⅓ the length of the dough, not too close to the ultimate edge, roll the strudel, and brush with melted butter. Sprinkle with powdered sugar and serve warm with whipped cream.

TYROLESE STRUDEL

Make and stretch the strudel dough and brush it well with melted butter.

Cream together ⅔ cup butter and ½ cup sugar until the mixture is light and fluffy. Stir in 6 egg yolks, well beaten, ⅔ cup chopped walnuts or almonds, 1 cup chopped raisins, ¼ cup each of sliced dates and figs, the grated rind of 1 lemon and ½ teaspoon cinnamon. Fold in 6 egg whites, stiffly beaten, and spread the filling over ⅓ the length of the dough. Roll the strudel, brush it with melted butter, and bake until browned, basting frequently with melted butter. Sprinkle with powdered sugar, and serve warm with whipped cream.

PAKLAVA

The great Armenian dessert. A lot of bother, but worth it.

FILLING

1 cup walnuts, crushed
¼ cup sugar
½ teaspoon cinnamon

SYRUP

1⅓ cups honey
⅔ cup water
1 teaspoon lemon juice

Mix the ingredients for the filling thoroughly. Mix the ingredients for the syrup. Heat and allow to cool to lukewarm.

Select a medium-size baking dish (I use one 2×7×11½ inches). Butter it.

Make and stretch strudel dough on a large (3×6 feet, or so) table. Brush the entire surface with melted butter. (Start with ½ pound. If you have done a good job of stretching, however, you will probably be able to use ¾ pound before you finish.)

Begin at the narrow end of the table and fold the dough over on itself at 7-inch intervals. As each fold is made, brush some more butter on the unbuttered parts of the dough. Continue until you have a strip of folded dough as long as the width of the table and 7 inches wide. Cut this into three 11½-inch lengths. (In any case, be sure that at least two of them are as long as your baking dish; on the other hand, if you have any extra dough, by all means include it somewhere in the *paklava*.)

Place one of these pieces in the bottom of your baking dish. Cover it evenly with the filling of crushed walnuts, cinnamon, and sugar. On top of this, place the remaining pieces of folded dough (saving the best for the top), and brush well with melted butter.

With a sharp, wet knife, cut the paklava into serving size (1½×3-inch) wedges. Be sure to cut right through all the layers to the bottom of the pan.

Bake in a 350° oven for 15 minutes.

In the meantime, measure 1½ cups of fresh, clear, tasteless cooking oil (Crisco oil, for example). At the end of 15 minutes, heat ⅓ of this oil in a saucepan until it is a good, hot frying temperature. Open the oven and carefully pour this oil all over the paklava. It should sizzle and puff as soon as the oil hits it.

Repeat this at 10 minute intervals with the remaining thirds of the oil. Lower the heat as necessary to keep from burning. Do not let the paklava get too dark. A light golden brown should be the goal.

Bake 10 minutes more (total time, 45–55 minutes) approximately—or until the oil has pretty much stopped bubbling, remove from the oven, and pour off all excess oil. (Be careful not to let the paklava fall out of the dish; use a cookie sheet, or something to keep it in the dish while you pour out the oil.)

When the paklava has cooled to lukewarm, pour the lukewarm syrup over it, and let it stand in the pan until needed.

One comment. As is obvious by now, this pastry is french-fried more than it is baked. Take pains, therefore, that even the center is crisp. Soggy paklava is a contradiction in terms.

PUFF PASTE

(See above, pages 161 ff.)

SACRISTAINS

Sprinkle your rolled puff paste with sugar and chopped almonds and run the pin over everything to embed it in the surface. Then, with a knife or pastry wheel, cut the rectangle into strips ¾ inch wide and 6 inches long.

Take each strip, twist it lengthwise 2 or 3 times into a corkscrew, and lay it on a baking sheet. Bake as for puff paste, at 450° and 350°, until done.

These are very good indeed. So good, that you may even be tempted to make an entire batch of puff paste into *sacristains*, and thus avoid the problem of scraps altogether. It is a temptation worth yielding to.

LANGUES DE BOEUF

Take your finished puff pastry from the refrigerator and roll it out into a large rectangle ³⁄₁₆ inch thick. Then, with a 3-inch fluted pastry cutter (or a plain round cookie cutter), cut out as many rounds as you can get.

Next, sprinkle a thick layer of sugar on one end of the pastry table. On this sugared surface, place the circles of puff paste one at a time and, making two deft but firm passes with the rolling pin (one away from you and one back), convert the circles into elongated ovals. Hence the name, beef tongues.

Place these on a cookie sheet, sugared side up, and bake until dry and a good color. (Begin with the oven at 450°, and, after the *langues* are puffed, reduce to 350°—or even lower—until well dried.)

TURNOVERS

Made with your own all-butter puff paste, these will be a million miles removed from the commercial cardboard pistol holsters which sometimes pass for turnovers among us. Filled with almond filling, they make a delightfully light and dry accompaniment to coffee at refreshment time.

Roll out puff paste into a rectangle ⅛ to ³⁄₁₆ inch thick. Cut this with a knife or pastry wheel into 4-inch squares.

In the center of each square, place a generous teaspoonful of filling (almond, prune or apricot lekvar, or any good jam or preserve).

Moisten the edges, fold neatly, and seal. Prick the top side a few times with a toothpick. (If you are careful to keep the filling away from the edges, you will have less of a problem with leakage. If you want to avoid leakage even more, let the turnovers chill for an hour or so before baking.)

Bake in a hot (425°) oven for 8–10 minutes, lower heat, and continue baking until crisp and golden.

Remove from oven, place on rack, and, while still hot, brush well with confectioners'-sugar icing.

NAPOLEONS

Bring your Napoleon to the table whole on a large bread board and slice it with the point of a sharp knife right before your guests' eyes. After all, how often can they see that much goodness in one piece?

Roll out puff paste into a large rectangle ⅛ to ³⁄₁₆ inch thick. Cut this into 3 equal rectangles and place them on baking sheets. Prick well and bake, beginning at 400° and turning heat down after 5 minutes or so. (These thin sheets will burn faster than most pastries, so keep an eye on things.)

Remove to rack and cool.

Take the second-best-looking piece, put it on a suitable dish or board and spread it very liberally with sweetened whipped cream. Place the worst looking piece on top of this and spread it, too, with a thick layer of whipped cream. Place the choicest piece of pastry on top and sprinkle it liberally with powdered sugar.

Cut into rectangular pieces just before serving.

CREAM ROLLS

These call for a little equipment, but, given that, they are not too much trouble.

Roll out puff paste ⅛ inch thick, cut it into strips 1×8 inches and wind each strip carefully around a cream roll form, making sure that each turn overlaps the previous one by a half-width.

Place on a baking sheet, brush with beaten egg or not, as you like (with it, they will be a richer color), and bake: 5 minutes or so at 400°; the rest of the time at a lower temperature, until crisp.

Remove from the oven, allow to cool, remove molds (carefully!), and fill with sweetened whipped cream piped in with a pastry bag. (If you use a star tube, the cream at the ends of the rolls will be specially attractive.)

RHUBARB PIE

One of the great American pies. If you like a few straw-berries along with your rhubarb, go ahead and add them.

FOR ONE 11-INCH PIE:

4 cups rhubarb cut
   in ½-inch pieces
2 cups sugar
4 tablespoons flour

2 eggs
Plain pastry for 11-inch
   pie

Mix sugar, flour, and eggs in a bowl. Stir in rhubarb. Line an 11-inch pie plate with plain pastry, pour in filling, and make a lattice-strip top with the rest of the pastry.

Bake like any pie. Serve warm.

DANISH PASTRY

(See above, page 165 ff.)

PINWHEELS

Roll your Danish pastry into a large rectangle ¼ inch thick. Sprinkle it liberally with sugar, cinnamon, and raisins.

Roll it up, jelly-roll fashion, and seal the edge with a little water. Slice this into 1-inch widths and place the slices flat on baking sheets.

Let rise, brush with beaten egg, sprinkle with sugar, and bake. (Start out at 350° here. You don't want burnt sugar on the bottom of your pastries.)

Behold! You have just brought forth the most elegant plain Danish in the world.

SCHNECKEN

(*Schnecken* means snails. The pinwheels above are therefore Schnecken too. But in my family, the name is reserved for the following more elegant pan of buns.)

Take your finished pillow of Danish from the refrigerator after its night of nights and cut off not more than ⅒ of it.

Take this small piece and roll it into an incredibly thin sheet, large enough to cover the bottom of the baking pan you plan to use. If necessary, finish the rolling in the pan itself, patching where you must, so that the entire bottom surface of the pan is covered with pastry. (This insures that your Schnecken will never stick, and that none of your fillings will ever disgrace you by turning black.)

Then proceed as before with the rest of the dough: Roll it into a rectangle, spread it with filling (this time, almond), form it into a jelly roll, seal it, slice it, and place the slices flat on the pastry-covered bottom of the pan. (Don't crowd them in, however. They must have room not only to rise, but also to expand into the flaky layers you so painstakingly made by all that rolling. I never put more than nine Schnecken in a 12×12-inch space. Govern yourself accordingly.)

Let rise, brush with beaten egg, sprinkle liberally with sugar and bake at 375° until beautiful. They really are.

ADDITIONAL FILLINGS FOR DANISH SCHNECKEN

The cheese is fussy, but the rest are easy.

CHEESE FILLING WITH CHERRIES

Cream together 1 tablespoon butter and ¼ cup sugar. Beat in 2 eggs. Force ½ pound dry pot cheese through a sieve and add to egg mixture. Add the grated rind of ½ lemon, ¼ cup thick sour cream, and a pinch of salt.

Spread this filling evenly on rolled-out Danish pastry, roll up loosely, jelly-roll fashion, and cut into Schnecken (with a sharp knife and a quick, smart stroke—otherwise the filling will squirt all over).

Spread the thin sheet of dough in the bottom of the pan (see above, page 257), with a good amount of fine whole cherry preserves, arrange the Schnecken in the pan (with plenty of room for expansion).

Let rise, brush with beaten egg, sprinkle with sugar, and bake till a good color.

APRICOT OR PRUNE

Buy some good lekvar from a Hungarian store, spread it evenly on the dough to be rolled up, and proceed as usual.

ALMOND AND RASPBERRY

One of the great combinations. Roll up the Schnecken with almond filling but spread the bottom sheet with good raspberry jam.

THREE IN ONE

Spread the dough to be rolled up with 3 bands of filling (apricot, almond, prune). Roll up so that the fillings remain separate; that is, so that you get three distinct kinds of filling in one long roll. Cut into Schnecken and arrange in groups in the pan; apricot at one end, almond in the middle, prune at the other.

Proceed as usual.

MAZARIN CAKE

Not too fussy, but spectacular. A great, ordinary, fancy cake.

SHORTPASTE:

1⅔ cups flour	⅓ cup sugar
1 teaspoon baking powder	1 egg
½ cup butter	

Sift the flour and baking powder onto the pastry board—or into a bowl—and work in all ingredients in the order given, until you have a smooth paste. Set aside.

FILLING:

2 cups grated almonds	4 eggs
2 cups sugar	2 teaspoons almond extract
1 cup butter	

Work the first 3 ingredients together by hand and then beat in the eggs with a wooden spoon. Last of all, beat in the almond extract.

PREPARATION:

Roll out the shortpaste between layers of waxed paper and, by hook or by crook, line two shallow 9″ round cake tins with a thin layer of paste. Throw the paper away. (I am sorry for directions like that, but once a teacher, always a teacher.) All in all, it is a singularly unfussy piece of business. Short-paste handles as easily as toothpaste. All that matters is that the bottom and sides of the pans be covered.

Spread some good raspberry jam on the bottom crust, and add the filling.

Bake at 325° until a nice color (about 1 hour, give or take whatever is necessary). The filling should be well risen but not soggy. Test with a cake tester until nothing comes away. It will fall, of course, when it cools; but then, we all do, love. People who live in glass houses . . .

Serve in tiny wedges. Mazarin cake borders on confectionery. Each of the 9-inch tins will yield sixteen servings—making this the perfect dessert for a large buffet. With great coffee, it leaves nothing to be desired.

CAKE A LA BENNICH

Rather fussy, very sweet, and altogether different. My children call it "yellow pie." It is more a confection than a cake.

MACAROON

4 egg whites	1 cup sugar
1 cup grated almonds	1 teaspoon almond extract

Beat egg whites until stiff, and fold in almonds, sugar, and almond extract.

Butter and flour 2 cookie sheets, pour half the macaroon mixture on each, keeping it in 2 neat, equal rounds or squares. Bake in a slow oven (325°) until well set and fairly dry.

Remove carefully from sheet (a long thin knife is a help). Cool on a rack, and then chill in the freezer (to insure that filling, when applied, will set up nicely).

FILLING

4 egg yolks	4 tablespoons cream
¾ cup sugar	⅔ cup fresh butter

Whisk yolks, sugar, and cream in a saucepan over a slow fire until well thickened. Do not let them boil. When thick, back away from the stove, still whisking, and whisk in the butter a few pieces at a time. Cool completely, but do not chill.

Place 1 of the macaroon rounds on a serving dish, spread it with ½ of the filling, place the other round on top, and spread it with the remainder of the filling. Sprinkle with lightly toasted almond strips. Keep cold, but allow it to lose a little of its chill before serving.

ICE BOX CAKE

The traditional birthday cake in my family. You should be so lucky.

1 pound dark sweet chocolate melted in 3 tablespoons boiling water	9 egg yolks
	9 egg whites, beaten stiff
	3 dozen ladyfingers, split
2–3 tablespoons confectioners' sugar	1 pint cream, whipped
	2 tablespoons sugar
1½ teaspoons vanilla	1 teaspoon vanilla

Melt chocolate in water. Add sugar and vanilla, and stir well. Remove from stove. Add egg yolks one at a time, beating thoroughly after each addition. Fold in egg whites.

Line 2 long bread pans with sheets of waxed paper (to facilitate removal). Put a layer of split ladyfingers in the bottom and pour on some of the chocolate mixture. Put in another layer of ladyfingers at right angles to the first and add more chocolate. Continue until all the chocolate is used up. Finish with a layer of ladyfingers.

Chill well (overnight is best), unmold, and cover thickly with sweetened whipped cream. Serve in slices.

ZABAGLIONE

For each serving, take 1 egg yolk, and for each egg yolk, add a tablespoon of cream, 1 of sugar and 1 of Marsala (Sherry, Madeira, Cherry Heering, Swedish Punsch, Grand Marnier, or even Drambuie make superb substitutes).

Put all ingredients in a bowl and whisk well; strain into a saucepan.

Then continue whisking, on and off the fire, until it approaches the consistency of custard.

Back away without stopping till you reach the small Sherry or cocktail glasses into which you plan to pour it.

Fill, chill, and serve.

CRÊME CHOCOLAT

Chocolate pudding gone to heaven.

1 pound grated sweet chocolate
1 pint milk
8 egg yolks, lightly beaten in a bowl

Scald milk in a saucepan, add chocolate, and whisk until chocolate is melted. Bring to a boil.

Pour over egg yolks, beating constantly until smooth. Strain through a fine strainer and pour into small ceramic cups or small wine glasses (3 or 4 ounces). Chill.

Serve with whipped cream.

STEAMED CHOCOLATE PUDDING

A hearty, no-fooling dessert; yet one with great finesse.

3 tablespoons butter	4½ teaspoons baking powder
⅔ cup sugar	1 cup milk
1 egg, well beaten	¼ teaspoon salt
2¼ cups flour	2½ squares bitter chocolate

Cream butter, sugar, and egg. Sift flour with baking powder and salt. Add alternately with milk to first mixture. Melt chocolate over hot water and add to flour mixture.

Pour into buttered mold (fill only ⅔ full). Steam for 2 hours. Serve warm with cold, stiffly whipped cream.

FOUR HOLIDAY COOKIES

These, together with the breads I gave you above (pages 195–200) and the Plum Pudding immediately following, will give you a hint of what Christmas is like where I live. (The dinner, by the way, is always Standing Ribs of Beef, Yorkshire Pudding, Wild Rice, Mashed Potatoes, Creamed Onions, Cubed Turnips, Buttered Carrots, Green Beans, Pan Gravy, and several bottles of Chambertin. As you see, we celebrate not only the Word, but the flesh He came to save.

SPRITZ

2 cups butter
2 cups sugar
2 eggs, well beaten

4 cups sifted flour
2 teaspoons almond extract

Cream butter and sugar. Add eggs, beating thoroughly. Add flour and flavoring. Put through a cookie press. Decorate or not. Bake at 350° until a delicate color (about 10 minutes).

RUSSIAN TEA CAKES

½ pound sweet butter
6 tablespoons confectioners'
  sugar
2 cups sifted cake flour

1 cup pulverized nuts
  (filberts or walnuts)
1 teaspoon vanilla

Mix completely by hand. Shape into ¾-inch balls. Bake at 350° until light and delicate. Roll in confectioners' sugar.

SWEDISH JUDEBRÖD

1½ cups butter
6 cups flour
2 eggs

2 cups sugar
¾ teaspoon baking soda
½ teaspoon ground cardamom

Mix with hands. Roll out very thin. Cut into various shapes with cutter. Brush with beaten egg. Sprinkle with cinnamon and sugar. Bake at 350° until light and delicate.

HERMITS

1 cup butter
1 cup sugar
2 eggs, beaten
¼ teaspoon baking soda
1 teaspoon cinnamon
1 teaspoon ground cloves
¼ teaspoon nutmeg

¼ teaspoon salt
1 cup seeded muscat raisins
1 cup coarsely chopped
  walnuts
1¼ cups flour
  (approximately)

Cream butter and sugar. Add eggs. Add remaining ingredients, using just enough flour to make dough easy to handle. Make into balls the size of walnuts.

Bake at 350° well apart on greased cookie sheets for 10 minutes.

Open the oven twice during the baking and bang the sheets to make the cookies fall and spread out.

MY GRANDMOTHER'S PLUM PUDDING RECIPE "JOHN BULL'S OWN"

A great recipe. Served with her sauce, it makes the Christmas feast complete. The finished pudding, if kept in a dry place, will keep for over a year.

1 pound kidney suet (membranes removed), chopped fine

1 pound ground dried bread crumbs

1 pound sugar (brown and white, mixed)

1 pound muscat raisins

1 pound seedless raisins

1 pound currants

1 pound candied peel (orange, lemon, and citron) chopped fine

1 teaspoon cloves

1½ teaspoons cinnamon

2 teaspoons salt

1 large cup ground apples with juice

1 cup flour

8 eggs, slightly beaten

1 wineglass Cognac

Mix all ingredients in a large bowl by hand.

Select a number of bowls sufficient to accommodate the recipe. Fill them ⅔ full, cover with clean, white cloths and tie well. (It's a good idea to use bowls of different sizes: That way you will have puddings of varying magnitudes to choose from.)

Steam for 6 hours. Dry and store.
Before serving, steam for 1 hour.

MY GRANDMOTHER'S OWN PLUM PUDDING SAUCE

For a medium-size plum pudding, take 4 egg yolks, 4 tablespoons of sugar, 2 of cream, and 2 of Cognac;

Place in a pot and whisk well—away from the fire;

Then whisk on and off the fire, until the custard stage is reached;

Back away, whisking, and add 8 tablespoons of butter. As with Hollandaise, when the butter is blended in, the sauce is finished.

(Other proportions of Cognac to cream are, of course, possible—as are other flavorings than Cognac; the main secret, however, is in your hands. If you thank me for nothing else in this book, you will thank me for this.)

VII *BEVERAGES*

MY GRANDFATHER'S CHAMPAGNE COCKTAIL

In each glass, put a lump of sugar which has been flavored with *a few drops* of one of the following: good Cognac; Benedictine; Pernod; Angostura bitters (gently, unless the Champagne is dreadful).

Fill with cold Champagne and serve.

SWEET MARTINI

I told you there was one, Virginia. Here it is.

2 parts dry gin
1 part sweet Vermouth
Twist of orange peel

Stir with ice and serve.

MOTHER'S RUIN

The housewife's noonday pick-me-up. In the old days, they used to explain mother's protracted stays in her room by saying she was "upstairs with the vapors." Now we all live on one floor, have hardly any doors at all, and see grim clinicians lecturing us in our sleep. Brazen it out then: Find some company to share your drop of the milk of human kindness with you and drink in public, like a man.

1 part orange juice   ½ part sweet Vermouth
1 part gin   Dash Cognac

Shake well with ice.

FISH HOUSE PUNCH

*If you serve punch at all, make sure you serve one with real
muscle. There is nothing worse than trying to launch a party
on a gallon of seltzer and a fifth of gin.*

*Here, then, is the original iron fist in the velvet glove—for
fifty persons, all at once.*

1½ cups plain sugar syrup   1 bottle ***Cognac
1½ cups lime juice   1 cup peach brandy
1½ bottles dark Jamaica rum   4 bottles Champagne

Put large chunks of ice in the biggest punch bowl you can
find. Add above ingredients, stir well, and add 4 bottles of
good domestic Champagne.

Serve and stand back.

(Everything but the Champagne, of course, can be mixed
beforehand and stored in a suitable jug until the last minute.)

BOWLE

*The perfect drink for a slightly shirtier party. Encouraging
but not compelling.*

Put a quart of hulled strawberries in a bowl, sprinkle on 1
cup sugar and pour in 1 cup good Cognac. Mix well, cover
with plastic wrap and refrigerate overnight.

Chill 3 bottles of good May Wine and add to the strawberry mixture. Put in no ice at all.

Stir and serve with a few berries in each glass.

(Bowle can also be made with good ripe peaches—and with inexpensive Moselle or Rhine wine.)

GLÖGG

Here are two recipes for the great Swedish winter drink. Just the thing on a bitter cold night.

GLÖGG I (GENTEEL)

Take a gallon of California Sherry and pour a quart into another bottle. Drink it in your spare time.

In a saucepan, put:

3 1×2-inch pieces of orange peel	5 slim pieces stick cinnamon
3 1×2-inch pieces of lemon peel	10 cloves
¾ cup blanched almonds	5 whole cardamom seeds
	1 cup raisins

Add to these a cup or so of Sherry from the gallon jug and boil the spices in it (covered) for 15 minutes.

Pour this infusion (peel, seeds, and all) back into the jug, fill it up with decent domestic brandy, screw on the cap, shake well and allow to sit for a few days. Agitate 3 or 4 times in the first 48 hours. After that, it will keep indefinitely.

When you are ready to use it, heat it on the stove in a large pot (don't boil), and pour it into a metal or enamel bowl to serve. Ignite just before serving. (The way to do this and not burn the hair off the backs of your hands is to take up a dipperful, light that, and lower the dipper into the liquid to set it afire. To put the fire out, blow very hard—or if you are short-winded or stuffy, hold a suitable lid over it for a moment.)

GLÖGG II (POTENT)

1 bottle domestic brandy	10 whole cardamom seeds
1 wineglass good Port or Madeira	10 cloves
1 cup sugar	Handful of raisins and blanched almonds
Small piece stick cinnamon	

Pour a glassful of brandy out of the bottle and have a drink with your wife.

Put the sugar in the bottom of a saucepan. Add a cup of brandy, heat slightly, ignite, and ladle constantly until the sugar is completely melted. Extinguish the fire, add the rest of the spices, etc., and pour all back into the brandy bottle. Fill up with Port wine, and reseal.

To serve, heat gently in a saucepan on the stove top (don't boil), transfer to the serving bowl, add a little more Port, ignite, ladle awhile, and serve. Be flamboyant but not reckless. (Whatever you do, never pour wine or spirits into flaming dishes direct from the bottle. Use a ladle as an intermediary, or you will get an explosion and some nasty cuts.)

SWEDISH PUNSCH

The end at last. It has been lovely knowing you. My parting gift is princely: It makes one case of Punsch.

6 bottles (fifths) water
6 pounds sugar

Put water in a very large soup kettle (at least 12 quarts —but 20 is easier to work with). Note level of water. Add sugar, and boil syrup down to near the original quantity of the water. Allow to cool well.

Then stir in the following:

3 fifths best arrack	1 fifth good Cognac
2 fifths best 100-proof vodka	2 tablespoons glycerine

Stir and ladle the *punsch* for at least a half hour. Bottle and seal. It improves greatly with time, but can be used after a few days.

The taste is rather like rum, and it is, of course, very sweet. Serve ice cold (but without ice) in liqueur glasses—after dinner.

(Arrack is hard to come by. German and Scandinavian neighborhoods, however, will usually have at least one liquor store that carries it. I buy mine in Yorkville in Manhattan. The glycerine can be bought in any drugstore. For heaven's sake, though, don't send your teen-age son for it: After the saltpeter, the pharmacist will be sure he is hatching a bomb plot.)